Omowale Pert-em-Hru ~ Afrikan People Abolished the 'Slave Trade'

Submission presented in Parliament Tuesday 17 January 2017

Memorial to the Afrikan Maroon Warriors – Roseau, Dominica

Omowale Ru Pert-em-Hru

Afrikan People Abolished the 'Slave Trade'

Incorporating
An Updated Version of

Horrors, Responsibility and Origin of Slavery

Roseau's Old Market, Dominica – Afrikan People were sold there on arrival

Omowale Ru Pert-em-Hru

Afrikan People Abolished
the
'Slave Trade'

Incorporating its companion book

The Horrors, Responsibilities and Origin of Slavery

Omowale Ru Pert-em-Hru
Founder of
Ukombozii

Copyright © 2017
Omowale Ru Pert-em-Hru

All rights reserved.

ISBN-13: 978-1543057195

ISBN-10: 1543057195

Published by
Omowale Ru Pert-em-Hru

Ukombozii@gmail.com
00 44 (0) 7914 750 753

Printed in Europe by CreateSpace.com

Afrikan People Abolished the 'Slave Trade'

Tribute to our Ancestors

Special tribute to ancestors of:
The *Pan-Afrikan Society Community Forum (PASCF) and GACuk*

Brother Omowale

• *Brother Ras Lloyd* (aka Lloyd Johnson) the first *Chair of the PASCF* – Born 17th August 1956, crossed to meet the ancestors 20th December 2011;

• *Brother Oxalando Efuntola* (aka Andrew Navarro Smith) the first *Director of Communications and Organisational Priest* of the PASCF – Born 29th January 1957, crossed to meet the ancestors 16th September 2014. Son of Mr Kenneth and Mrs Enid Smith;

• *Sister Mawasi Bojang* (aka Patricia Presilla Chambers) the first *Deputy Chair of the PASCF*, who took up the role of *Chair of the PASCF* on the passing of Ras Lloyd – Born 8th February 1965, crossed to meet the ancestors 11th May 2016; and

• *Mama Gee Bernard* the *Joint Chair of GACuk* – Born 29th December 1935, crossed to meet the ancestors 6th December 2016.

Though our comrades did not necessarily describe themselves as socialists, they were all ardent, committed and active anti-imperialists. They all gave selflessly to the struggle against capitalism and made important dedicated contributions to our people's advance towards socialism within the disciplined framework of organised resistance. They will always be remembered by Ukombozii, the PASCF and GACuk.

Omowale Ru Pert-em-Hru

PASCF, NUSBSC, Momentum Black Caucus & GACuk invite you to
Piracy, Slave Trade, Slavery and Colonialism

International Speaker:
Bob Brown – A-APRP (GC)
& former founder of the Black Panther Party (Chicago Chapter)

Coming to Parliament

Tuesday 17th January
5.30pm prompt Start
Committee Room 18
Houses of Parliament
Westminster
London SW1A 0AA
NB. Cromwell Green Entrance

We pose these questions to the British State:
1 Who abolished the 'slave trade'?
2 When, where and why were piracy, human trafficking, the slave trade, slavery and colonialism declared crimes against humanity?
3 Why were they not always declared crimes against humanity especially with respect to Afrikan people?

Please aim to *arrive at 4.30pm* to allow for queues and security

Incorporating a special tribute to PASCF and GACuk Ancestors (overleaf):
Ras Lloyd, Brother Oxalando Efuntola-Smith, Sister Mawasi Bojang & Mama Gee Barnard

Supported by: Pan-Afrikan Society Community Forum * RMT Black Workers * MGOC* AAPRP (GC) * GAC (UK) *
Haiti First! Haiti Now! Reparations Campaign * NUSBSC * Momentum Black Caucus
www.pascf.org ; pascfevents1@gmail.com; 07914-750-753   nus *black students*
www.a-aprp-gc.org; info@a-aprp-gc.org; (202) 719-0529 (USA)

Click the link: https://www.eventbrite.co.uk/e/piracy-the-slave-trade-slavery-and-colonialism-tickets-31005929570

Table of Contents

PREAMBLE I XVII

MY VISION FOR AFRIKA AND HER PEOPLE XVII
    Our capacity to create, produce and build as our contribution to a better world for humanity xvii
    Driven by our capacity to govern a just society for Afrikan people xviii
    Driven by our capacity to build respectful relationships for the achievement of happiness xix
    Driven by a humble and respectful relationship with our environment for the achievement of higher understanding xx
WHY PARLIAMENT? XXII

1 AFRIKAN PEOPLE HAD A HISTORY BEFORE SLAVERY 3

1.1 THE CONTEXT AND IMPORTANCE OF THE ENSLAVEMENT ERA 3
    1.1.1 Contextualising the enslavement era in Afrikan history 3
    1.1.2 The deployment of aspects of Afrikan history 4
1.2 THE ENSLAVEMENT ERA IN THE FULLNESS OF AFRIKAN HISTORY 5
    1.2.1 Afrikan people have the longest history of all the human family 5
    1.2.2 The enslavement era as an historical blip 7
1.3 AFRIKAN PEOPLE ADVANCED HUMANITY 7
    1.3.1 Some ancient achievements of Afrikan people 7
1.4 AFRIKAN EXPANSION AND DOMINANCE OVER EUROPE 9
    1.4.1 Afrika's ancient empires 9
    1.4.2 Afrika's conquests over Europe 9
1.5 THE AFRIKAN ROOT OF WORLD CULTURES 10
    1.5.1 Afrikan culture gave rise to modern European culture 10
    1.5.2 Contact between Afrikan and European cultures immediately prior to slavery 12

2 THE HORRORS OF SLAVERY 17

2.1 REPAIRING IMPERIALISM'S ANTI-AFRIKAN DAMAGE 17
    2.1.1 Anti-Afrikan Terrorism and Afrikan resistance 17
    2.1.2 Economics drove slavery and slavery drove racism 18
    2.1.3 Truth for justice: The horrors must be revealed 18
    2.1.4 The scam 'legality' of slavery 20
2.2 TERRORISM: KIDNAPPING AFRIKAN PEOPLE IN AFRIKA 21
    2.2.1 Avoiding cannibals 21
    2.2.2 The disorientation of Afrikan people 22
    2.2.3 The treatment of kidnapped Afrikan people 23
2.3 THE SEABOARD JOURNEY: A RECONSTRUCTION 24
    2.3.1 Conditions for kidnapped Afrikan people 24

    2.3.2 The violation of Afrikan women 28
    2.3.3 Punishing resistance on board 31
  2.4 ANTI-AFRIKAN GENOCIDE IN THE AMERICAS 33
    2.4.1 Terrorism on the forced labour camps: The killing fields 33
    2.4.2 The sexually abusive torture of Afrikan women 37
    2.4.3 Rape as evidence of the triple oppression of enslaved Afrikan women 41
    2.4.4 Triple terrorism: The physical torture of enslaved Afrikan women .. 43
    2.4.5 Beyond the records 45
    2.4.6 Other forms of anti-Afrikan terrorism 47
    2.4.7 Afrikan heroism in a climate of murderous terrorism 49
  2.5 CONCLUSION 50

3 WAS SLAVERY REALLY OUR OWN FAULT? 57

  3.1 IMPERIALISM'S FALSE ACCUSATION AGAINST AFRIKAN PEOPLE 57
  3.2 OUR RESPONSE 59
  3.3 ALLEGATION 1: WE ENSLAVED OURSELVES BEFORE EUROPEAN IMPERIALISM CAME ALONG 60
    3.3.1 Imperialism did not copy chattel slavery from Afrikan societies 60
    3.3.2 The Afrikan form of 'slavery' was less draconian 60
    3.3.3 Slavery is integral to European imperialist culture 61
    3.3.4 Imperialism created the market for enslaved Afrikan people 62
  3.4 ALLEGATION 2: WE SOLD OUR OWN PEOPLE INTO SLAVERY 64
    3.4.1 Human trafficking and the 'Triangular trade' 64
    3.4.2 The hypocrisy of British imperialism – The worse kidnappers 67
    3.4.3 An honest reflection – Afrikan people fought against kidnapping and deportation 69
    3.4.4 Afrikan people in Afrika were the first to abolish the 'slave trade' . 70
    3.4.5 British imperialism used a divide and rule approach to reinstating slavery 71
    3.4.6 Afrikan people in Afrika battled against the 'slave trade' 74
    3.4.7 European imperialism a common denominator in chattel slavery .. 78
    3.4.8 Other peoples collaborated with oppressors 79

4 WILL THE REAL WILLIAM WILBERFORCE PLEASE STAND UP? 85

  4.1 THE PROCESS OF DECEPTION 85
    4.1.1 Trickery in the name of Wilberforce 85
  4.2 THE REAL WILBERFORCE 87
    4.2.1 Wilberforce: a man of class 87
    4.2.2 Wilberforce a drug addicted late comer to the abolition cause 89
  4.3 WILBERFORCE: GOVERNMENT AGENT AND BOGUS ANTI-SLAVERY 'LEADER'? 91
    4.3.1 Thwarting the abolition process 91
    4.3.2 Hidden motivations behind Wilberforce's duplicity 93
    4.3.3 Wilberforce wreaks the Abolition Society 95

- 4.4 WILBERFORCE THE RACIST MISOGYNIST 98
  - 4.4.1 Racist Wilberforce opposed the abolition of slavery 98
  - 4.4.2 Racist Wilberforce delayed the abolition of slavery 100
  - 4.4.3 Sexist Wilberforce opposed women's groups advocating the abolition of slavery..102
- 4.5 THE REAL WILBERFORCE – STOOD UP 106
  - 4.5.1 Failure as a human being 106
  - 4.5.2 Wilberforce – Underhanded saboteur of the abolitionist cause 107
  - 4.5.3 Imperialism's distortion of history 108

5 AFRIKAN PEOPLE ABOLISHED THE 'SLAVE TRADE'..113

- 5.1 INTRODUCTION...113
  - 5.1.1 British imperialism: Unrepentant for its crimes against humanity 113
  - 5.1.2 Wherever there were Afrikan people there was resistance to imperialism's chattel slavery system..114
- 5.2 NARROW PERSPECTIVES ON ABOLITION AND RESISTANCE.....................................116
  - 5.2.1 Wilberforce: The bogus 'king of abolition' 116
  - 5.2.2 Imperialism's other contenders for the bogus 'abolition crown' ...118
  - 5.2.3 'Abolition' and the British working classes.......................................119
  - 5.2.4 Afrikan people in Britain drove the diplomatic front for 'abolition' 120
- 5.3 BROADENING THE SCOPE 124
  - 5.3.1 Thinking outside of imperialism's ideological box – The Abolition Matrix..124
  - 5.3.2 The value of the Abolition Matrix framework and beyond 129
- 5.4 SOURCES OF AFRIKAN PEOPLE'S ABOLITION ON AFRIKAN SOIL 130
  - 5.4.1 Levels of Afrikan abolition of the so called 'slave trade' 130
  - 5.4.2 Afrikan people in Afrika were the first to abolish the 'slave trade' 131
  - 5.4.3 British imperialism abolished Afrikan abolitions of the 'slave trade' 133
  - 5.4.4 Afrikan national resistance to the so called 'slave trade' 136
  - 5.4.5 Coastal battles to defeat the so called 'slave trade' 137
  - 5.4.6 Consequence of Afrikan people's homeland resistance to the 'slave trade'..140
- 5.5 SOURCES OF AFRIKAN PEOPLE'S ABOLITION IN THE ATLANTIC...............................141
  - 5.5.1 Kidnapped Afrikan people commandeered the human trafficking ships 141
  - 5.5.2 Uprisings that did not take control of the ship................................142
  - 5.5.3 Ships successfully taken and later recaptured 144
  - 5.5.4 Triumph: Conquered ships sailed back to Afrika 146
- 5.6 SOURCES OF AFRIKAN PEOPLE'S ABOLITION IN THE CARIBBEAN............................148
  - 5.6.1 Afrikan victories against great odds 148
  - 5.6.2 Internal and external stimuli to Afrikan people's resistance..........148
- 5.7 HAITI: EPICENTRE OF REVOLUTIONARY UPSURGE 150

5.7.1 The magnitude of the Haitian Revolutionary victory *150*
5.7.2 The Haitian revolution ignites *151*
5.7.3 The beginning phase of the revolution *152*
5.7.4 Afrikan revolutionaries defeat multiple enemies *153*
5.7.5 Settling internal disputes *154*
5.7.6 Toussaint takes firm control *155*
5.7.7 The arrival and impact of the French invasion force *156*
5.7.8 The French lust for Afrikan women *160*
5.7.9 Satisfying the Frenchman's lust for a higher cause *161*
5.7.10 Henriette St Marc – heroic self-sacrifice *162*
5.7.11 Afrikan Revolutionaries triumph in Haiti *163*
5.8 CARIBBEAN-WIDE REVOLUTION AND THE HAITIAN CONNECTION 165
5.8.1 Jamaica *165*
5.8.2 Guadeloupe *168*
5.8.3 Dominica *170*
5.8.4 Saint Lucia *174*
5.8.5 Barbados *176*
5.8.6 Saint Vincent *178*
5.8.7 Grenada *178*
5.9 REVERBERATIONS OF THE HAITIAN REVOLUTION BEYOND THE ISLAND OF HISPANIOLA
.... 179
5.9.1 The Haitian revolution brought Britain to its knees *179*
5.9.2 The language of a regional revolution *181*
5.9.3 The French empire on the brink of collapse *182*
5.9.4 French imperialism abandons the Americas *184*
5.9.5 Trafalgar Square or Haitian Revolution square *186*
5.9.6 Haiti and the Bolivarian revolution *187*
5.10 ADDITIONAL AND BROADER LEVEL FACTORS 188
5.10.1 Afrikan military victories: Impact on the 'abolition' of the 'slave trade' *188*
5.10.2 Afrikan People's resistance took every conceivable form *190*
5.10.3 Afrika's abundant riches superseded Caribbean slavery *191*
5.10.4 World military, political and economic forces overwhelmed the institution of slavery *192*
5.10.5 Afrikan people abolished the 'slave trade' *197*
LIST OF MENTIONED SOURCES 202

6 A BRIEF INTRODUCTION TO AFRIKAN LIBERATION 209
6.1 A SNAPSHOT OF AFRIKANS IN THE WORLD 209
6.1.1 The historical assault on Afrika and Afrikans *209*
6.1.2 The contemporary assault on Afrika and Afrikans *212*
6.1.3 The contemporary assault on Afrikans in Britain *222*
6.2 A COLLECTIVE PURPOSE FOR AFRIKANS 228
6.2.1 A basis for Afrikan unity *228*

    6.2.2 Neo-colonialism: Afrika's principle enemy 230
    6.2.3 Afrika: Our centre of gravity 234
  6.3 UKOMBOZII STATEMENT ON REPARATIONS 238
    6.3.1 They all owe us..238
    6.3.2 A business case for reparations...239
    6.3.3 The first instalment is 243 years overdue 240
    6.3.4 Reparations is one small 'r' in the 'Revolutionary armoury' 244

7 DECODING SLAVERY & ANTI-SLAVERY SYSTEMS: 251

  7.1 THE FUNDAMENTAL BASIS OF HUMAN RELATIONSHIPS 251
  7.2 HUMAN BEINGS CANNOT EXIST OUTSIDE OF NATURE 252
    7.2.1 Nature has four elements...252
    7.2.2 Land is unique amongst nature's elements.....................................253
  7.3 PEOPLE, LAND AND THE DEVELOPMENT OF PRINCIPLES...254
    7.3.1 Some characteristics of land 254
    7.3.2 The establishment of the true principles of humanity....................256
    7.3.3 The change to anti-human patriarchal principles 257
  7.4 THE ORIGIN, DEVELOPMENT AND METHODOLOGIES OF SLAVERY 259
    7.4.1 Exploitation – the common denominator of slavery......................259
    7.4.2 Women were the first 'slaves': Exploitation and its impact on Afrikan women 260
    7.4.3 How exploitation led to oppression...262
    7.4.4 How oppression led to domination 262
    7.4.5 How domination led to humiliation 262
    7.4.6 How humiliation led to alienation..263
  7.5 LINKING EXPLOITATION AND DIVISIVE BARRIERS AMONGST AFRIKAN PEOPLE............264
  7.6 PROPERTY RELATIONS: THE SOURCE OF ALL SYSTEMS OF SLAVERY.........................264
  7.7 SLAVERY AND ANTI-SLAVERY SOCIAL SYSTEMS 265
  7.8 AFRIKA'S EXPERIENCE OF SLAVERY - IN BRIEF 266
  7.9 DEFEATING SLAVERY – A BRIEF NOTE ON THE FUTURE 267
  7.10 THE AFRIKAN PERSONALITY AND ITS HUMANIST IDEOLOGY AND CULTURE 270
  7.11 AFRIKAN PEOPLE WILL ABOLISH SLAVERY FOR EVER..273

Omowale Ru Pert-em-Hru

ACKNOWLEDGMENTS

To the Charles, Peltier, Emmanuel, Daniel, Lewis, Michel, Pascale, Bougyne, Ramey lines and all of our unknown ancestors right back to our origin in Afrika. Without all of you and each of you individually, our present day lineage could not exist; nor could anything that we've produced, including this book. Though I can never repay my debt to you, I can contribute to the recovery of Afrika by passing your gift of life to the next generation in a manner that will make us proud. Thank you for life and much, much more.

I would also like to say a special thank you to the late historian, lawyer and activist Richard Hart. Richard kindly provided me with a copy of his notes, rich with facts, that helped me unearth the real character of one of imperialism's false 'saints'.

Omowale Ru Pert-em-Hru

Preamble I

My Vision for Afrika and her people

Our capacity to create, produce and build as our contribution to a better world for humanity
I want every Afrikan person on earth to be an effective contributor to the technological advance of humanity and the production of ever more effective and efficient tools. What we are going to achieve with our mastery of new technology is beyond anything that we can currently imagine, but some of the indicators of our advance will include:
- The reproduction of ever healthier people symbolised by 100% live women and babies emerging from the birthing process and Afrikan babies born with an average life expectancy in excess of 100 years;
- The production of ever more intelligent/productive people symbolised by:
    - The understanding that Afrika – the richest land in the world – will remain under the exclusive sovereign control of Afrikan people at home and abroad collectively into eternity;
    - Afrikan children's complete mastery of the history/geography of Afrika and the world;

- o Afrikan children's complete mastery of the secrets of quantum physics;
- o Afrikan children's complete mastery of the ability to bring the past and future into the present and work on them to create an optimally better future;
- o Afrikan children's complete mastery of the languages and techniques of efficient and effective communication;
- o Afrikan children's complete mastery of managing our continent and the world for the greater good of humanity and Mother Nature;
- The production of ever higher and better technology i.e. tools in service of and in harmony with the best interests of humanity and Mother Nature, symbolised by an ever cleaner planet, in turn symbolised by the ability to produce and reproduce an abundance of:
  - o The purest and freshest possible air;
  - o The purest and cleanest possible water;
  - o The healthiest and most nutritious foods;
  - o The most robust travel vehicles facilitating the movement of Afrikan people through the universe at speeds faster than the speed of light;
  - o The most efficient and effective long and short distance communication tools;
- By living in a world where:
  - o We fully deploy the creative genius of Afrikan people to produce all that we need (and surplus) so effectively, efficiently and speedily that we create more time for us to respectfully engage with each other, Mother Nature and our ancestors; and
  - o The most advanced technologies flourish in service of Afrikan people as part of greater humanity and Mother Nature.

Driven by our capacity to govern a just society for Afrikan people
I want every Afrikan person on earth to understand that the most effective method for governing our homeland and people at this point in history means:

- Afrika, including her surrounding islands, must be united and governed as one continental-wide super-state, freed from all internal 'national' boarders;
- The super-state must be created by and be under the collective control of all Afrikan people – those at home and those abroad – and predominantly managed by women;
- The land and resources of Afrika must be under the exclusive sovereign control of Afrikan people at home and abroad collectively and used for the benefit of all Afrikan people in the first instance, making us the richest, most powerful people and humble leaders of the world for the greater good of humanity;
- We must develop a military capability sufficient to defend our homeland from any foe;
- Our continental-wide super-nation-state - the most powerful in the world - is constantly ready, willing and able to protect any and all of her children whether based at home or abroad;
- Our continental-wide super-nation-state is a means to a greater end. It is tasked with laying the foundation for a continent and by extension a world so supportive and in tune with the best interests of the people, Mother Nature and our ancestors, where truth, freedom, justice and peace are so inculcated into human existence, that all states become unnecessary, are removed from the world and become relics of history.

Driven by our capacity to build respectful relationships for the achievement of happiness
I want every Afrikan person on earth to understand, adopt and apply in the modern world the principles underpinning the tendency towards healthy relationships found typically in Afrikan village culture. Namely that:
- Human beings are fundamentally humble and respectful of other human beings, Mother Nature and their ancestors;
- Every human being is more important than property, money or profit and therefore an end in their own right, not a means to somebody else's end;
- The benefits to the 'we' are usually, but not always, prioritised over the benefits to the 'me' and when the benefits to the 'me' are given higher priority, that is decided by the 'we'; and

- Whilst all human beings are unique have differing qualities, attributes and abilities, we are all equal in essence;

Driven by a humble and respectful relationship with our environment for the achievement of higher understanding
I want every Afrikan person on earth to understand that:
- Mother Nature is composed of antagonistic opposites held in unison;
- The never ending engagement of opposites is the source of perpetual change in Mother Nature and everything in her;
- Mother Nature was there before us and gave us space within her;
- We are a part of Mother Nature;
- We are absolutely obliged to engage with Mother Nature;
- Spirit is inside Mother Nature;
- Spirituality is the process of connecting with spirit, achievable only through a respectful engagement with Mother Nature;

Agreement/acceptance with/of the above vision will form part of the criteria for membership of Ukomozii. It is to be recited twice daily (first thing in the morning and last thing at night) by all members and their families as a constant ongoing reminder of the future that unites us.

Omowale Ru Pert-em-Hru
19th January 2018

Afrikan People Abolished the 'Slave Trade'

Preamble II

Why Parliament?
We bring the issue of British involvement in slavery to Parliament in order to raise three important questions:

1. **Who abolished the 'slave trade'?**
2. **When, where and why were piracy, human trafficking, the slave trade, slavery and colonialism declared crimes against humanity?**
3. **Why were they not always declared crimes against humanity especially with respect to Afrikan people?**

We specifically seek answers to the first 2 questions from Parliament, its members and the government which controls it.

This booklet also addresses the first of the above questions as a stimulus to the discussion. This initial contribution will focus mainly on issues raised as a result of the first question. A later contribution will place its emphasis on questions 2 and 3.

We are specifically inviting MP's from a range of relevant All Party Parliamentary Committees to be a part of this discussion so that they can: (i) be further informed and encouraged to expose important contradictions in the portrayal of the history of abolition; (ii) raise and discuss these issues in their committees; and (iii) raise them for formal debate in Parliament.

To facilitate the Parliamentary and broader community debate we seek the disclosure of all the records and files: the files on the royal family; colonial files; piracy files; slavery files; slave trade files; military and intelligence files and all files relevant to the questions under discussion.

We seek a rigorous and thorough unearthing of the facts in order to change the narrative for the better. The achievement of the more historically and factually accurate narrative will and must positively impact Britain's educational curriculum from primary school all the way through to university. The story of the hunter is a distortion. It is the stories of the hunter and the hunted, combined with those of relevant third parties that will offer a truer more rounded account of the history.

Access to the requested files should not be limited to academics, but rather be open to any and all members of the public online. This will make a significant contribution to revealing the truth about this critically important aspect of history and facilitate important steps towards the advancement of humanity.

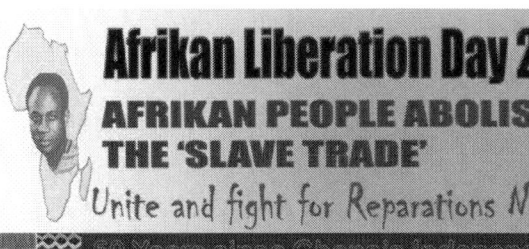

Afrikan People
Had a
History Before
Slavery

Omowale Ru Pert-em-Hru

Chapter 1

1 Afrikan people had a history before slavery

1.1 The context and importance of the enslavement era
1.1.1 Contextualising the enslavement era in Afrikan history

We open this book - *Afrikan People Abolished the 'Slave Trade'* - with a brief reminder that Afrikan people had a history before slavery. The reminder is important because it properly contextualises this very depressing part of our history as a mere moment in the eons of time that Afrikan history spans. Furthermore, there are many outstanding contributions that Afrikan people have made to the advancement of humanity which, along with all other peoples' contributions, ought to be recognised.

If we make the enslavement era our only focus, we are in danger of divorcing Afrikan people from the glorious and in fact dominant elements of our history. Even more damaging is the danger that we could leave Afrikan people and the rest of humanity with the wrongful impression that Afrikan people were never anything but 'slaves'. This would of course be an unmitigated lie. By contrast, a clear understanding of the great historic achievements of Afrikan people, in addition to emphasising the fact that we have achieved great things, makes clear that we are capable of repeating them now and in the future. It lays the foundation for a reclaiming of Afrikan greatness.

1.1.2 The deployment of aspects of Afrikan history

We must nonetheless be mindful that we are not seduced by the greatness of our past into doing nothing to solve our problems in the present. There is also the danger that by focusing on our historic great achievements and ignoring the material fact of our enslavement, we engage in escapism – simply romanticising the past and ignoring the present, not only wretched, but depressing condition.

The enslavement era is a critically important part of Afrikan history precisely because it is there that the lessons of how we got into our current mess lie. As depressing as it may be revisiting it, a full understanding of this part of our history is crucial for all Afrikan people. In order to solve our current problems, we must have a clear analysis of how those problems came about. It is only when we are clear about the root causes, that we can develop an effective strategy for solving them. Afrikan people must therefore take charge of this, as well as other parts of our history. Whilst keeping it in context, we must rewrite and relay it so that it is correctly delivered and use the corrected version to reorient us into plotting our path to liberation.

This essay focuses on keeping the depressing history of enslavement in context, it will:
- Briefly examine the archaeological history surrounding the origins of humanity and the place of Afrikan people within that historical process;
- Remind us of a tiny sample of the ancient, but nonetheless considerable achievements of Afrikan people which have helped to advance humanity;
- Touch on the development of ancient empires in Afrika highlighting the advanced state of these Afrikan cultures;
- Illustrate how Afrikan culture gave rise to modern European high culture; and
- Make the briefest of comparisons between the relative development of Afrikan and European cultures in the era immediately preceding European imperialism's enslavement of Afrikan people.

The essay is merely a superficial scan and under no circumstances should it be regarded or treated as a complete record of Afrikan people's pre-enslavement history.

In the fuller context, this book lays a foundation/starting point for explaining how Europe underdeveloped Afrika. That underdevelopment became entrenched by a prolonged European imperialist assault via the causal chain of slavery, colonialism and neo-colonialism. That 500 year unrelenting attack is at the heart of our current problems. When studying this book we are reminded, not only of how we became enslaved, but what we did to overcome it. It therefore provides a blueprint outlining the essence of what we need to do to overcome our current wretched circumstances.

1.2 The enslavement era in the fullness of Afrikan history
1.2.1 Afrikan people have the longest history of all the human family
The best archaeological evidence that we have tells us that Homo Sapien Sapien (the name for the full human being, distinguished from monkeys) is that humanity emerged in Afrika between 200k and 100k years ago. Between 40k and 20k years ago there was an ice age out of which emerged Europeans. Around 15k years ago Asians came into existence as an admixture of Afrikan people and Europeans. The American Indian is dated back to approximately 10k years ago when humanity crossed the Bering Straits (Diop, 1991, p. 11-23; Van Sertima, 1996, p. 288-307).

The archaeological evidence betrays the fact that two things happened simultaneously in Afrika 200k to 100k years ago: (i) the birth of humanity; and (ii) the birth of Afrikan people – which should not be confused. The other parts of humanity have their own distinctive points of birth. These birth points are different from Afrikan people's and what is more, they underwent one or more categorial conversions, ceasing forever to be Afrikan people and becoming what they are today. They are not Afrikan people and although some may try, they cannot reasonably claim to be. This truth does not in any way undermine their humanity – their late arrival makes them no less human than Afrikan people. They are full human beings in every sense - they are just not Afrikan people. From the above flow a number of other facts:
- Afrikan people were the first human beings;

- Afrikan people are the original human beings from which all other parts of the human family are derived;
- Afrikan people are the mothers and fathers of all other parts of humanity;
- All other parts of the Afrikan family are derived from Afrikan people;
- All other parts of the human family owe their existence to the Afrikan part, just as a child owes its existence to its parents;
- If Afrikan people had not existed, no other part of the human family as we know it today could have existed;
- In the sense that they are all derived from Afrikan people, all other parts of humanity owe, at the very least, a debt of gratitude to Afrikan people; and
- Afrikan people have by far, the longest history in humanity.

These objective facts do not mean that the Afrikan part of humanity is in any way superior to the other branches – humanity is one race and equal - but they do nonetheless highlight the contradiction that the part of the family to which all others are historically and biologically indebted, is arguably the most downtrodden on earth.

Origins and Migrations

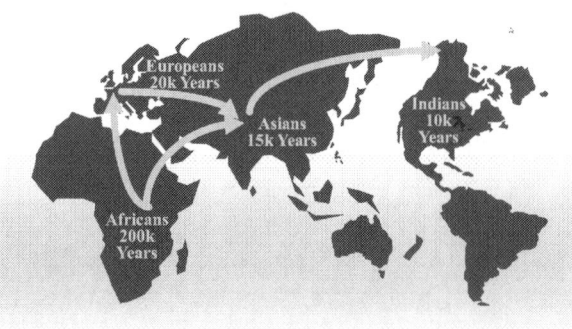

Brother Omowale

Furthermore, part of imperialism's assault against Afrikan people has been an attack on our identity, designed to make us ashamed of, or worse still even hate our Afrikaness. These objective factual observations also operate as a counter-balance allowing Afrikan people and the rest of humanity an opportunity to appreciate what an honour and blessing it is to be a member of the Afrikan part of humanity. It therefore positively impacts the pride and self-esteem of a people whose sense of worth has been severely and cripplingly undermined by European imperialism.

1.2.2 The enslavement era as an historical blip
Afrikan people have been on this earth for between 200k and 100k years. By contrast the enslavement era ran from approximately 1441 when the Portuguese first made contact with Afrikan people through sailing to the Afrikan continent, to 1888 when the Portuguese colonialism in Brazil were the last of the Europeans to formally claim that they had 'abolished' slavery. This makes 449 years a reasonable estimate of the total duration of European imperialism's anti-Afrikan enslavement era. By extrapolation, this amounts to less than one half of one percent (0.05%) of 100k years and less than one quarter of one percent (0.025%) of 200k years.

The enslavement era therefore constitutes something less than the range of a quarter to a half of one percent of Afrikan people's history. It constitutes little more than a drop in the ocean that is Afrikan history. Nonetheless, one of the reasons it remains so fresh in our minds, is that it is recent. Another is that its legacy firmly impacts on the lives of Afrikan people in the present day. Its impact has been so negative and so profound, that Afrikan people are still in the process of recovering from its affects in the contemporary world.

1.3 Afrikan people advanced humanity
1.3.1 Some ancient achievements of Afrikan people
In the 200k years that we have been on earth, Afrikan people have made some outstanding contributions to the advance of humanity. For instance, Afrikan people determined that it took 26k years for the whole universe to make a single rotation (Finch, 1988, p. 176). If we take a generation to equate to approximately 20 years, this means there is something in the order of 1,300 human generations to every rotation of the universe. This is an absolutely remarkable observation even by the standards of modern science. The fact that this knowledge was achieved as early as antiquity makes it all the more astounding.

We can perhaps only imagine the level of scientific discovery this achievement betrays. For instance, what kinds of instruments are needed to observe and measure universal rotation? What kind of record keeping system is necessary for relaying findings from one generation to the next over such a vast period of time? What infrastructure is necessary for verification of findings over such a time span? Even if we are unable to give detailed answers, we can assert that the people capable of making such an observation were highly advanced scientifically. We can further cement the significance of this achievement by observing that up until 500 years ago European culture had not even worked out that the world was round and spinning, let alone the rotation of the solar system, galaxy or universe.

500 or so years of the enslavement era has had a distortive, detrimental and damaging effect on the truthful presentation of Afrikan people's ancient historical achievements. In providing a sample summary Ivan Van Sertima makes the following observation:

> "Five centuries of these falsehoods have been exploded in just 5 years. These years have seen the discovery of Afrikan steel-smelting in Tanzania 1,500-2,000 years ago, an astronomical observatory in Kenya 300 years before Christ, the cultivation of serials and other crops by Afrikan [people] in the Nile Valley 7,000 years before any other civilisation, the domestication of cattle in Kenya 15,000 years ago, the domestic use of fire by Afrikan [people] 1,400,000 (one million four hundred thousand years before its first known use in China) the use of tracyclene by the ancient Afrikan population fourteen centuries ago, an Afrikan glider plane 2,300 years old, a probe by microwave beams of an American radar satellite beneath the sands of the Sahara, revealing cultures 200,000 years old and traces of ancient rivers running from this Afrikan centre. Some of these buried streams seem to be 'ancient connections to the Upper Nile Tributaries,' towards which [Afrikan people] migrated, later peopling Nubia and Egypt." (Van Sertima, 1985, p. 5)

Other examples include the world's oldest known counting system – the Ishango bone. It was excavated by European archaeologists in the Congo i.e. the heart of Afrika and dated 25k years old (Finch, 1998, p. 57). The Ishango site also reveals a relatively advanced Afrikan culture dating back 70k years. Europeans came into being between 40k and 20k years ago and all of the remainder of humanity came after them. It is therefore arguable that Afrikan people developed calculators even before any other part of the human family came into being.

The Afrikan continent is currently being ravaged 'to smithereens' by greedy capitalists out to make a quick buck, but mining is nothing new to Afrika and her people. There is anthropological evidence of systematic metal mining in Swaziland dating back 40k years. Nor is this an isolated case with similar findings in Zimbabwe and Zambia (Finch, 1998, p. 26 & 35)

1.4 Afrikan expansion and dominance over Europe
1.4.1 Afrika's ancient empires
As anti-imperialists we have no great admiration of empires, but for those who do, Afrika had its fair complement too. They included Nubia [East] – founded as Kush in 1,600BCE, it became Nubia in 800BCE; Kemet [North] – unified in 3,100BCE; Ancient Ghana [West] – ran from approximately 700 to 1100CE; Ancient Mali [West] – ran from approximately 800 to 1550CE; Songhai [West] – which ran from approximately 1300 to 1600CE; Borno Kanem [West] – which ran from approximately 700 to 1380CE; Ancient Zimbabwe [South] – which came into being in approximately 1,000CE; and Mutapa [South] – descended from the even more ancient Monomotapa, approximately 1430 to 1760CE (Du Bois, 1996, p. 209; Latif, 1994, p. 92; Finch, 1998, p. 26).

At the very least these empires demonstrate that Afrikan people were moving to larger and larger aggregates of living and organisation. The natural path of this development would obviously have been a united Afrikan continent, but for the unwelcomed disruptive interventions of retarding external cultures.

1.4.2 Afrika's conquests over Europe
Again, as anti-imperialists we take no pride in the conquest and theft of other people's land, but as a matter of mere fact these things happened. We note for instance that **Gourmond** king of Ireland was an Afrikan man (Van Sertima, 1996, p. 14 & 227). **Septimus Severus** the Roman emperor who conquered Britain in 211CE was Afrikan. His disparaging observation of the people that he conquered there was that they were so savage, they weren't even fit to be slaves. He died in Britain as its ruler, remains buries in York and was succeeded by another

Afrikan emperor his son **Caracalla** (Van Sertima, 1996, p. 223; Ben Jochannan, 1988, p. 119).

Other histories of Afrikan conquests of Europe are provided by the Blackamoors, who came from Afrika and are described as being descended from Black skinned Afrikan people (Du Bois, 1996, p. 221). They include **Hannibal** of Carthage (Van Sertima, 1996, p. 190). He roamed around Europe conquering everything in sight, using his Afrikan elephants to clear all obstacles from his path. His elephants, the prototype for modern day tanks, took him all the way up to the Alps. His efforts have the appearance of being something of an extension of the family business. The Afrikan conquest of Spain gave birth to the name Barcelona, the city named after **Hamilcar Barca** – **Hannibal's** father (Van Sertima, 1996, p. 190). We are also reminded of **Gibal Tarik** (Du Bois, 1996, p. 183), the Afrikan general who conquered Spain in the 8th Century. On route he took the island of Gibraltar, which bears his name to this day.

The Blackamoors (Van Sertima, 1996, p. 144-172) had achieved a high level of culture and education which they brought with them to Europe. In Timbuktu, Goa & Jenne they had departments of what some describe as the world's first university, named Sankora, where thousands of students studied law, literature, grammar, geography and surgery (Du Bois, 1996, p. 211). These were of course, long preceded by the halls of learning in Kemet, which were surely nothing less than universities. Regardless, the Afrikan Moors' conquest brought with it Europe's first university in Cordova – to which the origins of classical music can be traced – Yes, Afrikan people gave Europeans classical music!

1.5 The Afrikan root of world cultures
1.5.1 Afrikan culture gave rise to modern European culture
The modern world still marvels at the phenomenal achievement of the Kemetans in building the pyramids – a feat still beyond the capacity of the world's best contemporary scientists. It is less well known that they were preceded by the smaller pyramids of Nubia in modern Sudan (Diop, 1974, p. 158). This is an important part of the evidence demonstrating that civilisation migrated from the centre of Afrika to the North (Ben Jochannan, 1988, p. 474-5). **Nubian Culture gave rise to Kemetic culture.**

Kemet brought many profound contributions to humanity's advancement. The Hippocratic oath, traceable to Kemet betrays a deep profound impact on medical science – so deep, it is still sworn by contemporary doctors in the West (Ben Yochannan, 1984, p. 316). Modern day paper is a development on the Kemetic papris. It follows that reading, writing, books, libraries and all facilities for the cascading of documents owe their existence to Kemetic culture (Ben Yochannan, 1984, p. 356).

Route of Civilisation

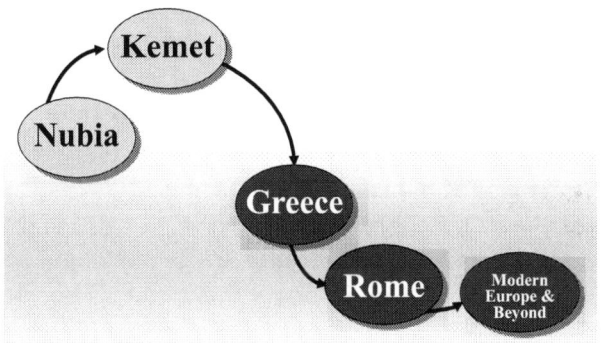

Brother Omowale

Added to this is production of the first calendar, bringing the codification of time (Finch, 1998, p. 188) and the fact that all of the Greek philosophers either directly studied in Kemet or were directly influenced by her:

> "The philosophers and mathematicians were in full agreement. Pythagoras spent no fewer than twenty-one years in Egypt [Kemet]. Aristotle said that 'Egypt [Kemet] was the cradle of mathematics', Eudoxus, Aristotle's teacher and a foremost mathematician of his time, had likewise studied in Egypt [Kemet] before teaching in Greece. Isokrates and Plato were profoundly influenced by Egyptian [Kemetic] philosophy. Euclid, again, learned mathematics in Egypt [Kemet] before applying them elsewhere. And who can be surprised? For the temples and the pyramids of the Nile were not built by guesswork or rule of thumb. They were built by the use of mathematical propositions which the Egyptians [kemetans] had discovered and proven. How otherwise could it have

come about that the difference in length between the shortest base-side of the Great Pyramid of Gizeh (c2,600BC) and the longest side (756.08 inches) is no more than a staggeringly 7.9 inches?" (Van Sertima, 1993, p. 44).

This provides another clue to the developmental route of civilisation. It travelled from Kemet to Greece, giving birth through Greece to Europe's classical high culture. **Kemetic culture gave rise to Greek culture** (James, 1992, p. 1-53)

There is little dispute that the cultural route travelled from Greece to Rome and from there to the rest of Europe through conquest. *Civilisation therefore travelled from the heart of Afrika (Nubia) to the North (Kemet), made a stop in Greece, before moving to Rome and on to the rest of Europe and beyond.* Not only are Afrikan people the mothers and fathers of humanity, but Afrikan civilisation is the mother and father of the other cultures in the world. Of course this includes even those European imperialist cultures that invented modern day anti-Afrikan racism.

1.5.2 Contact between Afrikan and European cultures immediately prior to slavery

European pirates, kidnappers, wicked enslavers and their ideologues made up all kinds of stories alleging a 'sub-human' status for Afrikan people. In part they did this by making up derogatory stories about how Afrikan people lived prior to the enslavement era. These myths can be contrasted with truthful accounts given by other European spies sent to our shores. Their written accounts demonstrate how they marvelled at the Afrikan matrilineal system and the high level of respect shown to women:

> "Their women are of surpassing beauty, and are shown more respect than men. The state of affairs amongst people is indeed extraordinary. Their men show no signs of jealousy whatsoever; no one claims decent from his father, but on the contrary from his mother's brother. A person's heirs are his sister's sons, not his own sons." (Du Bois, 1996, p. 208)

They were in awe of the high moral standards and exemplary sense of justice of Afrikan people:

> "[Afrikan people] possess some admirable qualities. They are seldom unjust, and have a greater abhorrence of injustice than any other people. Their sultan shows no mercy to anyone who is guilty of the least act of it. There is complete security in the country. Neither traveller nor inhabitant in it has anything to fear from robbers or men of violence. They do not confiscate the property of any white man who dies in their country, even if it is uncounted wealth. On the contrary, they give it into the charge of some trustworthy person among the whites, until the rightful heir takes possession of it. " (Du Bois, 1996, p. 209)

On the technological front, they openly admitted that Afrikan people had created techniques far in advance of anything that existed in Europe (Du Bois, 1996, p. 154). On the medical front, Afrikan people in Uganda were also successfully performing caesarean section for the protection of mothers and their unborn babies (Van Sertima, 1996, p. 152-155). Whilst attempts were being made in Europe to do the same, their imitation procedure resulted in the deaths of mother and child. They were merely aping the physical cutting element of the procedure and hadn't understood the need for a sterile environment. This turned the life saving caesarean section, when under their stewardship, into a death sentence.

These marvels occurred at the point in history when Europe was in/emerging from its dark ages 'full of robbers, fetishmen and slaves' (Du Bois, 1996, p. 207). Europe was an unsafe part of the world with a low moral standard. To get a bit more of an idea of the relative development of the two continents at that point, this was happening in Europe, Britain at least, when people were inadvertently tossing pales of their bodily waste onto passersby unfortunate enough to be under their window at the time. Hygiene and even basic cleaniliness appears not to have been Europe's forte.

The above is a very brief traverse through aspects of the pre-enslavement era of Afrikan people's history. It is necessarily shallow as it is designed to give nothing more than a snapshot of certain elements of that history as a counter-balance to this book's concentration on an altogether more depressing era of Afrikan history.

That snapshot is nonetheless sufficient to demonstrate that Afrika was ahead of Europe at the point of their pre-enslavement encounter. At the very least it must be conceded that it was at least on par with Europe and certainly not behind. The picture of Afrika painted by European imperialist enslavers and colonisers issued a pack of lies against Afrikan people. Those lies were specifically designed to character assassinate Afrikan people as a precursor to the greatest grand theft in the history of humanity – the stealing of Afrika and her people. That grand theft comprised what is arguably the worse genocide in the history of humanity i.e. the enslavement and colonisation of Afrika and her people.

References
1. Ben Jochannan. Yousef, (1988), *Africa: The Mother of Western Civilisation*, Black Classic Press
2. Diop. Cheikh Anta, (1974), *The Afrikan Origin of Civilisation: Myth or Reality*, Lawrence Hill Books
3. Diop. Cheikh Anta, (1991), *Civilisation or Barbarism: An Authentic Anthropology*, Lawrence Hill Books
4. Du Bois. William, (1996), *The World and Africa: An inquiry into the part which Africa has played in world history*, International Publishers, New York
5. Finch. Charles, (1988), *The Star of Deep Beginnings: The Genesis of Afrikan Science and Technology*, Khenti Incorporated
6. James. George, (1992), *Stolen Legacy: Greek Philosophy is Stolen Egyptian Philosophy*, Africa World Press
7. Latif. Sultan, (1994), *Slavery: The African American Psychic Trauma*, Latif Communication Group Incorporated
8. Rodney. Walter, (1981), *How Europe Underdeveloped Africa*, Howard University Press
9. Van Sertima. Ivan, (1985), *Blacks in Science: ancient and modern*, Transaction Books
10. Van Sertima. Ivan, (1993), *Egypt Revisited*, Transaction Books
11. Van Sertima. Ivan, (1996), *African Presence in Early Europe*, Transaction Publishers

The Horrors Of Slavery

Omowale Ru Pert-em-Hru

Chapter 2

2 The Horrors of Slavery

2.1 Repairing imperialism's anti-Afrikan damage
2.1.1 Anti-Afrikan Terrorism and Afrikan resistance

This document is intended to give the reader a snapshot of some of the horrific tortures that enslaved Afrikan people were subjected to during one of the most critical phases of the *Maangamizi* - imperialism's anti-Afrikan chattel enslavement era. Almost all of the examples provided are events that actually occurred; they have been compiled from a range of historical sources. In addition, there is also an element of reconstructing events based on facts extrapolated from both contemporary and historical sources. Together these examples paint a gruesome picture of overt terrorist activity that was waged and continues to be waged against Afrikan people.

Anti-Afrikan terrorism was a constant feature of the chattel enslavement era. It was exacted against Afrikan people at home in Afrika where the kidnapping phase took place and on the high seas during the compulsory deportation phase. However, the greater part of the terrorism took place on the forced labour camps in the Americas, where often unspeakable cruelties were relentlessly inflicted for hundreds of years. Examples of the torture employed are drawn from each of these phases in order to highlight the calculated nature of the acts of wickedness perpetrated against innocent Afrikan people.

Afrikan people did not simply cower and submit to imperialism's campaign of evil. Even though they were operating against overwhelming odds they resisted - every step of the way. Part of their resistance included acts of great heroism in the face of the most brutal brand of anti-Afrikan terrorism. Examples are included to illustrate the strength of character of Afrikan people in the face of adversity.

2.1.2 Economics drove slavery and slavery drove racism

Imperialism's system of chattel slavery terrorism was motivated by economic factors rather than by the rancid brand of anti-Afrikan racism which followed in its wake. European imperialism first tried to enslave the American Indians. This led to a process of genocide that came close to wiping them out (Ferguson, 1999, p. 20). Then European 'indentured servants' were targeted (Honychurch, 1995a, p. 66), but proved too weak and few in number to satisfy demand. It was only afterwards they turned to the systematic theft and compulsory deportation of Afrikan people.

The violent ill-treatment of enslaved people is to enforce their conformity. Enslaved people are subjected to wicked acts of terror in order to crush their resistance. In the case of European imperialist agents in the Caribbean, their first priority was ensuring their own survival since they were massively outnumbered. However, the level of anti-Afrikan terrorism went beyond brutality, seeking to actually dehumanise Afrikan people.

European imperialism's profit motive does not mean slavery was a matter of 'pure' economics devoid of other cultural factors such racism. Whilst it was economically driven in the first instance, racism was inextricably inculcated into the system. It led to the lie that Afrikan people were sub-human, which in turn fostered an environment where anti-Afrikan racism flourished. Racism became the mechanism used by European imperialism to justify the unprecedented level of terroristic evil perpetrated against Afrikan people.

2.1.3 Truth for justice: The horrors must be revealed

The gross barbarism of imperialism's chattel enslavement of Afrikan people makes for uncomfortable reading. Some of the murders, mutilations and other horrific forms of torture were so disgusting that they make it difficult to broach the subject even today. This raises the question of whether the terrorism of the *Maangamizi* should be highlighted to the general public. These grotesque horrors happened a long time ago, is it counterproductive to bring them up now? The individuals responsible are long since dead. Can a new generation with apparently 'nothing to do with it' to be asked to take responsibility?

We are dealing with systems which are distinct from and beyond the level of individuals. For instance, the British army and navy both played and continues to play a direct role in the terroristic atrocities of the *Maangamizi*; Britain's parliament planned and continues to plan the whole thing – including the atrocities and as the 'sovereign' legislative body sanctions the alleged 'legality' of slavery; Britain's monarchy officially sanctioned and profited from the whole sordid affair and this still continues today; many of British capitalism's trans-national businesses such as Tate & Lyle, Lloyds of London and Barclay's Bank benefited and continue to profit from the proceeds gained directly from the blood of Afrikan people right up to the present day. They are all culpable for unquestioningly accepting the profits from the ongoing *Maangamizi* which is still costing the lives of millions of Afrikan people. These entities were all there participating in chattel slavery terrorism and its associated horrors and they are all here right now. They must make proper recompense.

Our ancestors were forced to go through a catalogue of gruesome tortures in the *Maangamizi*. The least we can now do to honour them is remember and talk about the terrorism that happened. Furthermore, it is imperative that Afrikan people and others are woken up to the scale of the terroristic crimes against humanity inflicted against us. It is only possible to do this by remembering and talking about what happened, even the gruesome details.

Slavery has not ended; instead it has transformed, firstly into colonialism and now neo-colonialism, so its terrorism and associated problems remain. For instance, the wealth stolen from Afrikan people is still in the hands of the thieves' descendents – through their institutions. If we want justice for our ancestors, ourselves and our descendents we must expose the terrors and horrors as part of a process of uncovering the truth.

It is imperialism that must bow its head in shame for treating a part of humanity in such a despicable and disgusting manner. Far from being a source of shame or disgrace for Afrikan people, the horrors represent the ultimate confirmation that Afrikan people vigorously resisted enslavement. Our resistance was so profound, that it succeeded in overturning both chattel and colonial enslavement. Our resistance will also defeat neo-colonialism, which **Kwame Nkrumah** reminded us is the last stage of imperialism (Nkrumah, 1974, p. xvi); and when that happens, our just reparations will follow as a matter of course.

2.1.4 The scam 'legality' of slavery
Britain's racist Prime Minister Anthony 'Liar Blair' refuses to apologise on behalf of British imperialism for its part in the *Maangamizi* – an obvious crime against humanity. Instead he has been propagating the ludicrous idea that 'slavery' was legal at the time. More recently he made the 'concession' that if 'slavery' happened now it would be a crime against humanity.

Anybody who argues that slavery was legal at the time or that Afrikan people were legitimately 'property' or that it was legitimate for Afrikan people to be disqualified from testifying in court is automatically racist. These ideas rest on the false notion that Afrikan people were less than human - a racist lie having no basis in reality. It follows that the very act of advocating this bogus idea is proof conclusive of racism in operation.

Reducing our ancestors to 'property' was a pretext for dehumanisation; dehumanisation was a pretext for treating Afrikan people in the most savage, brutal and demeaning ways. When an Afrikan person was murdered by a European, as frequently happened, this was not treated as a crime. Furthermore, Afrikan people were not permitted healthcare, education, decent housing or even to testify in court.

The false notion that slavery (and presumably all the actions contained within it) was legal, rests on the lie that Afrikan people were sub-human. Once that argument is dismissed, the 'legal' notion falls flat on its face. Homo Sapien Sapien, which scientists generally agree constitutes the full human being, emerged in Afrika 150,000 years ago

(Diop, 1991, p. 11). This fact makes Afrika the birth place of humanity and Afrikan people the mothers and fathers of humanity. Since the emergence of Homo Sapien Sapien, there has never been a time when Afrikan people, or any other people on the planet, were not human. If imperialism's law makes claims to the contrary, then it is imperialism's law that is wrong.

The dilemma facing imperialism is that its law must either adjust to conform to reality or it must be swept away. The idea that reality must adjust itself to conform to imperialism's laws is completely untenable. The laws of Afrikan people, the American Indians and Aboriginal people have never made the fundamental error of classifying human beings as sub-human. They are obviously morally superior to imperialism's laws in this respect and therefore provide the basis for a more appropriate framework for the replacement of the corrupt national and international legal systems which imperialism has imposed on the world.

The British public is ignorant about the true horrors of slavery. Imperialism has a vested interest in concealing the truth about its role and purpose in inflicting chattel slavery terrorism onto Afrikan people. The true horrors are deliberately concealed, sanitised and even trivialised. To help overcome widespread ignorance, it is vital that the full horrors of slavery are thoroughly exposed to all. With the grotesque truth exposed, the lies will be swept aside by a conscious public.

2.2 Terrorism: kidnapping Afrikan people in Afrika
2.2.1 Avoiding cannibals

The concept of chattel slavery was so alien to Afrikan people that it did not necessarily occur to them that they were being hunted and captured for enslavement. In Afrika hunting was not a practice ordinarily carried out for fun or financial profit, it was primarily a method for feeding the community. Since the purpose of hunting was to procure food, there were those, such as **Olaudah Equiano** who assumed that the Europeans hunters of Afrikan people were cannibals with a particular taste for Afrikan flesh (Shepard, 2000, p. 825). Afrikan people were therefore living in a constant state of terror. They feared that being captured was the first step in a trail that would end with them being cooked in the pots and digested in the stomachs of cannibalistic Europeans. The objective of many terrified Afrikan people was to avoid being eaten.

2.2.2 The disorientation of Afrikan people
The objective of imperialism operating through its fleet of pirates, was to kidnap as many Afrikan people as possible. Imperialism specifically employed divide and rule tactics designed to compel Afrikan nations to supply fellow Afrikan people for compulsory deportation into enslavement. It created proxy states which were used to decrease the region's stability by starting wars and terrorising all of the Afrikan nations around. It further stimulated wars by using rumours, trickery and fear to pit Afrikan nations against each other. An important part of imperialism's divide and rule strategy was to flood Afrikan nations with guns and alcohol. To stimulate the kidnapping process, the imperialists ensured that guns could only be bought if Afrikan people were used as currency (Fryer, 1989, p. 10).

This strategy proved to be a great catastrophe for Afrika. British imperialism alone dumped 394,000 guns in West Afrika annually as a stimulus to inter and intra-tribal war and the general political destabilisation of the region (Justice, 2005, p. 142). Another 50,000 guns were dumped in the Loango-Congo area every year (Justice, 2005, p. 143). Other European imperialist nations assisted Britain in this process. For instance, in the case of the Gold Coast, guns were supplied to the Ashante by the Dutch, while the British armed their southern cousins the Fante (Justice, 2005, p. 127). Imperialism's destabilising processes were so devastating that they effectively ended up disempowering and destroying all of the Afrikan nations in the affected regions.

In that kind of dog eat dog environment, someone who was your friend whilst sober, could be your enemy when seeking their next 'fix' to quench their alcoholic addiction. Many other pirates i.e. prospective kidnappers were armed, dangerous and motivated by greed, wars and misguided notions of self-preservation. They would go to almost any length to kidnap Afrikan people. A trip to the river to drink water or to bathe could end with abduction. Afrikan people were left with no sense of safety, no sense of security; family and friends who were there one minute could be absent the next, presumed stolen, dead or even eaten. Afrikan nations, communities and relationships were destroyed; mothers were separated from their children and visa versa.

2.2.3 The treatment of kidnapped Afrikan people
Those Afrikan people who were unfortunate enough to be caught were at the beginning of an ordeal that was worse than anything they could imagine. The kidnappers totally lacked mercy:

> "Many of the [kidnapped Afrikan people] would waste away, only to be thrown out to the edge of town by the [kidnappers] and left to die. The vultures [and] other animals would begin eating them while they were still alive. In some cases, the [kidnapper], finding no potential money in them, would shoot them or club them to death in full site of other captives. This was a warning to the healthier captives: If you get sick or fake it, your fate is death." (Anderson, 1995, p. 64).

Kidnapped Afrikan people were taken to any of a number of dungeons, forts, castles and baracoons on the coast that were used as concentration camps prior to deportation. Between the 16th and 19th centuries, there were 48 major concentration camps on the west coast of Afrika (Anderson, 1995, p. 67). Inside these structures, Afrikan people were packed like sardines in highly cramped conditions. There was no sanitation, which meant that the kidnapped Afrikan people were left chained in a rank mixture of human waste. In addition to the squalor, the physical discomfort in the concentration camps was horrendous. In the worse cases the ceilings were only three to four feet (ninety to one hundred and twenty centimetres) high, making it impossible for either adults or children to stand up properly (Anderson, 1995, p. 61).

The human carnage caused by these conditions is beyond calculation:

> "Over the centuries ... hundreds of thousands of [kidnapped Afrikan people] died while they were languishing in dungeons and baracoons waiting for their death ship to arrive." (Anderson, 1995, p. 65).

The conditions were so awful that some of the kidnapped Afrikan people committed suicide in a drastic attempt to escape their ordeal. The kidnappers were so cruel and sadistic that they responded by publicly decapitating the dead bodies as a deterrent to others that might harbour similar ideas (Breaking the silence).

It is for Anthony 'the liar' Blair, the British government and their fellow apologists for slavery to explain when where, how and in whose jurisdiction: piracy, kidnapping, false imprisonment, compulsory deportation, torture, murder, the destruction of the Afrikan family and the destabilisation of Afrikan governments became legal activities.

2.3 The seaboard journey: a reconstruction
2.3.1 Conditions for kidnapped Afrikan people

Despite the way things are sometimes made to appear, Afrikan people were reluctant to sell their sisters and brothers into enslavement. This was one of the factors that contributed to the extremely long journey times suffered by those people unfortunate enough to be captured. For instance, the human trafficking ship *The Afrikan Queen* was left waiting on the coast of what is currently called Nigeria for 7 to 8 months (Portcities Bristol). This was how long it took before the captain was able to fill its hull with a sufficient number of kidnapped Afrikan people to make the journey 'viable'. Another important factor affecting the duration of the journey was that ships often spent several weeks stopping at different ports along the Afrikan coast. This was done in order to pack their hulls with kidnapped Afrikan people before embarking on the main journey across the Atlantic (Honychurch, 1995, p. 87). In addition, the journey from Afrika to the Americas took from 6 weeks to 3 months (Portcities Bristol) and sometimes even longer.

This meant that the first Afrikan people to be Kidnapped and imprisoned in the concentration camps and human trafficking ships could be held captive in chains for up to a year. They would have been locked up in total darkness for most of that period. By the time the ship was full, they would have been packed by their hundreds in tightly confined spaces. They:

> "... were chained in compartments only three feet three inches high and sometimes no more than eighteen inches to prevent their sitting erect. Forced to lie spoon fashion to increase carrying capacity and prevent any defiance, the [kidnapped Afrikan people] were often rubbed raw by rolling ships ..." (Karenga, 1993, p. 137).

The result was that:

> "Each [enslaved Afrikan person] had less room than a man in a coffin." (Williams, 1997, p. 35). To make matters even worse: "It was normal for the captain to pack more [kidnapped Afrikan people] than the ship was registered for." (Anderson, 1995, p. 94).

Clearly, there was no possibility of a comfortable journey for the human beings subjected to the perilous conditions below deck.

Profits were imperialism's motivating force and in order to maximise them, all moral standards were pushed aside leaving unrestrained cruelty and general evil to reign supreme. The ships' captains were fully aware from the outset that a proportion of the imprisoned Afrikan people were bound to die. Instead of improving the inhumane conditions to stave off these expected deaths, they responded by cramming extra people on board to ensure that they had a relatively full load at the end of the journey. Armet Francis highlighted the rate of deaths on what were in effect floating dungeons come graveyards. The disregard for human life was such that:

> "Probably every [enslaved Afrikan person] imported represented on the average, five corpses in Afrika or on the high seas." (Anderson, 1995, p. 2).

Ironically, if the kidnappers had demonstrated just a little compassion, the majority of these cruel deaths could have been prevented.

Shipping conditions that were not fit for animals contributed to the alarmingly high death rate. On top of that culture of violence, brutality and wickedness the kidnapping process meant that captured Afrikan people suffered cuts, bruises, wounds and injuries of the most hideous kinds. Inevitably, the putrid mixtures of blood, puss and exposed flesh created a deadly environment - where disease and infections flourished. Added to this was a toxic cocktail of other bodily fluids: the obvious sweat in the constant heat; excretion mounting at a rate of hundreds of loads a day; vomit brought about by the vile atmosphere; the exposed monthly cycles, broken waters, aborted foetuses, still born babies and afterbirths of Afrikan women totally stripped of their dignity often through rape; snot from the noses and wax from the ears of human beings denied all opportunities to clean and relieve themselves in privacy; even dandruff from the hair must have mixed with the human sludge; their urine may have provided a sense of relief by washing some of the sewerage mixture away, but any relief was soon dampened by the stench that it added to the already rancid atmosphere. The urine compounded the environment of misery by showering and drenching their sisters and brothers as it sprinkled down to the lower decks. Perhaps the symbol of rock bottom was the addition of rat faeces and their other deposits to the grotesque mixture, whilst they feasted on the chained, defenceless Afrikan prisoners as read meals.

With hands and feet in chains, there was nothing to prevent flies and maggots, lice, flees, ringworm, insects and other larvae setting up home in the noses, ears and open wounds of the kidnapped Afrikan people. With their noses blocked, their last ditch attempts at breathing in order to survive meant that they had to open their mouths – an invitation to those same creatures to set up home in there also. Instinctively, they would clear their airways by spitting the intrusive vermin from their mouths as a last line of defence. Their spit had nowhere else to go other than on to their chained sisters and brothers.

The unbearable smell coupled with the total lack of ventilation added to the body count. Innocent Afrikan people died as a direct result of the cruelty of this feature of the human trafficking process. The captain of one human trafficking ship admitted that poor ventilation led to a:

> "... loss of one-fourth of those valuable [kidnapped Afrikan people] in the long passage from Afrika to the French plantations ..." (Anderson, 1995, p. 99).

Some of those that survived the foul air died by drowning or dysentery as the vile, poisonous mixtures of bodily fluid formed a shallow lake around them. Their decomposing bodies, still chained to their live compatriots, added to the deadly mixture of human waste chemicals whilst further perpetuating a vicious cycle of deadly contagious diseases.

In modern British hospitals all materials contaminated with bodily fluids are incinerated as part of a standard health and safety code designed for the preservation of good hygiene. Also in prisons the practice of 'slopping out' where prisoners were required to empty their pails full of human waste each morning, was banned because it was too foul. These modern examples provide a yardstick against which to measure the quality of hygiene endured by the kidnapped Afrikan people who were trying to exist in an environment awash with ever mounting levels of contaminated human waste. This totally disgusting environment was their bedroom, which obviously meant that it was impossible for them to get any meaningful amounts of sleep; they were therefore weakened by insomnia. If sleeping was a problem then it was only surpassed by the fact that this most grotesque of environments was also their dining room.

Under these unbelievably horrifying and nasty conditions, it is understandable that many of the kidnapped Afrikan people decided to abstain from eating. They obviously reasoned that a slow gruesome death through starvation was preferable to eating food 'seasoned' with a mixture of vile human bodily fluids. Reality was worse for them than any nightmare; kidnapped Afrikan people found that they were deprived even of the option of this wickedly slow death. Instead:

> "... in 1674, a captain of the ironically named *Black Joke* flogged to death a one-year-old child for refusing food. Its mother was forced to throw the corpse overboard." (Dennis, 1988, p. 16).

Those that escaped with their lives did not necessarily fare much better, it was standard practice to break the teeth of those who refused to eat in order to force feed them (Anderson, 1995, p. 3).

Even those kidnapped Afrikan people who survived all of these hideous ordeals could find their slender hold in life extinguished at the whim of the ship's captain. For instance, on 29th November 1791, 44 kidnapped Afrikan people were thrown into the sea from the human trafficking ship *The Zong*; the next day 42 more were murdered in the same way; this was followed the next day by 26 more murders carried out in the same manner. The Afrikan witnesses on deck were so petrified by the thought of their own impending murders that 10 of them took their lives into their own hands and jumped overboard. One person actually survived but the 9 others committed suicide to prevent themselves from being murdered. These were just some of the 131 innocent Afrikan people relentlessly slaughtered like animals (Walwin, 1993, p. 17). Ironically, this act of merciless genocide was carried out because, Captain Luke Collingwood's shipping:

> "... insurance covered death by drowning, but not from starvation" (Anderson, 1995, p. 100).

2.3.2 The violation of Afrikan women

Some of the women were spared the indignity and sheer misery of being bound and chained in the stinking cocktail of human swill below deck. They were 'fortunate' enough to be held on deck in the fresh air, kept clean, sometimes not even chained and allowed to 'exercise'. Theirs would have been an altogether more pleasant experience but for the fact that their 'exercise' included being rape fodder for their sexually depraved kidnappers. From the point of view of the kidnappers, the rape experience was 'enhanced' when the defenceless Afrikan women and girls were clean, fresh and agile.

It was these women's misfortune to be thrown down onto their backs often on the open on deck, pinned down with several men to a limb, if need be, and then mercilessly gang raped at the whim of their misogynistic, racist abusers. The raping of pregnant women was a particular speciality because it ensured that the rapist would not be burdened with an 'unwanted' child (Walwin, 1993, p. 218). Many Afrikan women died as a result of their injuries. Those that did not die physically, died emotionally with some even committing suicide (Anderson, 1995, p. 52, 68 & 122).

Afrikan women who dared to defend their honour were subjected to the most heinous forms of punishment. A fifteen year old Afrikan virgin who refused to be violated was hoisted up-side-down by her ankle, stripped naked, lashed to submission with a whip and then raped on top (Howarth, 1773, p. 456). This represented only the lighter end of the punishment regime. As unbelievable as it may seem, even more horrifyingly torturous ordeals awaited those Afrikan women that fearlessly fought against the sexually perverted molestations of their European kidnappers and captors. Afrikan warrior women who defended themselves to the point of injuring or maiming their would-be rapists were subjected to one of the most sadistic practices ever employed against human beings.

The public stripping and gang raping of the Afrikan warrior woman who defended their virtue was the crew's foreplay. It was followed by her gruesome public mutilation which included hanging her by a hook through her mouth (Anderson, 1995, p. 113). An essential ingredient in the masochistic mutilation process was the hook itself. It was brought to notoriety amongst the modern public by the fictitious captain Hook of Peter Pan fame. Its real purpose was to securely hold the sails of ships so that they could be propelled securely and speedily during heavy winds. The hook was razor sharp at its point and being made of metal, it was incredibly strong.

The torture required that the razor sharp point of the hook be rammed into the upper pallet of the Afrikan woman's mouth and wedged securely so that its sharp point protruded through the bridge of her nose or out of her eye socket, with eyeball impaled. The most effective way of minimising the Afrikan woman's screams was to ensure that the hook was first jammed through her tongue, sealing it firmly and tightly to her upper pallet. To do this with any precision, it was necessary to break the lower jaw in order to make enough space for the operation.

Obviously, no human being would sit patiently for this level of mutilation to be exacted upon them. They would, no doubt have kept their mouths firmly shut, bit anyone that tried to prize it open and generally fought to defend themselves. They had to be beaten to the point where they were unable to put up any resistance; until their consciousness had been temporarily impaired and their mouths fell open limp and ready for the obtrusive procedure. With the gory incision complete, the other Afrikan people below deck could be brought up to witness the performance. The muted Afrikan woman unable to utter, speak, shout or scream could now be hoisted up by the hook in her mouth and suspended in mid-air. All of this took place in full view of traumatised Afrikan children, women and men; they were being taught the new value of Afrikan life through the debasement of Afrikan womanhood.

Still their collective ordeal was nowhere near its climax. The terrified Afrikan woman together with the reluctant Afrikan audience would then be put through the ripping apart of her body. Her orifices would be sliced open with sharp implements; this was a warning and a lesson to the other women about the consequences of impeding their predators' sexual abuses and perverted fantasies. It was also entertainment for the crew. The Afrikan woman would be mercilessly disembowelled leaving her belly sliced wide open for all to see. If she was pregnant, her child's foetus would be cut out and left dangling by their umbilical cord. If she was not, her intestines would be left dangling on display instead. An important part of the disembowelling process was the need to ensure that she did not die immediately. It was vital that she suffered intensely, but she must be kept alive for as long as possible.

Next was shooting practice, an opportunity for the 'sailors' to practice their marksmanship using the suspended Afrikan woman and her foetus as their targets. She would first be shot in the arms and legs only; to ensure that she suffered, but did not die immediately. Her immediate death would bring a premature end to the entertainment and lessen the impact on the mesmerised Afrikan people on deck. Long ago she would have begged for death, but for the fact that her mouth and tongue were locked together to silence her screams. Her ordeal would end with the order to shoot to kill; an order which 'ideally' was given before she bled to death. This marked the end of the sailor's entertainment and the beginning of the kidnapped Afrikan people's full realisation of the kind of existence they could expect in future.

No woman that valued life or feared the most painfully grotesque and humiliating forms of torture would dare resist the future 'advances' of any kidnapper, no matter how detestable he may be. Afrikan women were being programmed through this and similar tortures to submit to the unrestrained sexual fantasies of their depraved kidnappers. The most traumatised of these women were now trained to rush to give up, to any European man that 'requested' it, the most private and precious parts of their being.

This calibre of punishment was not reserved for Afrikan women only. Though not on the same scale, Afrikan men and boys were similarly raped. They also underwent similar anti-human punishments. However, because of their inability to produce foetuses that could be cut from the bellies, their genitals were mercilessly severed from their bodies during the hook hanging torture (Anderson, 1995, p. 117). Public castrations and similar acts of wickedness were conducted in full view of Afrikan children and were used as a key tactic for quelling future rebellions and keeping 'order'. The underlying message of this unlawful orgy of evil torturous persecution was resoundingly clear, kidnapped Afrikan people must not resist their enslavement.

2.3.3 Punishing resistance on board

It was the most oppressed group i.e. Afrikan women, that led the resistance against imperialism's seaboard atrocities. In between the episodes of rape that they were forced to endure, they organised to liberate their children, their brothers and themselves. For instance in 1797 on the human trafficking ship *The Thomas,* some of the Afrikan women on deck noticed that the musket chest was left unlocked. They managed to capture some guns, overpowered the crew, released their sisters and brothers below deck and took charge of the ship (Beckles, 1993, p. 37).

According to one historian a total of:

> "382 [seaboard] revolts have been recorded ..." (Breaking the silence).

Many ships were commandeered by the kidnapped Afrikan people in their bids to liberate themselves from their obscenely cruel bondage. The takeovers had varying degrees of success: in some cases such as *The Marlborough* in 1752 (Martin, 1999, p. 79) they simply turned the ship around and sailed back to Afrika; Others such as *The Neptunius* in 1795 were blown out of the water by British warships as they attempted to return to Afrika (Breaking the silence); in other cases they were eventually overpowered by imperialists' warships and sold into slavery as happened with *The Thomas* (Beckles, 1993, p. 37); or they were released after court cases as was the fate of Sengeh Pieh and the other Afrikan people who overpowered the crew on *The Amistad* in 1839 (Anderson, 1995, p. 86).

Seaboard rebellions were acts of extreme bravery on the part of kidnapped Afrikan people. The odds were completely stacked against them. Furthermore, there was an absolute guarantee of the gravest of consequences for Afrikan people involved if the rebellions did not succeed. The punishments were often continued until the kidnapped Afrikan people were unable even:

> "... to groan under the misery." (Walwin, 1993, p. 234).

They included:

> "Sexual assaults, cuffs, blows, thorough beatings ... in addition to the formal institutional violence." (Walwin, 1993, p. 236).

On top of this there were:

> "... whippings, hoistings by the thumbs [and] mutilations ..." (Martin, 1999, p. 81).

Afrikan people fighting for their freedom were subjected to: being made to eat the organs of dead kidnappers as happened on *The Rupert* in 1721 (Walwin, 1993, p. 236); being made to eat the dead bodies of their own sisters and brothers (James, 1963, p. 9); the castrations of Afrikan men (Anderson, 1995, p. 117); the chopping off of their limbs over a period of days (Breaking the silence); having their hands chopped off and bleeding to death (Breaking the silence); the cutting out of pregnant Afrikan women's foetuses (Anderson, 1995, p. 117).

There were also a variety of forms of hideous execution including: being shot dead (Walwin, 1993, p. 235); being thrown overboard to drown or be eaten by sharks as happened in the case of *The Sally* in 1765 (Breaking the silence; Anderson, 1995, p. 114; Walwin, 1993, p. 40 & 58); being disembowelled (Anderson, 1995, p. 113); being hung by the feet and whipped to death (Breaking the silence); being subjected to hook hangings (Anderson, 1995, p. 117); being beheaded sometimes before death but also after (Breaking the silence); and having cannons fired on them whilst on deck (Breaking the silence).

It is because Afrikan people constantly and courageously resisted the imposed kidnapping, deportation and enslavement process that this array of gruesome inhumane tortures were devised and inflicted upon them. It was typical for these unbelievably wicked torturous punishments to be carried out in front of other kidnapped Afrikan people. This was done deliberately to deter the others from exercising their legitimate right to fight for their freedom. The morally bankrupt punishments continue to the present day with deaths in custody being the current equivalent. The European murders of Afrikan people in Britain's state institutions invariably go unpunished – just as their ancestors and counterparts were left unpunished during slavery. All that has happened is the oppression, together with the inevitable resistance that it generates, has changed form. Afrikan people have never stopped fighting for justice and will never stop so long as the objectives of freedom and justice have not been achieved.

2.4 Anti-Afrikan genocide in the Americas
2.4.1 Terrorism on the forced labour camps: The killing fields

Matters did not improve for Afrikan people following their arrival in the Caribbean and other parts of the Americas. Those Afrikan people that survived were sold, branded with a hot iron, held prisoner, exploited, repeatedly whipped as standard and continuously and mercilessly oppressed on the forced labour camps. They were made to work from 5am until 11pm on a daily basis – a working day of 18 hours (James. 1963. p. 10). The sheer relentless brutality of life in these forced labour camps killed Afrikan people off fast. The wicked enslavers deliberately and mercilessly carried out a policy of working enslaved Afrikan people to death. They continuously brought in new 'supplies' of Afrikan people to replace the murder victims rather than attempt to develop them as a long or medium term skilled labour force (James, 1963, p. 14).

This level of calculated inhumane brutality meant that once Afrikan people had landed in the Caribbean, they did not have long to live. For instance, in Haiti, the average life span for newly arrived Afrikan people was 7 years (Carruthers, 1985, p. 24). In Barbados there was an expectation that 1 in 3 or 33% of Afrikan people enslaved on the island would die within 3 years (Beckles, 1993, p.19). During the enslavement period as a whole, Jamaica suffered a net loss of over 600,000 Afrikan people out of a total of 1 million; 200,000 Afrikan people were re-exported, with 400,000 apparently remaining on the island. Given that the net number of kidnapped Afrikan people remaining on the island amounted to 800,000, the extrapolated population figures suggest a premature death rate amongst Afrikan people in Jamaica of 1 in 2 or 50% (Hart, 1998, p. 23). This rate must also take into consideration the fact that the lives of all enslaved Afrikan people were already automatically shortened by the fact of their enslavement. These were therefore premature deaths against a background of the already shortened life expectancy of Afrikan people enslaved on the island.

The following horrors represent a brief summary of the grotesque variety of tortures that awaited the newly arrived kidnapped Afrikan people. They give a clear indication of why life expectancy was so short on the forced labour camps. Enslaved Afrikan people were subjected to a range of hideous tortures, including:

> "... irons on the hands and feet, blocks of wood that the [enslaved Afrikan people] had to drag behind wherever they went, the tin-plate mask designed to prevent the [enslaved Afrikan people] eating the sugar cane, the iron collar. Whipping was interrupted in order to pass a piece of hot wood on the buttocks of the victim; salt, pepper, citron, cinders, aloes and hot ashes were poured on the bleeding wounds. Mutilations were common, limbs, ears and sometimes even the private parts, to deprive them of the pleasures which they could indulge in without expense. Their masters poured burning wax on their arms and hands and shoulders, emptied the boiling sugar cane over their heads, burned them alive, roasted them on slow fires, filled them with gunpowder and blew them up with a match; buried them up to the neck and smeared their heads with sugar that the flies might devour them; fastened them near to nests of ants or wasps; made them eat their excrement, drink their urine, and lick the saliva of other [enslaved Afrikan people]. One colonist was known in moments of anger to throw himself on [enslaved Afrikan people] and stick his teeth into their flesh ... all the evidence shows that these bestial practices were normal features of [the enslaved Afrikan person's] life." (James, 1963, p. 12/13).

Sadistic tortures of all kinds were dreamt up and ruthlessly carried out against Afrikan people. For instance, the blowing up of an enslaved Afrikan person was such a regular way of committing cold blooded murder that it had its own name:

"to burn a little powder in the arse of a [n****r]" (James, 1963, p. 13).

The process would have required that the Afrikan person was first stripped naked and this was likely to have been followed by a severe beating. The other Afrikan people: children, women and men on the forced labour camp would have been specifically rounded up and compelled to view the staged spectacle of sordid humiliating terrorism.

The enslaved Afrikan person would have been beaten to a pulp and then bound or even chained. A favoured method of brutalisation involved tying the enslaved Afrikan person with a piece of wood passing behind their knees whilst simultaneously passing in front of their elbows. This would leave the Afrikan person clamped into a ball like shape with their back passage protruding.

At this point gun powder would have been mercilessly rammed into the back passage of the Afrikan person who was about to be murdered. If the Afrikan victim was lucky the instrument used to carry out the mutilation would have been an old style metal musket loader. This was designed for ramming gun powder into the barrel of early style single shot rifles as part of the reloading process. If a musket loader was not available, then a piece of metal or a sufficiently durable piece of wood could be used instead. Regardless of which particular torture tool was used, the pain for the Afrikan person being mutilated would have been indescribable. The gunpowder phase of the torture would have been completed with the ramming of the gunpowder fuse into the Afrikan person's back passage using one of the same devices. In order to affect maximum humiliation, the enslaved Afrikan person about to be murdered would have been left with the fuse protruding from their back passage in a manner resembling the way in which the tail would protrude from an animal.

The bounding and savage mutilation of the enslaved Afrikan person meant that there was no prospect of them running away or removing the gun powder. There was therefore no reason why the Afrikan person should be blown up immediately, so they could be left for a few hours, or even over night to contemplate their doom. There was no need to feed them because they were going to die anyway. A warning speech would have been made to deter other Afrikan people from resisting their enslavement, before the fuse was lit. The Afrikan people looking on would no doubt have been made to stand close enough to the explosion to ensure that bits of the disintegrated blood, flesh and other gory remains of their murdered sister or brother splashed onto them.

There is no history of even animals being killed in this way. It certainly is not necessary to publicly sexually mutilate and humiliate an already disempowered and wholly defenceless person before blowing them up - in order to murder them. The manner in which these executions were carried out meant that there was something much deeper than mere punishment going on. This calibre of ill-treatment implies a level of hatred which surpassed the level of oppression necessary for economic gain. It follows that part of the object of the unfettered cruelty being exercised was the evil racist agenda of attempting to dehumanise Afrikan people. This wicked attempt to dehumanisation was just an element on the process of devaluing the lives of Afrikan people; a process which continues in the world to the present day. Perhaps Anthony 'liar Blair' and the other apologists can explain which part of this process was legal.

Ben was an enslaved Afrikan man who made the mistake of imitating the behaviour of his wicked enslaver's son. The son was in the habit of secretly 'stealing' rice from his father's storage site, but when Ben did the same, he was caught. As punishment for taking and eating food, he was hung up by his hands, left dangling for a long period of time and sporadically beaten (Shepard, 2000, p. 850). Ben was in such excruciating pain that in mitigation he pleaded that he had only copied the wicked enslaver's son. This exposure created problems for the son who became so enraged that he rammed a bayonet through Ben's leg who was already in abject agony from the ongoing, prolonged suspension supplemented by multiple whippings. In another situation bearing some similar characteristics, an enslaved Afrikan man was sent by his wicked enslaver to steal from his enslaver's neighbour's garden. He was caught and brought back to the same wicked enslaver who had only a few minutes before ordered him to commit the theft. The same wicked enslaver then ordered that he be punished with a life threatening torture of 100 lashes (James, 1963, p. 15).

Man eating dogs were brought in as a military weapon designed to contain Afrikan people's most effective uprisings. Under British imperialism, they were used as a kind of last resort to contain Afrikan people who, against all odds, continued to defy its control. The beasts were so fierce that the only defence for enslaved Afrikan people when the savage dogs were let loose was to lock themselves in their homes (Robinson, 1993, p. 225). Packs of vicious blood hounds were specifically trained to hunt down Afrikan human beings literally in order to tear them to pieces (Robinson, 1993, p. 244). This was considered a sport, in much the same way that fox hunting is carried out today. In addition to the hunting 'games', arenas were created where Afrikan people's bellies were coldly cut open as enticement for the savage dogs. At the sight of the blood, the dogs would throw themselves on the unfortunate defenceless Afrikan victims and devour them instantly. The dogs were 'fed' in this way on a daily basis. This was part of the dogs' 'training'; it was designed to ensure that whenever there was a battle the dogs would see Afrikan warriors as ready meals and attack them mercilessly (James, 1963, p. 360). It is testimony to the commitment and strength of the Afrikan revolutionaries in Haiti and the Afrikan Maroon community in Jamaica that they were never defeated by the tactic of employing savage man eating dogs.

2.4.2 The sexually abusive torture of Afrikan women
The deadly journey across the ocean had so viciously brutalised their wombs that after landing, Afrikan women were usually sterile for a period of two years (James, 1963, p. 14). Perhaps this mutilation of their reproduction capacity contributed to the failure of the enslavers to regard Afrikan women as the 'gentle sex'. There seems to have been no limit to the severity of the level of torture that Afrikan women were forced to endure. Some Afrikan women are known to have been savagely burnt alive, whilst others were deliberately inoculated with small pox to ensure a slow painful death (James, 1963, p. 102). Imperialism ensured that Afrikan women were regularly subjected to being publicly stripped naked, beaten and mutilated. In addition to all of this bare faced brutal terrorism, Afrikan women were regularly, mercilessly and repeatedly raped by their enslavers and whosoever they assigned; hung naked by their limbs on trees, to be eaten alive by crows for daring to refuse the rape violation of their enslavers and assignees; the same enslavers that advanced the lie that Afrikan people were not human beings.

In her biography, **Mary Prince** gave an indication of some of the abuses that were imposed upon her by one of her wicked enslavers. She said:

> "He had an ugly fashion of stripping himself naked and then ordering me to then wash him in a tub of water. This was worse to me than all the licks. Sometimes when he called me to wash him I would not come, my eyes were so full of shame. He would then come to beat me." (Shepard, 2000, p. 851)

Mary Prince's testimony is not only important in terms of what is revealed, but also in terms of what is almost certainly left out. It is completely understandable that a woman who has suffered multiple bouts of rape would not necessarily want to relive those despicable experiences. It is equally understandable that a rape victim might not want the full extent of the horrors carried out against her to be published and dispersed to the general public. However, neither of these possibilities appear to be the reason for the failure to disclose the full horrors of **Mary**'s experience. **Mary** dictated her story to Susanna Strickland who wrote it down and arranged for it to be published. It is almost certain that Strickland sanitised and censored the information for reasons that remain unspecified. It is therefore highly likely that **Mary Prince's** written history did not reveal the full extent of the inhumane sexually exploitative horrors perpetrated against her by this evil man.

It is highly unlikely that it was the nudity issue alone that was the real source of disturbance for **Mary**. For instance, nurses bathe naked men as a standard part of their duties and even women who are not nurses may wash naked men from time to time without generating this level of disgust; there had to be more to it. These 'baths' were obviously systematically calculated episodes of rape which **Mary** was forced to endure. Furthermore, since the abuse and violation of the mouth can play such an important role in the confirmation of one person's domination over the other, it is likely that she would have been thoroughly abused to the point where she would have been forced to engage in all of the unwelcome processes necessary to ensure that she drank the semen of her sexually perverted rapist enslaver. He would also have used these bouts of rape to force her to perform any other lewd acts that titillated his fancy. It was in these 'baths' that he could exercise the full extent of his power over her; so full and so wickedly cruel was his rapist abuse of her that she openly states that she would have preferred to have been savagely beaten than undergo that level of sexually sadistic torture. These rape episodes were so distressing for **Mary** that even from her totally disempowered position she mustered up enough courage to defend herself; openly asserting her right not to live with him on the grounds that he was 'too indecent' (Shepard, 2000, p. 851).

Mary Prince was not alone in being exposed to repeated vicious sex attacks at the hand of the wicked European enslavers. Thomas Thistlewood, who enslaved Afrikan people in Westmoreland Jamaica, was a self confessed serial rapist of defenceless disempowered enslaved Afrikan women. Recording the gruesome details of his merciless sex attacks against Afrikan women in his diary effectively became his lifetime pursuit. His rape attacks were so frequent that no Afrikan woman was safe in his presence. The Afrikan women on his forced labour camp frequently ran away in order to protect themselves from his ravages. However, even when they successfully manage to get away and escape their ordeal, Thistlewood would have them hunted down, brought back and flogged so that he could continue his relentless sex attacks against them.

Thistlewood was such an obscene character that he even kept a record of the rape experiences that he felt delivered 'good' and 'bad' sex. This sex maniac was effectively rating the Afrikan women's rape ordeals as though they were performing in an ice skating championship. So prolific was his anti-Afrikan misogynistic raping spree that on 30th September 1752 he reported in his diary the discovery of 'yellowish greenish matter' running from his genitals (Beckles, 1999, p. 43). This unrepentant sex maniac then had the audacity to claim that the Afrikan women that he had raped gave him the venereal disease. The mind boggles at this totally corrupted line of reasoning. He carried out hundreds of separate acts of rape against defenceless Afrikan women, spreading diseases in his wake and then claimed that these defenceless Afrikan women, whom he had ruthlessly subjected to the most inhumane sexual ordeals, gave him diseases. In addition to being a terrorist in the midst of Afrikan women, this man was obviously stark raving bonkers.

The most prolific of the known rapists in the history of Britain are Jack the ripper and Peter Sutcliff, the Yorkshire ripper. Terrible as they undoubtedly were, their combined record of rape attacks against women amounted to less than 40. However, Thistlewood boastfully testifies in his hand written diary to 265 individual rape attacks against enslaved Afrikan women. This shameful record only accounts for the women that he admitted to raping during the years 1751 and 1754. In other words, these systematic episodes of rape constitute only a sample of his unrelenting misogynistic rape attacks carried out against enslaved Afrikan women (Beckles, 1999, p. 45). The main difference between Thistlewood and Jack the ripper is that Thistlewood's position of power was so great that it was not necessary for him to murder his victims in order to avoid punishment. He was so untouchable that he could, and did, repeatedly rape Afrikan women without fear of being brought to justice.

J. Marion Sims was hailed by the enemies of Afrikan people as the 'father of medicine'. He was given this title for mercilessly launching totally unprovoked vicious attacks against Afrikan women using what he claimed to be 'medical' experimentation as his excuse. He devised a torture instrument which he called the 'virginal speculum'. It was a device with a turning handle at one end and a number of moving finger like prongs at the other. Each time the handle was turned, the prongs would separate such that anything enveloping the outer perimeter of the prongs would be automatically expanded outwards.

Sims was in the habit of routinely inserting this instrument of torture into the most delicate parts of the bodies of innocent and defenceless enslaved Afrikan women. He would then turn the handle in order to stretch and expand the Afrikan woman's virgina to its point of maximum elasticity. In addition to the obvious humiliation caused, this was an excruciatingly painful ordeal for the Afrikan women, subjected to this sexually perverted brand of torture. However, even this level of pain and humiliation was not sufficient to suit Sims' agenda. He would continue the torture by turning the handle so that the Afrikan woman's genitalia were totally ripped open from the inside.

One of the consequences of this sadistic, inhumane level of abuse was that the Afrikan women who had been attacked in this way were left in a state where they could no longer control the flow of their urine. This meant that they constantly and repeatedly urinated on themselves as a direct result of their ruptured clitoris. Beyond that, there was the breach of the barrier between the Afrikan woman's virgina and anus, allowing urine and excrement to mix in the vicinity of the open wound. In addition to the discomfort caused by the ongoing mutilation coupled with the inevitable foul smells that these innocent women were left to endure, this created the circumstances for deadly diseases to flourish. It is therefore highly likely that some of his innocent unsuspecting Afrikan victims experienced slow and painful deaths as a direct result of this maniac's torture.

In 1857 a European woman approached Sims, seeking what would have, at the time, been experimental gynaecological surgery. Sims blatantly exposed his racism when he informed her that an untried 'procedure' could not be justified for use on one in her position in social life (Gavrus, 2005, p. 66). However, Sims had no qualms about practicing untried 'procedures' on Afrikan women. Without even the slightest consideration for their wellbeing he used many Afrikan women as guinea pigs in his 'experiments', dissecting their private parts with unrelenting vigour. One particularly unfortunate Afrikan woman had the unenviable misfortune of being systematically tortured and ripped apart by Sims on as many as 30 separate occasions.

2.4.3 Rape as evidence of the triple oppression of enslaved Afrikan women

When one section of humanity systematically steals the labour and resources of another, exploitation is the result. When the exploited group protest and resist the theft, the exploiting group must oppress the exploited group in order to retain and maintain the stolen wealth. Enslaved Afrikan women were the most abused group of people on the forced labour camps in that they faced the drudgery of triple oppression: firstly, they were subjected to Gender oppression where they were exploited because of their sex. Secondly, they were subjected to Nation oppression where they were exploited through racism; and thirdly, they were subjected to Class oppression where they were exploited on the basis that enslaved Afrikan women were automatically amongst the poorest people in the world.

Rape is the most wicked and dehumanising of thefts in that it is the theft of the most intimate part of a woman's being. Enslaved Afrikan women continuously suffered rape which, in addition to being an act of theft, is, and was unlawful as well as a direct act of oppression. When they dared to resist they were confronted with a second tier of oppressive consequences which came from a variety sources. The punishments that Afrikan women were faced with as a consequence of resisting rape or being 'caught' when subjected to rape, provide clear examples of the additional levels of oppression that they were forced to endure. For instance, if an evil European male enslaver decided to rape a defenceless enslaved Afrikan woman, she could expect to be mutilated and murdered for daring to resist. This is evidence of the class dimension where the rich oppress the poor. In addition, it highlights the gender dimension where men oppress women. Furthermore, it illustrates the race dimension where Europeans oppress Afrikan people.

Triple Oppression

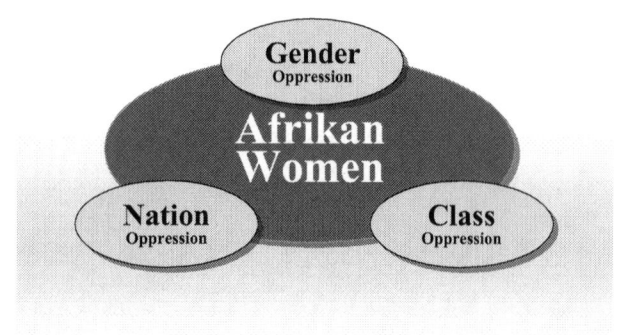

Afrikan Women at centre, surrounded by **Gender Oppression**, **Nation Oppression**, and **Class Oppression**.

Brother Omowale

If after having been raped by a savage enslaver husband his wife found out about it, the enslaved Afrikan woman could again expect to be mutilated and murdered on the orders of the jealous wife seeking vengeance. In Haiti for instance, an Afrikan woman by the name of **Coomba** was murdered because of her outstanding beauty. The wicked enslaver's evil wife, motivated by malice and a sense of revenge, mercilessly ordered the beheading of **Coomba** and had **Coomba's** head served on a plate to her husband because she suspected that he might have an interest in her (Hochschild, p. 262). It is difficult to imagine what would have happened had he actually acted on his alleged interest. **Coomba**, a completely innocent and defenceless enslaved Afrikan woman, was therefore subjected to the direct race and class oppression of her European 'sister'.

Furthermore, enslaved Afrikan women could find themselves being 'rented out' by their evil European enslavers as a means of gaining their enslavers a little extra income (Shepard & Beckles, p. 695). Obviously in this environment Afrikan women could find themselves also being 'rented out' to be used by Afrikan studs as part of the forced labour camp breeding process. The wicked enslavers would frequently instruct enslaved Afrikan men to rape enslaved Afrikan women in order to provide them with more 'stock'. These obscene rapes were often carried out with great enthusiasm by enslaved Afrikan men who could launch these attacks without fear of 'legal' or other sanction (Shepard & Beckles, p. 693). In this wicked system even their Afrikan brothers, who were also subject to enslavement and exploitation, were given the power to directly oppress enslaved Afrikan women on the basis of gender.

2.4.4 Triple terrorism: The physical torture of enslaved Afrikan women
Ordering the slow painful deaths of enslaved Afrikan women seems to have been a speciality of some of the more sadistic enslavers. For instance, two enslaved Afrikan women were subjected to, what can only be described as the most hideous of genocidal tortures. Their wicked enslaver ordered that their feet and elbows be roasted and this was carried out whilst they were still alive and conscious. The gruesome torture was obviously treated as a spectacle designed to completely terrify the gathering of Afrikan onlookers because it was supported by a process of alternately gagging the victims so that they were, each in turn, rendered speechless. The unhygienic and intrusive process of withdrawing the gag from one Afrikan woman's mouth and then ramming it into the other's, ensured that they would each scream out in turn rather than in chorus (James, 1963, p. 22). These Afrikan women's capacity for survival was incredibly strong because they were both still alive after the roasting of their limbs was completed. As a 'reward' for surviving that aspect of their terrifying and torturous ordeal, their elbows and feet were simply left to decompose before their very eyes.

On top of that, one of them had her neck so severely lacerated by the iron collar that she was forced to wear, that she could no longer swallow (James, 1963, p. 23). It is likely that this Afrikan heroine had resisted her enslavers by refusing to produce children, because the torture of the collar was especially reserved for women who were suspected of abortion. The wicked enslavers ensured that the collar never left their necks until they had produced a child (James, 1963, p. 13). Another sad irony was that regardless of whether they were wearing a collar or not, Afrikan women were forced to work in the fields and often outnumbered their male counterparts in that physically gruelling area of forced labour activity (Hart, 1998, p. 22).

Whilst some punishments were launched directly against the humanity of Afrikan women, other others were the specific domain of their pregnant sisters. In some cases the level of wickedness exercised during torture sessions was adjusted in a direct attempt to ensure that the children of pregnant Afrikan women survived to be born. For instance, one pregnant Afrikan woman was punished using the 'four post' whipping torture (James, 1963, p. 13). A hole was dug in the earth to accommodate her unborn child before she was mercilessly ravaged with the whip. In another case, the wicked enslaver went totally berserk to the point of ordering the cutting open of a pregnant Afrikan woman's belly, severing her child from her umbilical cord and then throwing her innocent unborn child into a fire (James, 1963, p. 102/3). Both of these grotesque forms of human torture were not uncommon. They were both examples of the anti-human genocidal practices which Afrikan women and their unborn children were forced to endure.

Strip beatings were clearly a regular technique of torture used against Afrikan men, women, pregnant women, children and even the elderly (Shepard, 2000, p. 847 & 857). For instance, **Sarah** who was an old, infirm, mentally confused and possibly senile Afrikan woman was the victim of one such outrage (Shepard, 2000, p. 850). According to her wicked enslaver's son, she committed the 'crime' of not wheeling the barrow that she was pushing quickly enough. As a result, this evil man got so angry that he stripped her naked and 'beat her severely'. He then picked her up and threw her into a sharp, venomous and prickly pear bush. **Sarah** was so grievously wounded by this act of abject wickedness that her body swelled and festered all over. A few days later, **Sarah** who was totally defenceless and never troubled anyone died of her injuries. This completely unprovoked and obviously unjustifiable act was nothing other than cold blooded murder. The onus must be on the apologists to explain how the rape, torture and mutilation of Afrikan women could ever have been legal.

2.4.5 Beyond the records

There are many aspects of the deplorable treatment of Afrikan people during the chattel slavery era that remain concealed. They are either too despicable to mention as some historians have claimed or documentary proof has been concealed or is otherwise unavailable. However, despite the lack of evidence, in some instances, there is still good reason to assert that ultra despicable abuses were carried out against Afrikan people. For instance, the film *Roots* (1977) depicts the humiliating abuse perpetrated on the wedding night of a newlywed Afrikan couple. Just as the couple retired to enjoy their wedding night, their wicked enslaver came along and effected entry into their living space. He then ordered the Afrikan man to wait outside by the door.

The wicked enslaver proceeded to mercilessly rape the newlywed Afrikan woman whilst her disempowered husband was made to wait immediately outside the door and listen to her ordeal. Part of his ordeal was hearing his wife being viciously raped whilst being unable to take effective action to protect her. After completely violating the humanity and dignity of the Afrikan family, the wicked enslaver compounded the humiliation by giving the Afrikan man permission to rejoin his wife. This deep sense of being disempowered would have affected both husbands and wives. For example, there can be little doubt that there would have been those wicked enslavers that would have ordered the wife to wait outside whilst they savagely raped the husband.

Furthermore, it is not inconceivable that there would have been those wicked enslavers that would have ordered both husbands and wives out of their homes so that they could practice the most despicable bouts of paedophilia against their defenceless Afrikan children. There would literally have been no limit to the extent of the diabolically abusive evils that would have been perpetrated. A modern example of the institutionalisation of this type of child sexual abuse happened in England. On 17th September 1987 a number of children from Cleveland in the north of England testified in open court that they were routinely and systematically subjected to rape by adults. Their stories were corroborated by medical evidence which was accepted as the truth by the court within which they testified (Cleveland Child Sex Abuse Scandal).

There may be those amongst us that might find it difficult to believe that under imperialism's chattel enslavement system, Afrikan men were forced to perform sex acts against each other. However, in addition to anal penetration they would have been forced to perform oral sex against each other to the point of being made to drink each other's semen. They would have been compelled to carry out these acts of self deprecation in front of all of their sisters and brothers on the forced labour camps and the children would not have been spared this sight.

The identification of this kind of sexually perverted terrorist activity might initially look like wild speculation, but even in the present day it is possible to see signs of these kinds of abusive sexual practices. For instance, on 11th January 2005 in a radio broadcast on BBC radio 4 (Sexual violence in prisons), an Afrikan man by the name of Roderick Johnson testified that whilst he was in a Texas prison, he and another inmate were forced to perform oral sex on each other for the entertainment of the other people present. Furthermore, in Iraq, men were stripped naked and made to prostrate themselves on each other in order to simulate group sex, of the homosexual variety. These abuses were forcibly carried out in front of TV cameras. Clips of these abuses were beamed into our homes for all to see, including our children.

There are now serious question marks surrounding the authenticity of a paper entitled *The Making of the Negro*. The paper outlines a process by which Afrikan people were 'broken in' or 'seasoned' into accepting chattel enslavement by using techniques normally applied to commanding the subservience of horses (Marrow, 2003, p. 23). It describes part of the process involving the brutal murder of the strongest Afrikan male on the forced labour camp. He would be severely beaten, tarred and feathered and then each of his limbs would be tied to a different horse. On the instructions of the wicked enslaver, the horses would be made to run off in different directions – tearing the Afrikan man's body apart in the process. This would be done in front of everybody in the forced labour camp, including the children. The object was to terrify every Afrikan person into a state total submission so as to enforce their conformity to the enslavement system. This kind of anti-Afrikan terrorism has not ceased. For instance, on 14th June 1998 three European men used a 24 foot 6 inch log chain to tie an innocent Afrikan man **James Byrd Junior** to the back of their motor vehicle (James Byrd Junior). They then drove off at speed, literally ripping the body of

James Byrd apart. Pieces of his body including his head and limbs were simply left dripping with his blood over a 3 mile stretch of road.

It is difficult to contest the fact that these unproven acts of cruelty actually happened during imperialism's chattel enslavement era when they can still be seen happening today. As obscene and perhaps unbelievable as these modern examples are, they provide powerful circumstantial evidence to support the notion that Afrikan people were subjected to these tortures and worse during the chattel enslavement era. The fact that they are happening now makes it more believable that these atrocities happened during the chattel enslavement era. There are currently national and international laws which are supposedly designed to protect today's victims of gross violence. Even though these official legal safeguards are in place, the sexual abuse of children, the public sexual abuse of grown men and the ripping apart of innocent Afrikan men's bodies have not been prevented from happening. It is therefore highly likely that such atrocities would have been more prevalent in the period when Afrikan people were officially regarded by imperialism as sub-human and therefore not afforded any 'legal' protection whatsoever.

2.4.6 Other forms of anti-Afrikan terrorism

Physical torture was not the only method of terrorism used to abuse and subdue Afrikan people. Afrikan people were also sold like animals and separated from their mothers, fathers and siblings; this cruel fate befell ***Mary Prince*** when her whole family were sold off separately to different enslavers on various forced labour camps (Shepard, 2000, p. 844/5). In ***Mary's*** case she even knew which forced labour camps her other family members were imprisoned on, but was prevented from visiting them or even having contact with them.

On one occasion after the enforced disintegration of her family, ***Mary*** was beaten and brutalised by her wicked enslaver until she could not stand and he was too weary to continue. As a direct result of this aspect of her torture, she ran away, eventually ending up at the forced labour camp upon which her mother was held prisoner (Shepard, 2000, p. 848). Her mother couldn't take her in, but nonetheless hid her and fed her (Shepard, 2000, p. 848). However when her father, who was imprisoned on yet another forced labour camp, learned of her whereabouts he came and got her. Rather than helping ***Mary*** to make good her escape, her father bought her back to the forced labour camp from which she had escaped and begged her enslaver/abuser for mercy. His begging seems to have had little in the way of a long term positive effect because **Mary** reports that she was abused almost every day for the next 5 years after which she was sent to Turks island.

Thomas Thistlewood, the wicked enslaver that was based in Westmoreland Jamaica, is also infamous for the wickedly grotesque nature of the tortures that he inflicted on enslaved Afrikan people. His hand written confession boastfully testifies to the fact that he used an enslaved Afrikan man by the name of Hector to totally humiliate any Afrikan person that exercised their legitimate right to resist their enslavement. In front of children, women and men alike Hector would be ordered, in the words of Thistlewood, to 'shit in [the] mouth' of Afrikan people who resisted the evils of his forced labour camp (Beckles, 1999, p. 52). On Thistlewood's command, Hector would shamelessly draw down his trousers in front of all of the other people on the forced labour camp, including the children. He would stoop over the open mouth of the Afrikan resistor and then mercilessly 'shit in [the] mouth' of his own sister or brother. Thistlewood would then give the order that a gag be fastened over the Afrikan resistor's mouth 'whilst full' so that the 'shit' could not be spat out and therefore had no place to go other than down the throat.

Obviously, no human being lays on their back with their mouths open patiently waiting for another person to 'shit in [their] mouth'. The Afrikan resister first had to be beaten into a state of total submission. They were mercilessly flogged to the point where they could hardly resist, then 'salt, lime juice and bird pepper' would be rubbed into the open wounds (Milwood, 2010, p. 25). This would have been done by fellow Afrikan people on the orders of Thistlewood. They would have then held their sister or brother down, forced their jaw open, possibly even breaking it in the process. Thistlewood gave the order to 'shit in [the] mouth' of Afrikan people, with the accompanying gag, on a regular basis. He boasts in his diary that he gave the order on 26th May and 25th, 26th and 31st July 1756. These examples are of course, only a tiny sample of Thistlewood's terrorist activity shamelessly carried out against innocent Afrikan people.

There seems to be no limit to the level of psychological torture that enslaved Afrikan people had to put up with. For instance, there is the documented case of an idiot by the name of Samuel Cartwright, who ran around calling himself a doctor. He was permitted to publish a paper in a so called 'academic' journal entitled *De Bow's Review*. In 1851, this fool diagnosed Afrikan people who ran away from the grotesque torturous horrors of imperialism's chattel enslavement, with a condition which he called *'Drapetomania'*. It is well known amongst practitioners of psychology and related disciplines that human beings (and other animals) instinctively respond to danger by either fighting it or removing themselves from the dangerous environment (Psychology of Stress). Afrikan people who ran away from the forced labour camps were obviously doing the latter. However, this brainless moron had the audacity to suggest that Afrikan people who responded to their gross ill-treatment by running away suffered from mental illness. He even went so far as to 'prescribe' whipping and the chopping off of Afrikan people's toes as 'remedies' for this 'perceived problem'. This man was obviously a dunce, because he seems to have been incapable of working out that those people who failed to absent themselves from an environment inculcated with the most hideous variety of gross torturous abuse were the ones more likely to have serious problems of mental ill-health (Drapetomania; Cultural Psychiatric Services).

2.4.7 Afrikan heroism in a climate of murderous terrorism

There are hundreds of eye witness accounts of the heroic actions of Afrikan people in the face of certain death. For instance, in 1767 in Ashantiland Afrikan people cut their own throats rather than allow themselves to be sold into enslavement. One Afrikan man even cut the throat of his wife before cutting his own (Breaking the silence). On the human trafficking ships used to deport Afrikan people from their own homes, Afrikan people courageously waved good-bye to their friends before jumping overboard to certain death (Bly, 1998).

On the island of Haiti, some outstanding acts of heroism are recorded. For instance one eye witness noted:

> "I have just heard of a bloody fight that general Boyer has experienced at Gros-Morne. The rebels have been exterminated; 50 prisoners have been hung; these men die

with an incredible fanaticism; they laugh at death; it is the same with the women ..." (James, 1963, p. 345).

In another case an eye witness informs us that:

> "While **Chevalier**, [an Afrikan chief], hesitated at the sight of the scaffold, his wife shamed him. 'You do not know how sweet it is to die for liberty!' And refusing to allow herself to be hung by the executioner, she took the rope and hanged herself." (James, 1963, p. 361).

Another astounding act of heroism was documented when:

> "Three [Afrikan people] were condemned to be burned alive. A huge crowd stood around while two of the men were consumed, uttering horrible cries. But the third a boy of 19, bound so that he could not see the other two, called to them in Creole, 'You do not know how to die. See how to die.' By a great effort he twisted his body in his bonds, sat down, and placing his feet in the flames, let them burn without uttering a grown." (James, 1963, p. 361).

Obviously these examples represent just a tiny sample of Afrikan people's acts of heroism during the chattel enslavement part of the *Maangamizi*.

2.5 Conclusion

Imperialism went to elaborate lengths in its attempts to dehumanise Afrikan people. Its pseudo scientists of the scientific racism school even separated humanity into races and declared themselves superior. With that they 'intellectualised' their own brand of racism. Since there is only one race i.e. the human race their nonsense obviously could not succeed. At the heart of their failure is the fact that humanity began in Afrika. That does not make Afrikan people superior to any other human beings. However, it does confirm that the mothers and fathers of humanity i.e. the givers of life to all of the other sections of the human family, cannot be sub-human.

The story that emerges from a review of the horrors of slavery is of an almost unbelievable concentration of evil acts of terrorism perpetrated under imperialism's chattel enslavement system. There was classifying human beings as sub-human, piracy, kidnapping, compulsory deportation, institutionalised cruel treatment, forcing people to eat food contaminated with urine, saliva and feces, torture, mutilation, disembowelling, applying hot wood on buttocks in between whipping, pouring burning wax and boiling sugar cane on people, involuntary human medical experimentation, public humiliation, dehumanisation, rape – even of pregnant women, castration, sexual molestation, paedophilia, murder, infanticide, burning people alive; feeding Afrikan people to animals, enforced cannibalism, chaining people to decomposing dead bodies, 'shitting' in people's mouths, shoving gunpowder into the 'arse' of a human being – inserting a fuse and blowing them to smithereens and the list continues.

It is a measure of the level of British imperialism's barbarism that it took over two hundred years for it to realise its anti-Afrikan reign of terror called slavery was morally wrong. Now over four hundred years later, British imperialism still hasn't even come to the understanding that these things were and are illegal acts. Imperialism has no shame. By what standard can this absolutely horrendous catalogue of genocidal scale anti-human terror be 'legal'? It is for the apologists to clarify when, where and under whose law and jurisdiction these atrocities were 'legal'.

References

1. Anderson. S. I., (1995), *The Black Holocaust for Beginners*, Writers and Readers Publishing Incorporated
2. Beckles. Hilary, (1993), *Afro-Caribbean Women and Resistance to Slavery in Barbados*, Karnak House
3. Beckles. Hilary, (1999), *Centering Women*, Ian Randle Publishers, Kingston Jamaica
4. Dennis. Ferdinand, (1988), *Behind the Frontlines: The Journey of Afro-Britain*, Gollancz Paperback
5. Diop. Cheik Anta, (1987), *Pre-Colonial Black Africa*, Lawrence Hill Books
6. Fryer. Peter, (1989), *Black People in the British Empire: An Introduction*, Pluto Press
7. Gavrus. Delia, (2005), *Gynaecological Surgery in the 19th Century: Diverging Historical Accounts*, University of Toronto Medical Journal, Volume 83, Number 1, December 2005

8. Haley. Alex, (1977), *Roots: The epic drama of one man's search for his origins*, Picador: Pan Books
9. Honychurch. Lennox, (1995a), *The Caribbean People*, Thomas Nelson and Sons Limited
10. Howarth. David, (1973), *The British Empire; Volume 2*, BBCTV Time Life Books
11. James. C.L.R., (1963), *The Black Jacobins*, Vintage Books
12. Justice. Prince, (2005), *The Blackworld: Evolution to Revolution*, AU Publishers
13. Karenga. Maulana, (1993), *Introduction to Black Studies*, University of Sankora Press
14. Martin. Steve, (1999), *Britain's Slave Trade*, Channel 4 Books
15. Milwood. Robinson, (2010), *Dis-empowerment and Engagement: Raising Consciousness*, TamaRe House Publications
16. Morrow. Alvin, (2003), *Breaking the curse of Willie Lynch: The Science of Slave Psychology*, Rising Sun Publications
17. Rodney. Walter, (1981), *How Europe Underdeveloped Africa*, Bogle-L'Overture Publications
18. Shepard, Verene & Beckles Hilary, (2000), *Caribbean Slavery in the Atlantic World: A Student Reader*, Ian Randle Publishers, Kingston
19. Sherlock. Philip & Bennett. Hazel, (1998), *The Story of the Jamaican People*, Ian Randle Publishers
20. Walwin. James, (1993), *Black Ivory: A History of British Slavery*, Fontana Press
21. Williams. Eric, (1997), *Capitalism and Slavery*, Andre Deutsch Limited

Internet references
1. Breaking the Silence – Learning about the Trans-Atlantic Slave Trade, www.antislavery.org/breakingthesilence
2. Cultural Psychiatric Services: Past, Present and Future, http://www.psychiatrictimes.com/p031057.html
3. Drapetomania: A disease called freedom, http://www.broward.org/library/bienes/lii13000.htm
4. James Byrd Junior, http://everything2.com/index.pl?node=James%20Byrd%2C%20Jr.
5. Portcities Bristol, http://www.discoveringbristol.org.uk/showNarrative.php?sit_id=1&narId=15&nacId=19
6. The Cleveland child sexual abuse scandal: An abuse and misuse of professional power, http://www.childrenuk.co.uk/choct2002/choct2002/pragnell%20cleveland%20abuse.html

7. The Psychology of Stress, http://www.guidetopsychology.com/stress.htm

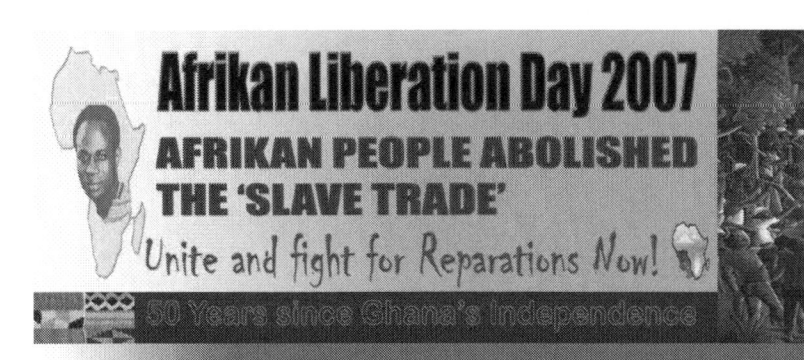

Was Slavery Really Our Own Fault?

Afrikan Liberation Day 2007
AFRIKAN PEOPLE ABOLISHED THE 'SLAVE TRADE'
Unite and fight for Reparations Now!
50 Years since Ghana's Independence

Ukombozii
Education for Liberation
Afrikan Freedom Means Defeating Neo-Colonialism
www.ukombozii.org

Chapter 3

3 Was slavery really our own fault?

3.1 Imperialism's false accusation against Afrikan people
In its attempts to hide and disguise its evil practices, imperialism tries to cover up its responsibility for the kidnapping, deportation and enslavement of Afrikan people by propagating the idea that the enslavement of Afrikan people was our own fault. The propaganda attack is divided into two parts. Imperialism attempts to indoctrinate the public by alleging that:

- We were in the habit of enslaving and selling ourselves before European imperialism came along, and
- The imperialists only bought Afrikan people because we enticed them by offering to sell our own people to them

The baseline of these arguments is that we deserve what we got because we brought it on ourselves. This wickedly misleading line of reasoning means that the imperialists, who planned and organised the most shamefully tragic episode in the history of humanity, get off 'Scot free'.

The situation is made even worse by a chorus of Afrikan people who spend their time shouting historically incorrect slogans like 'it's all our own fault' or 'we are responsible for our own enslavement' or 'we did it to ourselves'. They are displaying a lack of understanding of the history of how our people were stolen and compulsorily deported from Afrika into enslavement. Theirs is the behaviour of Afrikan people who have fallen for imperialism's classic blame the victim strategy.

It is the same strategy that the police use to cover up deaths in custody in the modern day. The idea is to isolate the potential threat resulting from the killing by vilifying the person whose life has been stolen. When this is done successfully there will be little or no public sympathy or support for the victims or their families and the problem confronting imperialism will be minimised. Afrikan *Maangamizi* victims suffer the same blame the victim attack *en mass*.

Propaganda Strategies

Culture or People		Activity		
		Kidnappers	Not Involved	Fighters
	Afrikan	Acknowledge / Centre Stage	Hightlight / Ignore	Highlight / Hide
	European	Highlight / Play Down	Disprove / Highlight	Contextualise / Exaggerate

Brother Omowale

It is clear that the so called 'slave trade' would have been impossible without the co-operation of a certain class of Afrikan people. Therefore in an attempt to deceive onlookers this is the factor that is given, not only centre stage, but the entire historical stage by imperialism. The fact that many Afrikan people had no part whatsoever to play in the so called 'slave trade' is given no attention. The fact that many Afrikan people actively fought against the so called 'slave trade' is completely concealed. Our ignorance of the details and incidents of our history is manipulated to trick us into incorrectly blaming ourselves for our own enslavement. Onlookers are then further disorientated when imperialism presents its own European candidates as the 'saviours and heroes' of enslaved Afrikan people.

The fundamental purpose of the blame the victim strategy is to protect imperialism itself. However, within that a tactical element of imperialism's plan is to launch a vicious attack against us by fostering divide and rule amongst Afrikan people. If Afrikan people in the Diaspora can be made to hate Afrikan people from home on the false premise that 'they sold us into slavery', then the ground will be set for damaging battles between Afrikan sisters and brothers and such battles are diametrically opposed to our need for unity.

Imperialism's aim is to literally augment bloody wars between us on a scale equivalent to the wars that caused the majority of Diasporan Afrikan people to be in the Diaspora in the first place. It hand picks Afrikan people from each side of the home/Diaspora divide, which imperialism itself created and uses them to hurl public insults at each other in order to fuel a climate of Afrikan self hate. As long as this strategy continues to succeed, imperialism will be safe from any meaningful level of destabilisation as a result of Afrikan resistance.

3.2 Our response
It must be acknowledge that some Afrikan people did behave in despicable, disgusting ways that contributed to our downfall as a people. There was a certain class amongst us that abandoned the Afrikan principles of: Humanism i.e. 'people before profits'; Collectivism i.e. 'we before me'; and Egalitarianism i.e. 'we're all equal in essence'. They instead adopted the alien principles of: Exploitation i.e. 'money before people'; Individualism i.e. 'me before we'; and Elitism i.e. 'I'm better than you'. In doing so they sold their own people into captivity for what they mistakenly thought would be their personal gain. The consequence of their errors was that all Afrikan people from that time to the present ended up losing out as a result.

Despite the fact that history has clearly proved these people wrong, some of their unprincipled behaviours still remain in our communities and continue to undermine the process of Afrikan liberation to the present today. It is vital that we unreservedly condemn these behaviours and fight for their total eradication. We must also investigate and learn from these behaviours so that:
- We stop them from occurring in our communities, and
- Once removed, never allow them to re-emerge

3.3 Allegation 1: We enslaved ourselves before European imperialism came along

3.3.1 Imperialism did not copy chattel slavery from Afrikan societies

If it is true that when European imperialists came to Afrika they found us busily enslaving ourselves, why didn't they stop it or try to persuade us to stop? They must have known that it as wrong, so why didn't they refuse to participate? Why did they join in? Why did they create a system of enslavement even worse than what they found? Why did they choose to profit from such an obvious wrong? In a nutshell, it is because they are lying. Any enslavement systems that might have existed in Afrika were not the motivating factor that caused the imperialists to enter into the habit of kidnapping, deporting and viciously enslaving Afrikan people.

Further doubts can be cast on the imperialist's line of reasoning by examining the consistency of their behaviours. For instance, the imperialists found Afrikan people practicing certain types of spiritual rituals, but they didn't copy them. Instead they set about destroying them. They found Afrikan people using particular names, they didn't copy those either, but set about destroying them too. They failed to copy Afrikan languages, methods of dress, cuisine or family patterns. In all these cases they tried to destroy them. Perhaps we can be forgiven for being just a little suspicious when they tell us that the only thing that we had worth copying was a system that they described as 'slavery'. Indeed, whether they forgive us or not, we must state categorically that they did not get the idea of enslaving Afrikan people from us.

3.3.2 The Afrikan form of 'slavery' was less draconian

Given the nature of the allegation, it is important to establish the type of so called 'slavery' the imperialists encountered in Afrika. The first revelation undermining their allegation of Afrikan 'slavery' is that before the coming of European imperialism 'slavery' was not widespread in Afrika (Fryer, 1989, p. 10). Next we discover that the system that existed in Afrika more closely resembled European serfdom or villienage than chattel slavery. The system seems to have emerged because in Afrikan societies there were no institutions such as prisons. The absence of such an institution raised the problem of what should be done with wrong doers and this is what led to a kind of 'Domestic slavery'. It was a kind of debt repayment through labour or penance for wrong doers and captured enemy soldiers etc. (Martin, 1999, p. 156).

It would be incorrect to attempt to claim that 'Afrikan slavery' was good and 'European slavery' was bad. All slavery represents the opposite of freedom which means that there is no such thing as good slavery – all slavery is bad. However, that does not mean that all systems of slavery exhibit the same degree of evil. It is clear that 'domestic slavery' in Afrika was significantly less draconian than European imperialism's 'chattel slavery' system (Diop, 1987, p. 152). For instance, under 'domestic slavery':

- Enslaved people were full human beings
- Enslavement was not usually a lifelong experience
- Enslavement was not usually passed from generation to generation
- Enslaved Afrikan people did not outnumber their enslavers
- Enslaved people were not generally sold
- No Afrikan economy was based on enslavement
- Enslaved people could marry into their enslaver's family
- Enslaved people could rise into positions of leadership
- Enslaved people had their own plots of land
- Enslaved people kept a proportion of the fruits of their labour (Fryer, 1989, p. 10)

Afrikan 'domestic slavery' was so different from European 'chattel slavery' that it would be completely false to suggest that the existence of 'domestic slavery' inspired European imperialists to engage in the chattel enslavement of Afrikan people. The Afrikan system obviously did not provide them with their blueprint. This then raises the question of where they really got the idea of chattel slavery from.

3.3.3 Slavery is integral to European imperialist culture

If it is true that European imperialism discovered slavery when it arrived in Afrika during the 15th to 17th centuries, then an examination of European history prior to that time will reveal no traces of slavery in European culture. This analysis provides yet another line of reasoning which helps to demonstrate that imperialism's bogus story, that Afrikan culture introduced it to slavery, does not fit the facts. On the contrary, from classical history right through to the present, European culture had and continues to have a variety of forms of slavery intimately bound up within it.

Any honest attempt at establishing the truth about the motivation behind chattel slavery must recognise that slavery was not the sole domain of Afrikan people. All peoples have been affected by slavery at some point in their history. Furthermore, there is an abundance of evidence which confirms that slavery is deeply imbedded within European culture. The first 'high culture' of Europe i.e. the Greeks had slavery as an integral part of their structure (Carruthers, 1999, p. 80). In addition, the greatest ancient empire of Europe i.e. the Romans was built and expanded on the basis of slave labour (Diop, 1991, p. 145). Even the word 'slave' is derived from the term 'Slav' which describes the Slavic people of Europe who were subjected to enslavement by their European kith and kin for centuries (Chandler, 1999, p. 167).

There is also documented evidence confirming that the British employed systematic processes of slavery in their own land long before any of their 'explorers' came into contact with Afrika. Bristol, for instance, was notorious white slave market in the 11th century (Fryer, 1984, p. 38). It is therefore wholly misleading to suggest that Europeans came to Afrika in ignorance of slavery and were somehow persuaded or corrupted by the systems practiced in Afrika into carrying out the chattel enslavement of Afrikan people.

3.3.4 Imperialism created the market for enslaved Afrikan people
In order to see through the lie of self inflicted slavery, observers need to be clear that there were no Afrikan people on the shores of Afrika waiting (with their sisters and brothers in chains) for foreigners to come along and buy them. Even if that had been the case, then there was certainly no external market for stolen Afrikan people to be deported to. In other words, since there was no demand, there would have been no internal basis for the kidnapping and compulsory deportation of Afrikan people.

European imperialist culture with its history of mass murder and mass enslavement created the market for enslaved Afrikan people when it committed genocide against the American Indians (Ferguson, 1999, p. 20). The process of genocide which was to have such devastating and traumatic effect on both American Indians and Afrikan people was officially sanctioned by the European Christian Pope Alexander VI when he signed the Treaty of Tordesillas on 7th June 1494 (Justice, 2005, p. 94).

After having wiped out the American Indians they initially imported European 'indentured servants' (Honychurch, 1995a, p. 66). However, European indentured servants proved to be too weak and too few in number to satisfy the European imperialists demands for labour. It was at this point that they turned to the systematic theft and compulsory deportation of Afrikan people to satisfy their lust for personal profit. This process was officially sanctioned by Britain's head of state Queen Elizabeth I when she granted her royal navy ship, *Jesus of Lubeck* with 300 crew, to Francis Drake (Fryer, 1984, p. 8). So pleased was she with his conduct that she later knighted him in reward for the profits he made for her through kidnapping and deporting Afrikan people from their homes (Fryer, 1984, p. 411).

The myth presented by imperialist 'historians' is that Afrikan people were responsible for the so called 'slave trade'. However, history reveals that the highest echelons of Europe clearly controlled and directed the 'trade' and made multi million pounds worth of profit from it. It is difficult to contest the fact that European imperialist involvement in the kidnapping and deportation of Afrikan people was wholly controlled, supported and sanctioned by their state and business mechanisms.

It is also important to note that when European imperialists finally decided to stop the trafficking, the compulsory deportation of Afrikan people dried to a trickle. If Afrikan people were the motivating and controlling force driving the kidnapping and deportation process, they would have built their own ships in order to continue to send their sisters and brothers overseas. They would have used their ingenuity to find ways around any ban that European imperialists had erected. As it happened, even those chiefs that wanted to continue to sell their own people were eventually compelled to stop, because the overall process was controlled from outside Afrika.

Furthermore, after the so called British abolition of the 'slave trade', the British deported Arabs, Chinese and Indians, on a voluntary basis, from Asia to the Caribbean. The reason that these people moved to the

Caribbean was purely and simply because of the demand for labour created by British imperialism. The whole trafficking process was organised and conducted by British imperialism in order to service its own need. Just as with Afrikan people before them, Asians did not control the trafficking process, it was the British who provided and peopled the entire infrastructure.

It is also important to note that there are no accusations of Afrikan people operating as middlemen in this period of the people trafficking process; they were not needed and therefore excluded by the British imperialists who had all the power. All of this evidence clearly illustrates that the reason for moving people from one part of the world to another was provided by imperialism's demand for labour and nothing else. The imperialists simply included Afrikan people in their affairs on an as and when needed basis – imperialism was always in overall control.

We can reasonably conclude that if Afrikan people had controlled the kidnapping and deportation of their own people, then they would have been in a position to control the secondary trafficking of Asian people also. History confirms that Afrikan people were not in control of either of these deportation processes. The truth is that the theft and compulsory deportation of Afrikan people started because European imperialists needed labour in the Caribbean. It was not because Afrikan people were previously enslaving themselves or because they had some kind of innate mystical desire to sell fellow Afrikan people to Europeans (Shepard & Beckles, 2000, p. 5).

3.4 Allegation 2: We sold our own people into slavery
3.4.1 Human trafficking and the 'Triangular trade'
If we take a panoramic view of the so called 'Triangular trade', we notice that all ships started their journeys in Europe; sailed south to Afrika and then west to the Americas, before returning to Europe. Their point of origin is the first clue as to who was in *control* of the trafficking process. European imperialism built the ships, owned the ships and *all* contents, staffed the ships and profited massively from the ships' voyages. European imperialists were obviously and clearly in total *control* of the 'transportation' process and therefore *responsible* for it. The kidnapping and deportation of Afrikan people was an integral part of that 'transportation' process.

If we look at the three points of the geographical triangle, we get another clue. Europe had 'free' people at all three points of the triangle. Afrikan people, by contrast, were enslaved in two points of the triangle i.e. the Americas and Europe and were either kidnapped or living in constant fear of being kidnapped in their own homeland. Only a 'free' people located at all three points of the triangle, working in a co-ordinated manner could *control* the destiny of those Afrikan people being trafficked around the triangle. In other words, only Europeans had the liberty and independently organised infrastructure necessary to be able to *control* the triangle. This is further proof that it was Europeans who were *responsible* for the kidnapping and deportation of Afrikan people.

Triangular Analysis

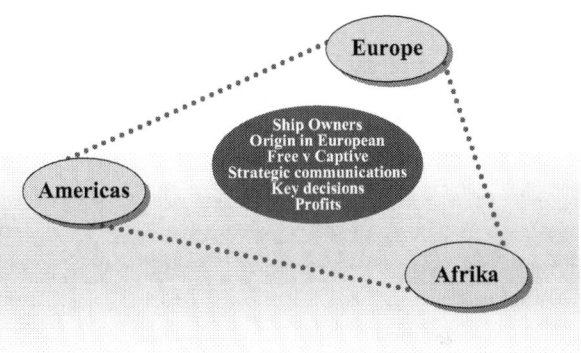

Brother Omowale

Europeans were also in *complete control* of communications throughout the triangle and were the only people to have a strategic knowledge of what was going on in all parts. Any Afrikan people colluding with the Europeans in the kidnapping and deportation process would have had no real idea about where their kidnapped countrymen were going or of the fate that awaited them. The ignorance of their position meant that there was no way that Afrikan collaborators could *control* the process. They could contribute to the process by capturing fellow Afrikan people, but only European imperialism through its communications network, had sufficient knowledge and understanding of the overall process to *control* it. Again it is obviously Europeans that were *responsible* for the system.

Eric Williams explains that Britain and other European states operated as the capital of the 'triangular trade'. All decisions affecting the whole triangle were made in Britain and other parts Europe. It was British and other European bankers that provided the subsidy needed in order to get the whole trade started. It was British and other European manufacturers that provided the products to 'trade' for Afrikan people and the bulk of the profits and industrial development went to Britain and their European allies (Williams, 1997, p. 51/52). Walter Rodney devoted a whole book to explaining how Britain and its European allies got rich by using slavery, colonialism and neo-colonialism to stifle the development of both Afrika and the Caribbean (Rodney, 1981). The whole 'triangular' process, together with the activities contained within it was designed by Europeans and centred on accruing benefits for those Europeans who *controlled* it and were *responsible* for it.

Another point that becomes clear from this triangular analysis is that some Afrikan people in Afrika did play a part in the kidnapping and to some extent, the deportation of fellow Afrikan people. However, it would have been impossible for Afrikan people in Afrika to have participated in the 'seasoning' or the actual enslavement of their sisters and brothers because those processes took place entirely outside the Afrikan continent. Afrikan people in the continent played no part in forcefully extracting labour, changing names, changing the belief systems of their deported sisters and brothers. This was organised entirely by European imperialism and any Afrikan people involved would themselves have been 'seasoned' outside of Afrika.

Chattel Slavery Components

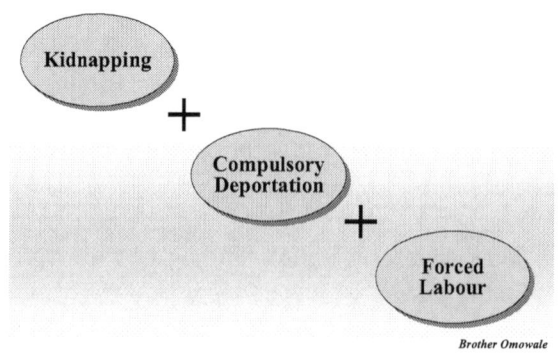

Kidnapping

+

Compulsory Deportation

+

Forced Labour

Brother Omowale

Through this triangular analysis we can reasonably conclude that some Afrikan people behaved badly towards their sisters and brothers and participated in the system created, controlled and organised by European imperialism. A minority of Afrikan people were complicit and colluded with the imperialists against the collective best interests of their own people. However, it is equally clear that no Afrikan person, group or nation can be held *responsible* for the institution of slavery. Both the *control* and *ultimate responsibility* for this institution rests entirely with European imperialism, with British imperialism claiming the lion's share.

3.4.2 The hypocrisy of British imperialism – The worse kidnappers

The British establishment shamelessly seeks to claim the credit for 'abolishing' what it calls the 'slave trade'. In this way it attempts to guide the public's attention away from its central role in the kidnapping, deportation and enslavement of Afrikan people. However, a closer examination of British imperialism's moral claims reveals the fact that the British were not rushing to 'free' enslaved Afrikan people.

The British historian Peter Fryer points out that:

> "Some Europeans raised their voices against the slave trade, though they did not begin to do so in Britain until the second half of the eighteenth century by which time it had been under way for some 200 years." (Fryer, 1989, p. 9).

The British were late in raising 'moral' objections even by European standards. Furthermore, whatever the stories propagated, it is obvious that British imperialists did not engage in the theft and compulsory deportation of Afrikan people simply for the pleasure of later abolishing that evil process.

An honest analysis of the history reveals that the British had an overarching role in the kidnapping and deportation of Afrikan people. Their role was so central that they operated as the supplier to the other main European imperialist nations of the time. For instance:

> "In 1701, the Spanish gave the French a contract to supply them with 4,000 [Kidnapped Afrikan people] a year, but the French didn't fulfil it due to their needs in Haiti and their other colonies, so the contract was awarded to the British." (Justice, 2005, p. 117).

Further details reveal how:

> "... in 1713, under the treaty of Utretch, Britain acquired the *assiento*, the official contract to supply 4,800 [kidnapped Afrikan people] a year to south and central America, the Spanish West Indies, Mexico and Florida." (Fryer, 1989, p. 8)

Furthermore:

> "A [British] government report of 1792 found that 50% of the [kidnapped Afrikan people] imported into the British islands were sold onto French [enslaver plantation owners]." (Ferguson, 1999, p. 131).

However, it was not just the Spanish and the French that came to rely on the British for their supplies of kidnapped Afrikan people:

> "The Portuguese, having the largest South American colony, were still the largest importers of [Kidnapped Afrikan people], but British merchants had taken over much of their importation volume." (Justice, 2005, p. 117).

The overall pattern of British complicity is revealed when we note that:

> "Until 1791, a quarter of the Atlantic slave trade was in British hands, and from 1791 to 1806 Britain's share was over half." (Fryer, 1989, p. 8 & 9).

If Afrikan people were really responsible for selling themselves and had a controlling interest in the so called 'trade', then all of the contracts mentioned above should have been developed and managed with Afrikan chiefs. The fact is that it was European imperialism, with Britain as its chief co-ordinator, that controlled the process of kidnapping and deporting Afrikan people from their homes. British imperialism has a 300 year plus track record of consistently coordinating the imposition of chattel enslavement upon innocent Afrikan people. This is unquestionably the worse national track record in the history of humanity. No Afrikan nation, anywhere on the continent can match that degree of complicity in the enslavement of any part of the human family. In short, no Afrikan nation has the blood of slavery on its hands to the extent that Britain has. We can honestly conclude that it was British imperialism, more than any other entity on earth that was responsible for the evil anti-human obscenity that it called the 'slave trade'.

3.4.3 An honest reflection – Afrikan people fought against kidnapping and deportation

European historians have been dishonest in so far as they have tended to concentrate the minds of the public on one tiny but important role played by Afrikan people at home in the enslavement of their Diasporan sisters and brothers. This propaganda strategy is designed to remove from vision the negative overarching role played by Europeans in the Afrikan *Maangamizi* i.e. the evil anti-Afrikan genocide. They were the driving force for the evil; even the Afrikan collaborators:

> "... had to be seduced ... [by them through] the dispensing of gifts and with bribes." (Walwin, 1993, p. 31).

In addition, it also hides the multitude of positive actions taken by Afrikan people in the continent, at great risk to themselves, specifically for the purpose of ending or hindering the enslavement of their sisters and brothers.

An honest refection reveals that not all Afrikan people were involved in the theft and compulsory deportation of their fellow Afrikan people into slavery; In fact a substantial proportion were most definitely not. It is true that some such as the Benin chiefs Tegebesu and Adandozan consistently participated in it (Martin, 1999, p. 30; Rodney, 1981, p. 119). However, it is also true that others such as the Benin chiefs **Agaja Trudo** and **Glele** participated in it at one point and then outlawed it and bravely fought against it, even achieving its abolition at another (Shepard & Beckles, 2000, p. 5; Barkindo, 1989, p. 92; Rodney, 1981, p. 81). Yet others such as warrior sisters **Nzinga** in Angola (Shepard & Beckles, 2000, p. 5; Rodney, 1981, p. 80) continuously fought against this illegal activity. In some parts of Afrika such as Zimbabwe, there does not appear to be a history of Afrikan people participating as agents of the trans-Atlantic kidnapping and deportation process at all.

Furthermore, it is also clear that some Afrikan people living in parts of Afrika affected by widespread kidnapping were themselves enslaved under the domestic system (Fryer, 1989, p. 10). It is highly unlikely that these relatively disempowered people would have been responsible for the kidnapping and deportation of fellow Afrikan people. At worse they may have been coerced into kidnapping others and even if that happened, it would be absurd to blame them for enslaving fellow Afrikan people.

3.4.4 Afrikan people in Afrika were the first to abolish the 'slave trade'

Afrikan people did not wait two to three hundred years to be persuaded that slavery was wrong; understanding that it was both immoral and illegal, we abolished it immediately. One example comes from the Bini people who abolished the 'slave trade' in their area from the early 1500's until the late 1600's. Unfortunately for us, their abolition of the 'slave trade' was itself abolished by European imperialism. Justice explains that:

> "Eventually, there was a foreign inspired civil war, at the end of which Oba Akensua won and reintroduced slavery" (Justice, 2005, p. 132).

A later example comes from **Agaja Trudo** who became the chief of Dahomey in 1708. He inherited a kingdom with an economy based on the kidnapping of Afrikan people, but came to the realisation that it was against the best interests of Afrikan people for the kidnapping and deportation to continue. In 1724 he declared the abolition of the 'slave trade', burned down European camps and deportation centres and blocked all so called 'slave routes' to the interior. It was a very successful abolition with the kidnapping and deportation of Afrikan people being ground to a virtual halt (Rodney, 1981, p. 81).

In 1725 he attempted to consolidate his abolition by sending an ambassador to Britain. The ambassador's remit was to inform the British authorities that Dahomey was willing to trade with them in goods and services, but the trafficking of Afrikan people would not be tolerated. His ambassador was ignored by the British establishment throughout the entirety of his time in London. No one would agree to see him or talk to him and his attempts at securing diplomatic consolidation of the abolition ended in failure.

Instead of co-operating with **_Agaja Trudo_**'s missionaries, British imperialism embarked on its own secret underhand 'diplomatic' mission. The British knew that there was a history of animosity between the Dahomey Empire and that of Oyo to the east. These differences were exploited by the British with the express intention of instigating wars between them so as to reintroduce the system of kidnapping and deporting Afrikan people into British enslavement – a process which was so lucrative for them. The British were eventually successful in abolishing this Afrikan abolition of the 'slave trade' and achieved this by instigating what were to become decade long wars between the two Afrikan nations. By 1730 the Dahomey abolition had been completely broken down by the secret British intrigues and a kidnapping spree ensued.

3.4.5 British imperialism used a divide and rule approach to reinstating slavery

It is important to understand the destabilising processes that were used to destroy both of the above mentioned Afrikan abolitions of 'slave trading'. In fact the destabilising processes were so devastating that they effectively ended up disempowering and destroying the Afrikan nations involved; reducing them to a shadow of their former power. British imperialism specifically employed divide and rule tactics designed to compel Afrikan nations to supply fellow Afrikan people for compulsory deportation into enslavement. It used Afrikan people to capture other Afrikan people, both within and beyond their own nation, and then cunningly blamed the capturers for the whole act of enslavement.

The first part of the destabilising process was to create an environment of fear amongst Afrikan nations by promoting total mutual mistrust. They did this by lying to each of the two or more Afrikan nations or sub-groups that they intended to trick and subvert. They simultaneously presented themselves as the friends of the Afrikan nations that they intended should war with each other. They secretly 'advised' each of the nations that the other was well armed and intended to attack them to take their lands and enslave them. They secretly 'offered to help' each of the nations by supplying them with the guns that they would need to fend off their supposed 'aggressors'. The catch was that guns could only be bought if Afrikan people were used as currency (Fryer, 1989, p. 10).

Destabilising Process

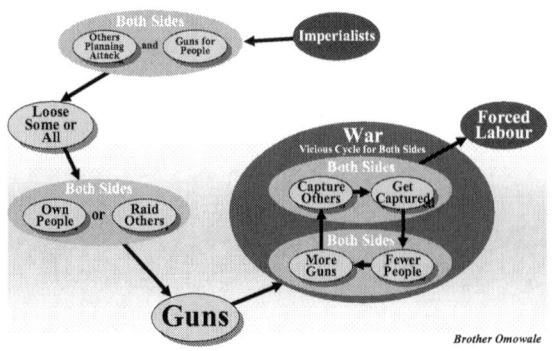

Brother Omowale

Once the Afrikan nations had been tricked, the choice that confronted them was to either: (i) give up a few of their people for the guns necessary for the survival of their nation, or (ii) refuse to sell anybody and be overwhelmed by their supposedly armed 'aggressor' nation, with the consequence that of all their own people would be defeated and sold into slavery. Inevitably, the Afrikan nations chose the former option in a desperate attempt to ensure their own survival. Some sold their own people, then organised raids on weaker neighbours to kidnap Afrikan people for whom the British would provide them with 'desperately needed' guns. When they felt that they had secured enough guns they would attack their supposed 'aggressor'. They would justify their own attack on the grounds that, in their view, it was a defensive tactic, designed to ensure that they themselves were not attacked and enslaved.

In addition to those Afrikan nations that were tricked into: (i) internal wars and (ii) warring against their neighbours to produce Afrikan kidnap victims for European enslavers, the imperialists used another devastating method. British and other imperialists set up their own proxy states. They were established for the specific purpose of destabilising Afrikan nations opposed to the kidnapping and deportation of Afrikan people. Again they armed them on the basis of guns being received in return for Afrikan people.

It is important to acknowledge that these proxy states which terrorised the Afrikan nations around them are guilty as charged for their part in the process of kidnapping Afrikan people. Their motives were purely and simply to make profits for themselves and they did this at the expense of the liberty of their own sisters and brothers. Their existence destabilised whole regions of Afrika and bred mistrust between hitherto peaceful neighbours. Formed in 1712, the Bambara state of Segu is said to have fulfilled this type of role (Breaking the silence).

Once the wars and raids had started some Afrikan nations became trapped in a vicious cycle where they felt forced to capture other Afrikan people in order to make themselves militarily strong enough in relative terms to avoid being captured. The more they captured fellow Afrikan people to obtain guns for their own protection, the more their fellow Afrikan people captured them in an attempt to protect themselves. The continuous escalation of this cut throat environment, where all other Afrikan nations were perceived as enemies, eventually meant that it was beyond the capacity of any single group of Afrikan people to stop the kidnapping. All of the Afrikan nations in the affected regions were caught in a downward spiral whether they wanted to be in it or not.

To get an idea of how successful these vicious underhand activities were, we must understand that British imperialism alone dumped 394,000 guns in West Afrika annually as a stimulus to inter and intra-tribal war and the general political destabilisation of the region (Justice, 2005, p. 142). Another 50,000 guns were dumped in the Loango-Congo area every year (Justice, 2005, p. 143). Other European imperialist nations assisted Britain in this process. For instance, in the case of the Gold Coast, guns were supplied to the Ashante by the Dutch, while the British armed their southern cousins the Fante (Justice, 2005, p. 127).

Another part of imperialism's strategy for kidnapping Afrikan people was to flood Afrikan nations with drugs. The drug used for this purpose was alcohol. There is little doubt that alcohol was sold to Afrikan nations (Rodney, 1981, p. 77), but its undermining and destabilising effects seem to have gone largely unrecorded by 'historians'. A speciality of the imperialists was to shower Afrikan people with alcohol and enter into 'agreements' and even 'treaties' with Afrikan leaders when they were drunk. It did not escape the imperialist's attention that it was easier to kidnap a drunken person than a sober one and they used that knowledge with deadly effect (Williams, 1997, p. 78-81). For addicted Afrikan people alcohol became a motivating force for kidnapping their sisters and brothers (Anderson, 1995, p. 60 & 78). Reduced to the mindset of a junkie, their personal 'fix' became more important to them than, either their own or their neighbours' national welfare.

Afrikan groups and individuals who actively participated in the kidnapping and deportation of their sisters and brothers cannot be absorbed of their personal responsibility for their part in undermining the future development of Afrika. However, history demonstrates that Afrikan complicity in the theft and compulsory deportation of fellow Afrikan people eventually became a matter of survival for participating Afrikan nations rather than a desire. All Afrikan peoples in the affected regions were, in fact, unwitting victims of a system of internal kidnapping that had been externally created by British imperialism and its allies. Once they had set up the system, all the British had to do was stand back, with their supply of guns and alcohol and wait for the captured Afrikan people to be brought to them.

The fundamental truth is that the majority of Afrikan people were against the kidnapping and deportation of their people. There were many attempts by Afrikan people to abolish the kidnapping because it so undermined Afrikan nations, Afrikan development and Afrikan culture. Every time Afrikan people abolished the kidnapping and deportation, the imperialists used secret underhand methods to abolish the Afrikan abolitions. It was the imperialists that started the whole kidnapping process and did everything in their power to ensure that it continued, because their interests were intimately bound up with it. Up until the birth of industrial capitalism, when their interests changed, they constantly supported, practiced and profited from their kidnapping, deporting and enslaving of Afrikan people.

3.4.6 Afrikan people in Afrika battled against the 'slave trade'

Part of the important information that remains largely concealed is the history of how Afrikan people on the continent courageously fought against those that kidnapped and deported their sisters and brothers. Some of them were particularly courageous because they were operating against a tide of kidnapping orchestrated by the imperialists in their regions of the continent. These Afrikan defenders of liberty and law employed a range of methods to fight against the kidnappers [both

Afrikan and European] operating in their lands. For instance there are historical examples of:

1. ***Afrikan people in the motherland physically battling with the imperialist, sometimes losing their lives in the process to defend their laws and prevent the kidnapping.*** For instance:

   > "...1767, when seven English ships - five from Liverpool, one from Bristol and one from London - were waiting [to receive kidnapped Afrikan people] on the Old Calabar River. A group of armed [Afrikan warriors] from Old Calabar attacked the English, but they were unsuccessful because the King's soldiers helped the English [kidnappers]. The leader of the Old Calabar warriors was then beheaded, and the survivors were sold into slavery in the West Indies." (Breaking the silence).

   It would be ridiculous to accuse these Afrikan warrior heroes, who gave up their lives and liberty, of selling other Afrikan people into slavery. It would be equally ridiculous to accuse other Afrikan people of selling these heroes into slavery. They understood that under Afrikan law kidnapping for enslavement was illegal and acted to defend that law.

2. ***Afrikan people in the motherland risking their lives in raids to release kidnapped fellow Afrikan people.*** For instance in 1758, Afrikan people in Gambia were so horrified when they witnessed their sisters and brothers being sold to William Potter, captain of the human trafficking ship *The Perfect*, that they attacked it. In the process of restoring Afrikan law, order and justice, they put the whole crew to death. These Afrikan heroes saved over 300 of their people from being deported into enslavement (Breaking the silence). It would be both harsh and incorrect to accuse these Afrikan heroes and their descendents of selling their fellow Afrikan people into slavery.

3. ***Afrikan people in the motherland refusing to 'trade' at all with the imperialists.*** In 1876, the tail end of the kidnapping and deportation process, the British sent a warship to carry out

'gunboat diplomacy' against **Glele** the leader of the people of Dahomey. They tried to steal money and other resources from Dahomey under the guise of what they called 'compensation'. Using cannons to assist 'negotiations', they blocked all trade from Dahomey. Undaunted, the people of Dahomey retaliated by using only local products and blocking all trade to the British. In the end, it was the British that had to come grovelling to **Glele** and the Dahomey people. They begged him to re-instate trade with them. He proved who the real masters were by forcing the British to pay heavy compensation, the legal fine for their arrogant illegal blockade of Dahomey's seas. Sadly, Glele will not be remembered as an Afrikan hero because of his earlier enthusiastic participation in the kidnapping and deportation of innocent Afrikan people (Barkindo, 1989. p. 92).

4. ***Afrikan people in the motherland shutting down the so called 'slave routes'.*** The example of **Agaja Trudo** has already been cited above. However around 1720 **Tomba**, one of the leaders of the Baga people in the Guinea-Conakry area of West Afrika, tried to build alliances amongst Afrikan people in the region with a view to enforcing Afrikan law and bringing an end to the illegal kidnapping and deportation of Afrikan people. It took an alliance between European kidnappers, mixed descendents of Afrikan people and Europeans and Afrikan people directly 'profiting' from the kidnapping to destroy his initiative (Rodney, 1981, p. 80). It would be absurd to suggest that **Tomba** and his descendents are responsible for the enslavement of Afrikan people.

5. ***Afrikan people in the motherland refusing to supply fellow Afrikan people to the European enslavers.*** Captain Samuel Stribling was captain of the Afrikan Queen a human trafficking ship which left Bristol in 1792. The ship docked at Old Calabar (now Nigeria) to illegally deport illegally kidnapped Afrikan people. He found little in the way of co-operation from Afrikan people in the region because:

> "At least 21 of the ship's crew died during the 7 or 8 months spent at Old Calabar waiting whilst the

captain purchased [illegally kidnapped Afrikan people]" (Portcities Bristol).

This was one of a number of incidents that caused James Rogers, the ships owner to go bankrupt. This example clearly demonstrates that Afrikan people were not habitually falling over themselves to break their own laws and kidnap and sell their sisters and brothers. Even this calibre of 'passive resistance' through non-cooperation with the kidnappers contributed significantly to the destruction of the so called 'slave trade'.

6. ***Afrikan people in the motherland sending diplomats to Britain to negotiate an end to the trafficking of their people.*** The example of ***Agaja Trudo***'s ambassador coming to London has already been cited above (Rodney, 1981, p. 81). This is an important example because whilst some of the violent resistance identified above has the potential to be (incorrectly) interpreted as spontaneous, ill-thought through reactions to injustice, international diplomacy cannot be belittled or dismissed in that way. Diplomats operate with the full force of their national law. This diplomatic initiative is clear evidence that the political and legal will to end the process of kidnapping, deporting and enslaving Afrikan people was clearly institutionalised in the societies of at least some Afrikan people in the motherland. Furthermore, this political will was sufficiently well organised to seriously seek the enforcement of its laws and the corresponding abolition of chattel slavery in the international arena. Abolition was therefore an official legal policy in Afrika over 100 years before Britain came around to practicing or even appreciating that level of civilisation and humanism. Indeed, the indictment against British imperialism is even more damning because of the way in which it passively and actively supported law breaking by opposing these anti-slavery initiatives.

If it is true that some Afrikan people from home were involved in the kidnapping and deportation of their own people, then it is equally true that many Afrikan people from home were actively involved in fighting against the same process. It does a great disservice to the many thousands of Afrikan people at home who were tricked into participating in the chaotic kidnapping situation orchestrated by European imperialism, together with those that actively fought against human trafficking to blame them for the plight of those Afrikan people who were unfortunate enough to be deported into enslavement. Perhaps there is a case for posthumously identifying, honouring and thanking our home based Afrikan anti-slavery hero warriors for their role in ensuring that the gruesome kidnapping and deportation situation was not made even worse.

3.4.7 European imperialism a common denominator in chattel slavery

The track record of European imperialism as it bullied its way around the world reveals an unmitigated pattern of genocide against other peoples which included enslaving them. If we take British imperialism as an example, everywhere it went it imposed some type of slavery system. In addition, to the genocides that it has perpetrated across north, south east, west and central Afrika there is the pattern of inter-continental genocide that it has left in its slip stream. No continent on earth has escaped its anti-human crusade of devastation against the peoples of the world. It is beyond the scope of this essay to fully examine the enslaving activities of British imperialism. Nonetheless, it is clear that British imperialism's worldwide track record of enslaving other people far exceeds anything to be found in Afrikan history or any other people's history for that matter.

Consider this tiny sample of the enslavement practices that Britain got up to. In its own native Europe, British imperialism invaded Ireland, enslaved the Irish people and stole their land with the result that we experience the so called 'Northern Ireland problems' today (Stewart, 1989, p. 21). It had to travel a little further to steal the island of Gibraltar from the Spanish and create a similar set of problems there also.

In Asia British imperialism attacked and enslaved the people of India in their own land (Chinweizu, 1987, p. 4). In China it used a cocktail of hard drugs to supplement their more conventional gun toting methods in order to steal Hong Kong and attempt to enslave the Chinese people (Executive Intelligence Review, 1992, p. 116). In Iraq it stole the people's land from under their feet, whilst in Palestine it took the additional step of giving the land away to its anti-human allies the

Zionists (Shlaim, 1988, p. 1). Again, the repercussions can be seen to the present day through wars which appear to have little prospect of early settlement.

In Oceania it managed to almost wipe a whole people i.e. the Aborigines, from the face of the earth (Cole, 1986, p. 35). To 'achieve' this level of completely unwarranted extermination of a people once might be considered 'poor judgement' or even 'bad luck', but these explanations can be ruled out because British imperialism repeated the whole process. It was the virtual extermination of the American Indians (Peiterse, 1986, p. 21) that created the labour vacuum that caused it to practice its genocide against Afrikan people.

It is the systematic pattern of enslaving different peoples across different parts of the world that reduces the argument that Afrikan people enticed British imperialists into engaging in slavery to the level of farce. There were no Afrikan people to entice British imperialism in Asia, Oceania, the Americas or its native Europe, but Britain and its imperialist allies practiced a variety of forms of slavery in those lands anyway. If imperialism could practice slavery everywhere else in the world without being seduced by Afrikan people, then obviously it could practice it in Afrika without being enticed by us to do so. That is exactly what happened. The truth is that the imperialists came to Afrika with a culture of practicing slavery, a proven track record of carrying out slavery and developed the intention of inflicting slavery on Afrikan people.

3.4.8 Other peoples collaborated with oppressors

Some Jews collaborated with the perpetrators of their holocaust, but we don't turn around and say that Jews caused their own holocaust and therefore deserved what they got. For instance, Chaim Weizmann described as one of the 'chieftains of Jewry' acted against the interests of his own people when he:

> "... pledged allegiance to the British war on the young Jews fighting for freedom." (Hecth, 1961, p. 5).

Furthermore, this architect and first 'Jewish leader' of the Zionist monstrosity known as 'Israel' actually refused German Jews immigration rights to 'Israel'. This refusal effectively condemned his fellow Jews to suffer the consequences of Hitler's extermination policy (Hecth, 1961, p. 19-22).

Yet another example of collaboration comes from the records of the Jerusalem District Court. The court testimony of another prominent Jew Rudolf Kastner confirms that in June 1944 he personally operated as an official of The Jewish Agency. He admitted that the agency actively participated in the process of killing his own Jewish people. In his official capacity he knowingly worked closely with Nazi Germany's SS to plan, round up and transport his fellow Jews to Auschwitz so that they could be killed (Hecth, 1961, p. 55-68).

Unfortunate as these behaviours are, we do not absorb the German Nazis of their responsibility for the genocide against the Jews on the grounds that some Jews collaborated. Nazi Germans have been correctly pursued, put on trial and convicted for their crimes. Furthermore, state and business institutions involved in the genocide have been compelled to apologise and make substantial reparation payments.

The argument suggesting that because some Afrikan people collaborated in the kidnapping and deportation of their own people, the imperialists have no case to answer is fundamentally baseless. It is borne out of a specific and rancid brand of anti-Afrikan racism i.e. *Afriphobia*, ultimately designed to shield the real culprits from answering for their illegal behaviours. The Afrikan *Maangamizi* is arguably the greatest catastrophe in the history of humanity. It was against Afrikan law and there is no moral reason why it should be treated less favourably than the Jewish holocaust. It follows that Afrikan people must receive full reparations for both historical and contemporary suffering and disadvantage resulting from the *Maangamizi*, caused by European imperialist lawbreaking.

References
1. Anderson. S.I., (1995), *The Black Holocaust for Beginners*, Writers and readers publishing incorporated
2. Barkindo. B. et al, (1989), *Africa and the wider world 1: West and North Africa since 1800*, Longman Nigeria
3. Carruthers. Jacob, (1999), *Intellectual Warfare*, Third World Press
4. Chandler. Wayne, (1999), *Ancient Futures*, Black Classic Press

5. Chinweizu. (1987), *The West and the Rest of us: White predators Black slavers and the Afrikan elite*, Pero Press, Lagos, Nigeria
6. Cole. Mike, (1986), *The Aboriginal Struggle: an interview with Helen Boyle* in *Race and Class*, Institute of Race Relations
7. Diop. Cheik Anta, (1987), *Pre-Colonial Black Africa*, Lawrence Hill Books
8. Diop. Cheik Anta, (1991), *Civilization or Barbarism: An Authentic Anthropology*, Lawrence Hill Books
9. Editors of Executive Intelligence Review, (1992), *Dope Incorporated: The book that drove Kissinger crazy*, Executive Intelligence Review
10. Ferguson. James, (1999), *The Story of the Caribbean People*, Ian Randle Publisher, Kingston Jamaica
11. Fryer. Peter, (1984), *Staying Power: The History of Black People in Britain*, Pluto Press
12. Fryer. Peter, (1989), *Black People in the British Empire: An Introduction*, Pluto Press
13. Hecth. Ben, (1961), *Perfidy*, Julian Messner Incorporated, New York
14. Honychurch. Lennox, (1995a), *The Caribbean People*, Thomas Nelson and Sons Limited
15. Justice. Prince, (2005), *The Blackworld: Evolution to Revolution*, AU Publishers
16. Martin. Steve, (1999), *Britain's Slave Trade*, Channel 4 Books
17. Peiterse. Jan Nederveen, (1986), *Amerindian resistance: the gathering of fires* in *Race and Class*, Institute of Race Relations
18. Rodney. Walter, (1981), *How Europe Underdeveloped Africa*, Bogle-L'Overture Publications
19. Shepard, Verene & Beckles Hilary, (2000), *Caribbean Slavery in the Atlantic World: A Student Reader*, Ian Randle Publishers, Kingston
20. Shlaim. Avi, (1988), *The politics of partition, King Abdullah, the Zionists and Palestine 1921 – 1951*, Oxford Paperbacks
21. Stewart. ATQ, (1989), *The narrow ground: The roots of the Ulster conflict*, Faber and Faber Limited
22. Williams. Eric, (1997), *Capitalism and Slavery*, Andre Deutsch Limited

Internet references
1. Africa and Slavery 1500-1800 in *Middle East and Africa to 1875* by Sanderson Beck, http://san.beck.org/1-13-Africa1500-1800.html
2. Africa's Contribution to European Capitalist Development — the Pre-Colonial Period in *How Europe Underdeveloped Africa* by Walter Rodney, http://www.marxists.org/subject/africa/rodney-walter/how-europe/ch03.htm
3. Breaking the Silence – Learning about the Trans-Atlantic Slave Trade, www.antislavery.org/breakingthesilence

4. FReeper Canteen ~ Part IV of Women Warriors: Africa ~ February 10, www.freerepublic.com/focus/f-news/1075043/posts
5. Internet Puppet Theater, www.internetpuppets.org
6. Portcities Bristol, http://www.discoveringbristol.org.uk/showNarrative.php?sit_id=1&narId=15&nacId=19
7. Wikipedia, http://en.wikipedia.org/wiki/Kaipkire
8. Women in power 1700 – 1740, www.guide2womenleaders.com/womeninpower/Womeninpower1700.htm

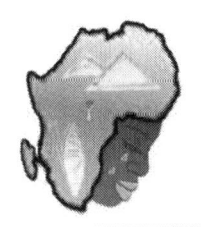

Afrikan People Abolished the 'Slave Trade'

Submission presented in
Parliament
Tuesday 17th January 2017

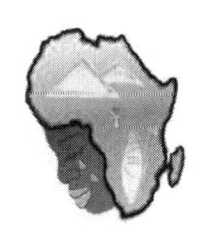

Will The Real William Wilberforce Please Stand Up?

Ukombozii
Education for Liberation
Afrikan Freedom Means Defeating Neo-Colonialism
www.ukombozii.org

Chapter 4

4 Will The Real William Wilberforce Please Stand Up?

4.1 The process of deception
4.1.1 Trickery in the name of Wilberforce
In its determination to lie to the British public by generally distorting the history of chattel enslavement, British imperialism has constructed a false saintly image around one of its own cadre. A character called William Wilberforce has been projected on to the centre stage of their interpretation of the history of the 'abolition of slavery'. In the worse cases of distortion, bogus 'historians' have deceived their readerships by giving Wilberforce the entire historical stage. He is presented to the people of the world as the person who 'abolished' the process of kidnapping and deporting Afrikan people from their homeland into slavery on the American continent. Wilberforce, raised to the status of superman, is presented as the individual (super hero) who single-handedly 'abolished' the whole institution of chattel enslavement. In this version of events, the fact that enslavement was imposed on Afrikan people by European imperialism is bye-passed and ignored. However, whilst it is true that Wilberforce took some actions that

affected enslaved Afrikan people, a closer examination of his activities reveals that he supported British imperialism's chattel slavery system by delaying and thwarting the progress of both the 'abolition of slavery' and the 'abolition' of the so called 'slave trade'.

British imperialism has cunningly used a set of hidden marketing techniques designed to trick all those who are ignorant or naive about the history of slavery. Their purpose is to mislead the public into believing that Afrikan people had no part to play in the destruction of the chattel enslavement system that was used to hold them in bondage. If they can maintain this false story, then it will help to disempower Afrikan people in the present day. Its constructed illusion contributes to Afrikan people believing that they do not have the power or ability to change current society for the better. Even those Afrikan people who feel a commitment to change, may be waiting for an individual super hero to come along and change society for them. Worse still they may be waiting for a non-Afrikan super hero, or more precisely a European imperialist super hero to sort their problems out. Certainly this is something that will never happen and any Afrikan people falling for this con trick will be contained just where British imperialism wants then - in a fantasy. In short, British imperialism would have successfully defended itself against any form of uprising or meaningful challenge from the Afrikan people that it has relentlessly and consistently oppressed for the last 400 years.

If we look behind imperialism's smoke screen, we find that the truth is very different. It was Afrikan people that abolished imperialism's system of piracy, kidnapping and deporting Afrikan people across the Atlantic and after that they went on to abolish the whole system of chattel enslavement. Afrikan people reached the point in struggle where their power simply could no longer be contained by imperialism. Their determined struggle for freedom burnt the fingers of imperialism so badly that it had to let go of the chattel enslavement system. Wilberforce's efforts were at best a side show in the process of this struggle. Imperialism's trick in ending chattel slavery, was that letting go of chattel slavery really meant transforming slavery into a form which for a while seemed more palatable to its victims. It is now becoming increasingly clear to Afrikan and other oppressed people that slavery still exists. The time has now arrived for current generations to master the historical truth so that they can use it to change British society for the better.

4.2 The real Wilberforce
4.2.1 Wilberforce: a man of class

Born in Kingston upon Hull on 24th August 1759 William Wilberforce was the son of a wealthy merchant (Web of English History). He was a Cambridge university graduate (Schama, 2006, p. 206) and clearly never knew poverty or even the nature of the hardships faced by ordinary working people; in colloquial terms, he was stinking rich. He inherited a landed estate from his mother (Web of English History), owned several properties and at one point was even landlord to the future Prime Minister of Britain (Howarth, 1973, p. 462). As a member of a family of wool merchants he also owned a chain of factories (Man's Unconquerable Mind). He was clearly a very busy man because on top of all of these interests, he was also a banker (Hart, 1998, p. 33). Wilberforce was truly representative of the elite class of British imperialism in that he was the embodiment of all of the sub-strata of the upper classes i.e. the aristocratic landed gentry, the factory owning industrial capitalists and the international finance capitalists.

Oppressor Class Cadre

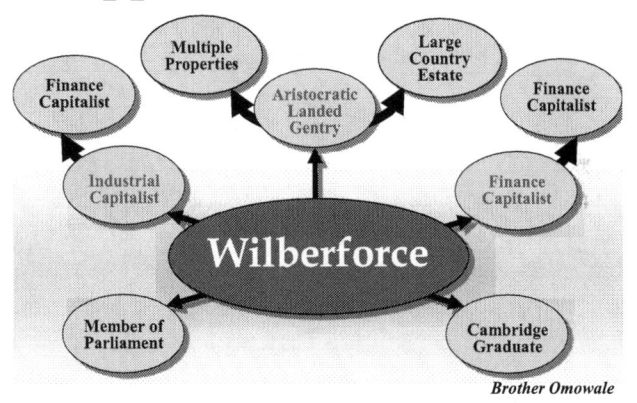

Brother Omowale

There was clearly no doubt that he was a member of the upper class elite and the evidence that we have confirms that his allegiance was firmly welded to the interests of his class. For instance he was the Tory MP for Hull at a time when the masses of British people were not even entitled to vote; needless to say this was prior to the existence of any form of working class political party (Ferguson, 1998, p. 132); so he could harbour no claims of representing the 'common man'. His family were land and factory owning wool merchants. There is no doubt that he took his family's interests seriously since he operated as the official Parliamentary spokesman for the wool industry (Williams, 1944, p. 160). This also makes it possible that he would have perceived the cotton industry, with its abundance of unpaid labour stolen from enslaved Afrikan people, as a rival with a competitive advantage that was unfair even by primitive capitalist standards (Martin, 1999, p. 71).

Whilst he looked after his own interests in Parliament, he was manifestly opposed to the interests of poor white people in Britain. For instance, he supported the introduction of the Corn Laws (William Wilberforce 1759-1833). These were the laws which protected the profits of the landed gentry by banning the importation of cheaper foreign corn. Whilst his actions were consistent with his own class interests, the problem for Britain's working people was that his actions meant that they were unable to pay the prices demanded by the British aristocratic farmers for their 'home grown' corn. His position on the Corn Laws meant that working people were literally expected to starve and did. He even supported the use of poor children in his native Britain as slaves (Milwood, 2010, p. 119). Wilberforce's body of upper class ideas, practices and decisions were so antagonistic towards the working classes in Britain that at one point his house had to be guarded by armed police in order to protect him from their wroth (Web of English History).

Wilberforce did not limit his oppressive ideas to the working class only, he repeatedly demonstrated that he did not have a high regard for women. He was blatantly against the interests of women to the point of even opposing their right to vote (Ligali, 6/11/2006). Another example of his antipathy towards women came in 1788 when he was part of a Parliamentary committee that decided that women sentence to death should be hung instead of burned (Web of English History). This 'commutation' or 'softer form of state sanctioned killing' was not for the benefit of the women themselves or their grieving families. Instead, it was so that their bodies could be donated to medical science; obviously the burnt bodies of the women killed would have been too badly damaged to be useful for medical research. These examples of Wilberforce's pattern of behaviour towards the 'less fortunate' reveals a man who appears to have quite casually exploited and oppressed anybody outside his class, without even a moments hesitation.

With such an indiscriminate track record of oppressing people 'below' his class, it is perhaps surprising that British imperialism asks us to believe that Wilberforce's Christian convictions inspired him to take up the cause of Afrikan people – the most exploited and oppressed group of all and furthest 'below' his class. The kindest assessment that we can make of this obviously false supposition is that it is patently ridiculous. To dismiss it all we have to do is ask a few simple questions. For instance: Was Wilberforce not a Christian when he voted in favour of the Corn Laws that, if he had had his way, would have led to the starvation of poor white people in Britain? Was he not a Christian when he supported the use of child slavery in Britain? Was he not a Christian when he determined that women should not be allowed to vote or that women 'felons' should be hung instead of burned? Did he lose his Christian convictions when he made these decisions and miraculously regain them when he heard about the suffering of Afrikan people?

Why should his Christian convictions cause him to suddenly spring to the assistance of a group of out of sight down trodden Afrikan people and at the same time, fail to cause him to assist his own people whose plight was immediately before him? In other words, why did his Christian convictions fail to begin at home? The reason is simple: It is because he was driven by the desire to amass profits for himself and his peers; he was not driven by Christian convictions at all. The story of his Christian convictions inspiring him to save enslaved Afrikan people from their suffering was a fake romantic cover story concocted to deceive the naive. The cover story is wholly inconsistent with his behaviour towards all other oppressed people, particularly those with whom he had direct contact. There is no truth in this concocted cover story whatsoever. The truth is that he was told to 'take up' the plight of enslaved Afrikan people by his boss the Prime Minister and the reason for 'taking it up' was so that he could underhandedly work to prolong the chattel enslavement system.

4.2.2 Wilberforce a drug addicted late comer to the abolition cause
Afrikan people resisted our enslavement from the very first day that European imperialism attempted to steal our people. However, it was not until 1776 that the world began to hear the first openly anti-slavery utterances of the British establishment. This happened when David Hartley condemned the 'slave trade' in the House of Commons (Hart,

2006, p. 1). It had taken British imperialism well over 200 years to begin to notice that there might be something wrong with piracy, kidnapping, deporting, holding in bondage, enslaving, murdering and otherwise abusing Afrikan people. Another initiative followed in 1783 when the Quakers petitioned Parliament against human trafficking (Hart, 2006, p. 1). Wilberforce was not involved in any of these early anti-slavery initiatives.

On 22nd May 1787 a group of British people gave themselves the official sounding title of 'The Abolition Society' and declared their existence to the British establishment. The society gave the outward impression that it was against the enslavement of Afrikan people, although its activities often suggested otherwise. Interestingly imperialism's 'great saviour and hero' Wilberforce was not amongst the original grouping (Hart, 2006, p. 1). Nor did he end up joining the society of his own volition or as a matter of conscience. Instead he was 'recruited' and sent into the abolition movement by the then Prime Minister William Pitt (Ferguson, 1998, p. 132; Williams, 1944, p. 123). The fake cover story about his moral and religious conviction compelling him to work for the abolition of slavery was made up later.

The choice of Wilberforce for the anti-slavery 'moral crusade' was an interesting one. Throughout his adult life, he is reported to have suffered significant health problems (Howarth, 1973, p. 463). This is hardly surprising given the fact that he was a known drug addict. Apparently he was a junkie, unable to wean himself off his reliance on hard drugs. British historians inform us that:

> "William Wilberforce ... took opium every day for 45 years."
> (Howarth, 1973, p. 562).

This evidence reveals the fact that Wilberforce demonstrated a greater level of commitment to the consumption of hard drugs than he ever did to the abolition of slavery. Evidence concerning whether he took hard drugs more often than he prayed is inconclusive. As if that was not enough, he was also known to indulge in drinking and gambling (Howarth, 1973, p. 457).

The appointment of a known drug addict and apparent drunkard as the champion of the abolition movement suggests that the British establishment had no real intention of abolishing its piracy, kidnapping, deporting and enslavement of Afrikan people. It also blows the cover off of the fake story that claims that he was inspired to save Afrikan people from slavery as a result of his Christian convictions. If Christianity was such an inspiration in his life, then why did it fail motivate and inspire sufficiently for him to refrain from hard drugs, gambling and alcohol?

4.3 Wilberforce: Government agent and bogus anti-slavery 'leader'?
4.3.1 Thwarting the abolition process

The recruitment of Wilberforce by the Prime Minister is an important clue suggesting that he may have been appointed to perform a subversive role designed to hold up the abolition process. Pitt was determined that Wilberforce, a backbencher, should be the official spokesman for the abolition society and in that role, present the abolition bill in Parliament. This is very surprising since the bill would have stood a much greater chance of success if the Prime Minister had taken it on as part of government business, headed and presented by a cabinet Minister. If he had really wanted to abolish the 'slave trade' he could have used the full power of his office to make it happen. The truth is that the Prime Minister's situation was delicate in that he wanted to appear to be in favour of abolition, whilst in reality being doggedly opposed to it.

Pitt was forced into giving the false impression that he favoured abolition because of the growing awareness about: (i) the barbarity, wickedness and general evil of slavery, and (ii) the large number of deaths of British seamen, soldiers and other personnel overseas. The resulting and ever growing outcry from the British public for the abolition of the 'slave trade' increased the pressure on him and his government to act. This then created serious problems for a government that relied heavily on the income that it received in the form of taxes from enslavers and others who profited from the human misery of enslaved Afrikan people. Pitt's tactical response was to send in his close and trusted friend Wilberforce; so close that at one time they even lived in the same house (Howarth, 1973, p. 462). Wilberforce's role was to function as the society's mouthpiece with the latent agenda of containing, stifling, thwarting, delaying and otherwise redirecting the pressure on government so as to stave off the abolition of slavery.

There are signs that initially Wilberforce was not quite up to the task of infiltrating and undermining the organised structures and processes developed to achieve the abolition of slavery. It evidently became necessary to coerce him into stepping more fully into the bogus leadership role ascribed to him because in 1787 Pitt found it necessary to warn Wilberforce that:

> "... if he did not bring the motion in [to the House of Commons], somebody else would ..." (James, 1963, p. 53).

The thought of somebody else stealing his limelight seems to have helped him overcome his reluctance.

Despite his shaky start, it did not take him long to blossom in his subversive role; there were deadly consequences for Afrikan people as Wilberforce used his position to destroy the 'Abolition Society's' infrastructure and stall the whole 'abolition' process. For instance, on 2nd April 1792 the House of Commons approved a bill, brought in by Wilberforce, for the 'abolition' of the practice of kidnapping and deporting Afrikan people across the Atlantic. This bill was consolidated on 23rd April 1792 when the House of Commons agreed and approved an exact date for the legal 'abolition' of British involvement in the kidnapping and deportation process (Web of English History). The date agreed for 'abolition' was 1st January 1796. In effect, the most difficult phase involved in enacting new legislation had been overcome and all that remained in Parliamentary procedural terms was approval from the House of Lords and Royal Assent.

It was at this point that one of the most amazing U-turns in the history of British politics happened. After having defeated all opposition in the House of Commons, a nearly complete piece of legislation lost the support of its supposed advocates. The result of this stand down was that the bill did not progress any further. The sovereignty of Parliament had already been established at this point in history and neither the House of Lords nor the Monarch could have prevented a determined House of Commons from carrying through this vitally important piece of legislation. It must therefore be regarded as extremely surprising that

Wilberforce and his friends chose this point to just pull the plug on the bill and drop it. One apologist for imperialism claimed that:

> "... the zeal of [Wilberforce and his friends] slackened ..." (Web of English History).

The historian Richard Hart gave a more honest appraisal when he explained that Wilberforce simply 'abandoned' the bill, leaving it to die an untimely death.

Imperialism's apologists excuse Wilberforce's abandonment of the bill on the grounds that he did not want to take an action that would be approved of by the Jacobins (Web of English History). However, the 'Black Jacobins' in Haiti had commenced their revolutionary war of liberation on 22nd August 1791 (James, 1963, p. 87). Furthermore, their European counterparts in France had started their activities aimed at changing the balance of power in their land even earlier on 14th July 1789 (Black, 1999, p. 87). The advocates of the bill were most definitely fully aware of the activities of the Jacobins at the time that they initially introduced the bill into Parliament. We can therefore reason that if the excuse given by the apologists was genuine and consistent, then the bill would never have been introduced in the first place. The truth is that the 'abolition' bill was only introduced as a public relations exercise and was never intended to succeed. Its advocates were caught by complete surprise when it reached as far as it did in the legislative process and responded by blatantly thwarting any further progress. If Wilberforce had been a genuine advocate for the 'abolition of slavery', then he would have increased his efforts during this critical Parliamentary phase in order to see the bill successfully through to legal enactment.

4.3.2 Hidden motivations behind Wilberforce's duplicity

When British imperialism abandoned its anti-Afrikan kidnapping and deportation racket, it was neither motivated by make believe Christian convictions nor philanthropy. Du Bois' observations expose some of its hidden agendas i.e. some of the real driving forces driving their actions:

> "Then came the French Revolution and eventually the revolt in Haiti. The British made every effort to seize control of this famous French colony. They tried both force of arms and bribery, but at last were compelled to

recognise the independence of Toussaint L'Ouverture, whom they tried to divorce from allegiance to the French.

Nevertheless, with Haiti out of the world market, the British could have retained their hold on the sugar industry had it not been for the continued cultivation of sugar in the Spanish and Portuguese colonies. So long as these colonies could obtain [cheaply priced kidnapped Afrikan people], they threatened and even destroyed the investment in [enslaved Afrikan people's] labour already made by British capital. Looked upon as machines or 'real estate,' as [enslaved Afrikan people] legally were, the investment in [enslaved Afrikan people's] labour was being undermined so long as cheaper [enslaved Afrikan people's] labour could be had from Afrika.

To keep the price of [enslaved Afrikan people] from falling, the [anti-Afrikan kidnapping and deportation racket] had to be limited or stopped. Otherwise the whole [investment in enslaved Afrikan people] would totter, and that is what England faced after the revolution from Toussaint. Early in the nineteenth century, therefore, she began to change, and ... philanthropists like Sharpe and Wilberforce came to the unexpected support of opportunist politicians like Pitt."
(Du Bois, 1996, p. 63)

In addition to the obvious benefit to Britain of cutting off reinforcements to the Afrikan Maroon warrior forces defeating them in the Caribbean, Du Bois illustrates how the cutting of new supplies of Afrikan people to competing wicked enslavers was also to Britain's advantage. The lie of philanthropy and Christian convictions motivating the likes of Wilberforce is completely exposed by those military and economic truths. , Britain eventually abolished its anti-Afrikan kidnapping and deportation racket on 1st January 1806. It saw no prospect of military victory over the Afrikan revolutionaries of Haiti and opted to give itself an economic competitive advantage over non British wicked enslavers. The undercover anti-abolitionist agent Wilberforce was nothing more than a distractive side show, there to give it a bogus philanthropic appearance.

4.3.3 Wilberforce wreaks the Abolition Society

After killing the bill, Wilberforce's next mission was to get rid of the 'Abolition Society' itself. Though he had hither to been working 'closely' with it, Wilberforce did not officially join the 'Abolition Society' until 1794 (Schama, 2006, p. 245). In retrospect, we can see that he joined the society in order to kill it off. He wasted no time in using the Afrikan revolution in Haiti as an excuse to wreck it. Wilberforce and his friends went so far as to cease virtually all 'Abolition Society' meetings. In their determination to ensure that the kidnapping and deportation of Afrikan people continued unabated, they deliberately did not meet regularly. Under Wilberforce's leadership, the society met only twice during the nine year period covering 1795 to 1804. The British historian Paul Foot explained that:

> "During this period the Abolition of Slavery Movement in Britain almost petered out." (Man's Unconquerable Mind).

In short, Wilberforce and his friends had reached the point of successfully achieving the Parliamentary 'abolition' of the process of kidnapping and deporting Afrikan people from Afrika and then jettisoned, not only the pursuit of the completion of the prospective Act of Parliament, but they also destroyed the whole organisational infrastructure that was supposedly designed to achieve 'abolition'.

Anti-Abolition Activities
of William Wilberforce

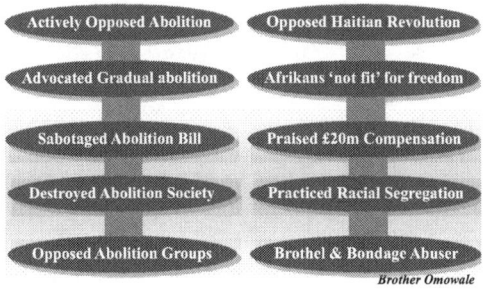

- Actively Opposed Abolition
- Opposed Haitian Revolution
- Advocated Gradual abolition
- Afrikans 'not fit' for freedom
- Sabotaged Abolition Bill
- Praised £20m Compensation
- Destroyed Abolition Society
- Practiced Racial Segregation
- Opposed Abolition Groups
- Brothel & Bondage Abuser

Brother Omowale

There can be little doubt that Wilberforce's actions were wholly inconsistent with the objective of abolishing the so called 'slave trade' and liberating Afrikan people from chattel enslavement bondage. Wilberforce was really a fake abolitionist and his actions directly contributed to delaying British imperialism's 'abolition' of the kidnapping and deportation process by British imperialism from 1st

January 1796 [when it was due to happen] until 25th March 1807 [when it eventually happened], a period of over 11 years. He stooped to even lower levels of deceit by using the Afrikan revolution in Haiti as a pretext for abandoning the 'abolition' bill designed to 'help' Afrikan people, a bill which had already successfully passed through the Commons (Hart, 1998, p. 62). The consequence for Afrikan people of Wilberforce's underhand delaying tactics was that British imperialism kidnapped and deported into slavery over a million more of our ancestors than would otherwise have directly suffered the human trafficking element of the *Maangamizi*. Given that 4 to 5 unsuspecting Afrikan people died for every one that made it across the Atlantic, we can reason that 4 to 5 million extra Afrikan people died needlessly as a direct result of his underhanded deceitful betrayal of the abolition cause. This evidence makes it clear that Wilberforce was no friend of Afrikan people; his actions were those of a blatant enemy.

Some readers might find it strange to think in terms of Wilberforce having operated as an undercover government spy working to subvert the abolitionist movement. However, we know that Pitt was really against the abolition of slavery because of his response to the Haitian revolution. When the world saw the Afrikan people in Haiti rise up and abolish slavery, Pitt failed to offer them either his government's support or even its official recognition. Instead he sent 60,000 British soldiers, mostly to die, in an unsuccessful attempt to crush the Afrikan people there in order to return them back into slavery (James, 1963, p. ix).

Pitt's actions must have been designed to maintain slavery, because he did not send his troops into nearby France to assist attempts to crush the revolutionary Jacobins who were fighting a similar cause. The British historian Paul Foot, himself the son of a former Leader of the Opposition, raises this analysis to an even higher level. He says that:

> "There was a chance that the French might be dislodged from the island by a slave revolt; and that the British might seize St Domingue, restore slavery there and make good British profits from it." (Man's Unconquerable Mind).

Foot makes it plain that the aim of Pitt was to reinstate the system of chattel slavery that Afrikan people had abolished of their own volition. As part of their cover up, Imperialism's bogus historians appear to be asking us to believe that the British government was going to reinstate slavery in Haiti so that they could have the pleasure of abolishing it a year or two later. This is obviously nonsense; the exposure of the latent objective of the British Prime Minister Pitt is crystal clear for all to see. Pitt was unequivocally an emphatic supporter of the idea that Afrikan people in the Americas should remain enslaved and his motivation for this was profit.

Instead of correcting his close friend the Prime Minister and championing the cause of the Afrikan people fighting for their freedom in Haiti, Wilberforce publicly supported Pitt's decision to send British forces into Haiti in order to fully re-instate slavery on the island and abandoned the abolition cause (Hart, 1998, p. 62). Historian Richard Hart explains that Wilberforce:

> "... did not wish the [enslaved Afrikan people] to participate in the abolition process as had occurred in Haiti, where [enslaved Afrikan people] themselves had brought their enslavement to an end." (Hart, 1998, p. 33).

There can be little doubt that Wilberforce's actions were specifically against the enslaved Afrikan people who were fighting for freedom. We know this because he had previously pronounced his opposition to Britain sending troops to fight against their own European kith and kin in North America (John Jay) and France (Howarth, 1973, p. 456). That they should be prepared to go to such lengths is proof conclusive that both Wilberforce and Pitt were unequivocally and fundamentally opposed to the abolition of slavery. Any other utterances that they made were just anti-slavery rhetoric designed to camouflage their real agenda. It is just not possible for an honest and objective observer to consider these facts and reasonably draw a contrary conclusion.

In addition, there is documented evidence confirming that governments of that period in British history actively used their own undercover agents as spies against groups that they did not approve of. Afrikan anti-slavery and anti-imperialist heroes such as William Davison (Fryer, 1984, p. 213) and William Cuffay (Fryer, 1984, p. 243) were executed or otherwise persecuted as a direct result of the subversive activities of government sponsored undercover agent provocateurs. The Briton Arthur Thistlewood suffered a similar fate (Foot, 2002, p. 149).

As will be seen, Wilberforce consistently behaved in ways that ran counter to the objective of abolishing slavery. It is his consistent pattern of blatant anti-abolitionist, blatant racist and blatant sexist behaviours that lay him open to the accusation of being a subversive government agent. It is also interesting to note that all the time William Pitt, the man who appointed him, was Prime Minister all bills to abolish the kidnapping and deportation of Afrikan people failed to make their way through Parliament. It was only after the death of Pitt in 1806 that the abolition of the slave trade bill finally made it onto the statue book.

4.4 Wilberforce the racist misogynist
4.4.1 Racist Wilberforce opposed the abolition of slavery
Another of the methods used by imperialism to propagate its lies is to create or control organisations that pretend to champion particular just causes whilst, at the same time, adopting the hidden agenda of derailing or containing that just cause. The actions of the so called 'Abolition Society' were consistent with that pattern in that despite its progressive sounding name, it openly boasted that it did not seek the abolition of the enslavement of Afrikan people. For instance, on 12th August 1788 just months after Wilberforce started operating as its 'quasi-official' Parliamentary spokesman, the 'Abolition Society' issued its first public statement:

> "... proclaiming that the abolition of slavery was not their objective' (Hart, 2006, p. 2).

The following year 1789, a Privy Council report concluded that free waged labourers were 3 times more productive than enslaved people (Ferguson, 1998, p. 132). There was an increasing realisation that enslaved people had no purchasing power and that this was as an obvious impediment to the development of the capitalist market system of distribution and exchange (Hart, 1998, p. 33).

The society appears to have been completely unmoved by the mounting sources of information and pressure supportive of the abolition of slavery. They still stubbornly refused to advocate for the abolition of slavery and on 31st January 1792 Wilberforce's friends in the 'Abolition Society' issued their second public statement:

"... proclaiming that the abolition of slavery was not their objective" (Hart, 2006, p. 2).

If these actions were not enough to demonstrate the desire of Wilberforce and his friends to hold back progress towards gaining the 'freedom' of enslaved Afrikan people then, on 29th March 1797 the case was sealed; three years after Wilberforce officially joined, the disingenuous nature of the 'Abolition Society' was confirmed when it issued its third public statement:

"... proclaiming that the abolition of slavery was not their objective" (Hart, 2006, p. 2).

From the point of view of Afrikan people, this is an aspect of Wilberforce's 'help' that we could have done without.

The success of the Haitian revolution and the Haitian declaration of independence in 1804 forced all of the imperialist nations to reconsider their approach to the enslavement of Afrikan people (James, 1963, p. 370). All of Pitt's and Wilberforce's attempts to support the maintenance of slavery on that island had ended in unmitigated disaster. The experience forced them and other imperialists to accept that they could be militarily defeated by enslaved Afrikan people. It also forced them to accept that if they continued to kidnap and deport Afrikan people to the Americas that they would be adding to the military might of the already powerful enslaved Afrikan people resisting their enslavers. This in turn would lead to the inevitable demise of their European kith and kin living in and colonising those lands.

Denmark wasted no time and abolished the 'slave trade' in 1802 (Greenwood, 1980, p. 64). Britain's response was slower: Since the 1790's the British Parliament had developed the habit of thwarting all attempts to abolish the kidnapping and deportation of Afrikan people into enslavement. Despite their military defeats at the hands of Afrikan people in Haiti. Some sections of the British establishment refused to accept the need to abolish. Over a period they began to accept reality, Britain changed stance and a bill for the abolition of the 'slave trade' was, though not for the first time, approved by the House of Commons in 1804. It was however, held up by the intransigence of the House of Lords (Hart, 1998, p. 63).

When in 1806 the House of Lords finally capitulated under the overwhelming pressure to abolish the practice of kidnapping and deporting Afrikan people, Wilberforce attempted to put the brakes on the Afrikan liberation process by publicly denouncing the idea of emancipating enslaved Afrikan people (Williams, 1944, p. 182). Following that, Wilberforce was to go on to prove just how reactionary he actually was when he and his friends advocated the 'gradual emancipation' of enslaved Afrikan people. If they had had their way, abolition would not have come into effect until 1923 (Hart, 2006, p. 2). That would have been 116 years after the actual abolition of the so called 'slave trade' or 127 years after the successful bill he 'championed', only to later sabotage. It is clear that he did not feel it necessary to consult with enslaved Afrikan people since he expressed the opinion that we were not yet:

> "... fit ... to bear emancipation ..." (Martin, 1999, p. 74).

Wilberforce's actions are clearly consistent with those of a person who was completely opposed to the idea of Afrikan people being freed from imperialist oppression – certainly in the short or medium term.

4.4.2 Racist Wilberforce delayed the abolition of slavery

After the abolition of the 'slave trade' in 1807, the next logical step for those in favour of Afrikan emancipation was the immediate abolition of the institution of slavery itself. However, Wilberforce found curious ways of showing his 'support' for the cause of immediate abolition. In addition to openly opposing immediate abolition, he practiced behaviours which did not fall far short of those carried out by the racist fascists who controlled the abhorrent anti-human Apartheid system in South Afrika. For instance in 1816, when he claimed to be advocating for 'equality' and the 'emancipation' of Afrikan and other oppressed people, Wilberforce chaired a dinner of the friends of Afrikans and Asians Society and:

> "... the token Afrikans and Asians invited to the gathering were separated from the other guests by a screen set across the end of the room." (Fryer, 1984, p. 234).

Wilberforce was not shy in demonstrating his apparent 'compassion' for enslaved Afrikan people in other ways. For instance, he advocated the idea that Afrikan people should only be whipped at night – presumably so as not to adversely affect production, which took place mainly in the day (Hochschild, 2005, p. 314). Furthermore our 'great hero and saviour', who openly opposed the abolition of slavery, failed to oppose his imperialist colleagues who recommended that Afrikan people be bred like animals as a substitute to boosting the Afrikan population in the Americas through the piracy, kidnapping and compulsory deportation of our people – otherwise referred to as the 'slave trade'.

Following the rebellion of enslaved Afrikan people in Demerara in 1823, calls for the immediate abolition of slavery once again grew amongst the British public. Wilberforce and his friends had successfully held back the aspirations of those people genuinely desiring the immediate abolition of slavery until that year, but the pressure was now becoming too great. The mounting public pressure compelled Wilberforce and his friends to launch the Society for the Gradual Abolition of Slavery (SGAS) (Hart, 2006, p. 3). They launched the society as a last ditch tactic to further delay the prospect of ending the institution of slavery. Since it was becoming clearer that they could not stop the progress towards abolition, they would drag it out and delay it for as long as possible. The SGAS advocated ideas and policies that would help slavery to survive for a further 100 years. Its members openly boasted that they wanted slavery to *gradually*:

> "… die away and to be forgotten …" (Williams, 1944, p. 182).

Wilberforce's anti-abolition position was completely out of touch with the will of the British people and diametrically opposed to the majority of the membership of his own organisation. In May 1830 the SGAS passed a resolution for the immediate abolition of slavery against the wishes of its 'leadership' i.e. Wilberforce and his new side kick Buxton (Hart, 2006, p. 3). This was an important catalyst in the history of the abolition movement. Wilberforce and his friends had successfully delayed, suppressed and contained the demand for the immediate freedom of enslaved Afrikan people for over 40 years.

At the age of 74 when Wilberforce was bed bound and close to death, he mustered up the strength to say:

"Thank God that I should have witnessed the day in which England is willing to give £20m sterling for the abolition of slavery" (Howarth, 1973, p. 474/5).

This statement betrayed the truth about where and with whom his real interests were aligned. He was thanking God for the fact that members of his class would not lose out financially as a result of British imperialism's enforced abandonment of the chattel enslavement system.

If he had genuinely supported the abolition of slavery as a means of achieving the emancipation of Afrikan people, Wilberforce would have openly rejoiced at the freedom of Afrikan people from enforced labour bondage. He would have insisted that £20m was paid to the 'newly freed' Afrikan people who for generations had had their labour stolen by the imperialists. However, instead of showing his gratefulness for the freedom of Afrikan people and seeking compensation for them, he expressed his gratefulness for his imperialist friends and allies receiving their £20m slush fund. A slush fund that they used to create and maintain a new style wage slavery system to replace the chattel system. Wilberforce's display of overt loyalty to his class even at the point of his impending death added to the overwhelming body of evidence that goes to prove that he was a covert enemy of Afrikan people, not a friend.

4.4.3 Sexist Wilberforce opposed women's groups advocating the abolition of slavery

In Britain, women were, after the Afrikan community itself, the most radical advocates for the abolition of slavery (Martin, 1999, p. 109-112). Whilst Wilberforce was openly advocating against the abolition of slavery, women's groups were actively campaigning to achieve immediate abolition. One example comes via Elizabeth Heyricke who wrote a pamphlet entitled, *Immediate Not Gradual Emancipation* (Martin, 1999, p. 110). Women were also prolific in the amassing of millions of signatures for anti-slavery petitions. More importantly, they led the mass boycott campaigns that damaged the economic interests of the plantation enslavers and their allies. Peckham Ladies Anti-Slavery Association is an example of a women's group that contributed to the organisation of the campaign to boycott West Indian sugar (Williams,

1944, p. 184).

Wilberforce actively opposed female anti-slavery associations and their role in organising boycott campaigns (Williams, 1944, p. 182). Wilberforce refused to accept women's signatures on anti-slavery petitions (Martin, 1999, p. 109). He tried to discourage and silence the political activities of women's groups working for the anti-slavery cause. If he was genuinely in favour of the abolition of slavery, he would have thanked and encouraged the various women's groups for the sterling work that they were doing to advance the cause that he claimed to stand for. In failing to do so he was demonstrating his overt sexism, whilst simultaneously harming the prospects of Afrikan people being freed from the bondage of imperialism. His undermining behaviour was clearly inconsistent with that of a person sincerely working to achieve the abolition of slavery.

Furthermore, Wilberforce's personal treatment of women also leaves a lot to be desired. For instance, there is information suggesting that Wilberforce engaged in adulterous activities with at least one woman; a woman by the name of Agnes Bronte. We are informed that she:

> "... moved to Whitby, where she soon became the mistress of William Wilberforce ... They used to spend Tuesdays together in his small fishing boat in Whitby Bay, when he used to demonstrate how [enslaved Afrikan people] were kept in chains on the long Atlantic crossing." (Agnes Bronte).

After graduating from her lessons in the sexually perverted and racist mockery of Afrikan people's suffering under the stewardship of Wilberforce she turned into a sexual misfit. The same author also informs us that:

> "It is believed that Agnes Bronte's lifelong love of bondage derived from this period." (Agnes Bronte).

Wilberforce was married to Barbra Ann for over 30 years and they had 6 Children. Not only did Wilberforce's 'affair' with his 'mistress' Agnes Bronte constitute adultery, but it is also clear, unmitigated evidence confirming that he was little more than a 'dirty old man'. We are informed that Wilberforce was giving his perverted lessons to Agnes Bronte in 1833 (Agnes Bronte). At that time he was over 70 years old, whilst at only 20 she was young enough to be his granddaughter.

No evidence is provided indicating how old she was when their encounters began. Her father is said to have been a long time friend of Wilberforce's, leaving open the possibility that she was a child and he a paedophile. Though this is not proven, it equally cannot be rule out. In any event, Wilberforce's sex bondage training sessions with Agnes Bronte must have contributed to her becoming a prostitute specialising in sexual bondage. Worse still she eventually moved beyond personal prostitution and became a 'high class' pimp, in her own right. She was the founder and manager a prostitution racket; her London based 'top people's' brothel colloquially known as 'the Bronte Dungeon', was a place where women were made to sell their bodies to men in order to make her a profit.

Whilst Wilberforce vociferously denounced the idea of women being involved in open political activity aimed at abolishing slavery, he made no such condemnation of the public exploitation of women as prostitutes in brothels. During the anti-slavery agitation period innocent Afrikan women were kidnapped, transported from their homes and held captive as sex slaves in British brothels. If he was genuinely against the enslavement of Afrikan people, he would have used his position in Parliament to help outlaw this most despicable of human abuses. However, instead of condemning this outrageous practice as a crime against the humanity of Afrikan women, he joined the exploitation process. He personally participated in systematically organised episodes of rape perpetrated against these defenseless Afrikan women, whose misfortune it was to be imprisoned in British imperialism's brothels. This aspect of his behaviour was brought to the attention of the public by cartoonists in the national press (Howarth, 1973, p. 456).

Wilberforce does not appear to have denied these public accusations, nor did he take legal action to protect his 'good name'. He would have had some difficulty defending himself given the fact that he was reported to have had at least one secret 'mistress' who was herself a prostitute. It is also worth noting that Wilberforce never ever claimed that Christianity 'inspired' him to engage in 'intimacies' with prostitutes. This should come as no surprise, because it is blatantly obvious that Christianity did not 'inspire' him to conduct himself in this despicable and immoral way. It should be equally obvious that Christianity did not 'inspire' his alleged anti-slavery activities either. In both cases he was motivated by non-religious factors: The first was 'inspired' by lust and the second by greed. Yet another weakness in Wilberforce's 'inspiration' argument is that his belief in Christianity did not 'inspire' him to restrain from raping defenseless Afrikan women who were imprisoned and enslaved. The fake story of his Christian 'inspiration' fails on the grounds that it is simply too inconsistent to possibly be true.

Behind Closed Doors

Brother Omowale

Perhaps one reason why Wilberforce was so openly against the abolition of slavery is that it could have led to a personal 'loss of privileges' on his part, by denying him his unrestricted access to the group of disempowered Afrikan women whom he used as sex toys. Afrikan people have already suffered on an unprecedented scale as a result of slavery and other aspects of the *Maangamizi*. On top of that catastrophe, derisory insults are then added when characters such as William Wilberforce a rapist, 'dirty old man' and anti-woman moral tyrant are held up as the saviours and heroes that Afrikan people should be grateful to. It is obvious that Afrikan people are best placed to choose their own heroes and imperialism insults, not only Afrikan people, but all of the peoples of the world by holding up this calibre of anti-human beast as an object of admiration. In short, Wilberforce's perverted, misogynistic and racist behaviour falls significantly short of that which should be expected of anybody posing as an 'Afrikan liberator, hero and saviour'.

4.5 The real Wilberforce – stood up
4.5.1 Failure as a human being

With the benefit of hindsight supported by the evidence above, it becomes possible to piece together a truer/more accurate picture of Wilberforce's and Pitt's subversive anti-abolitionist role in relation to the so called 'slave trade' and 'trans-Atlantic slavery'. By the same token it becomes possible to unmask at least one of the underhanded processes used by the British state to take over and derail progressive movements for change – a techniques still used in contemporary society.

Failure as a Human Being

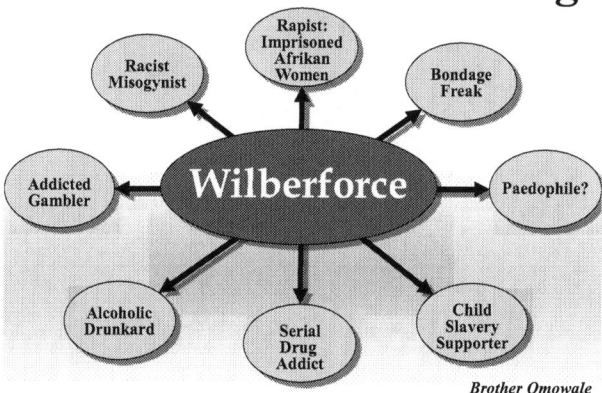

Wilberforce — with surrounding labels: Rapist: Imprisoned Afrikan Women; Racist Misogynist; Bondage Freak; Addicted Gambler; Paedophile?; Alcoholic Drunkard; Serial Drug Addict; Child Slavery Supporter.

Brother Omowale

Wilberforce who cared nothing for ordinary folk including women and children of England was a hated and despised figure – so much so that his house had to be protected by armed police guards. He was a failure as a human being – a serial rapist of Afrikan women imprisoned in brothels; a bondage freak; supported the death penalty as a medium for providing bodies for medical research; possibly a paedophile, but definitely a supporter of child slavery; a racist; a junkie; and alcoholic with an addiction to gambling. These aspects of his character are generally masked over by his class position as a member of the aristocratic landed gentry, with industrial and banking interests.

Wilberforce was effectively able to buy his way into parliament as a result of being well connected. In fact he was so well connected that that his best friend William Pitt was the Prime Minister. He was a useless character, a failure, a complete waste of time, or at least incompetent, which explains why he was a backbench MP, unable to secure even a junior position in his best friend's cabinet.

4.5.2 Wilberforce – Underhanded saboteur of the abolitionist cause
As a result of the rising number of deaths of British seamen as well as overseers and others in the Caribbean resulting from Afrikan people's anti-slavery and anti-trafficking uprisings and revolts, Pitt came under intense pressure to put a stop to the kidnapping and compulsory deportation elements of Britain's anti-Afrikan slavery racket. Pitt who was really an avid supporter of the anti-Afrikan slavery racket, came up with a plan designed to give the appearance that he was doing something to stop the racket, whilst in fact underhandedly but actively supporting its continuation.

He by-passed the obvious option of making it government business, because to do so would have guaranteed the racket's abolition. Instead, he sent in his best friend – useless William Wilberforce. It would give him something to do and naturally, Wilberforce the imbecile was bound to fail. Pitt would then be able to claim that he made a sterling effort to abolish the racket, whilst accomplishing his latent, but real objective of keeping it going.

The bottom fell out of Pitt's plan when against all expectations Wilberforce 'succeeded' in getting the bill through its second reading in the Commons – a feat that was not supposed to happen. This was a profound 'success', it meant that there was no further constitutional obstacle to prevent the abolition of Britain's anti-Afrikan kidnapping and deportation racket – the bill was effectively law with its starting date already agreed.

At this point the best friends agreed to sabotage the bill using the only means available to them – turn their backs on it, jettison it and ensure its failure by withdrawing the support of its supposed advocates. Not only did they kill off the bill, but did the same to the Abolition Society as well – reviving it only after Afrikan people in Haiti militarily defeated slavery, at which point they used it to condemn the greatest anti-slavery achievement in the history of humanity.

Both Wilberforce and Pitt were avid anti-abolitionists faking support for the abolitionist movement. They tried to subvert it by taking it over, becoming its public face and directing it away from its abolition

objective. Wilberforce was in truth an anti-abolitionist subversive agent. He wilfully took on this role because he was:
- Pro-slavery
- Opposed to and oppressive towards any and everyone 'below' his class

Of course Afrikan people were, in his order of things, the furthest 'below' his class.

4.5.3 Imperialism's distortion of history
It is the logic of imperialist operations that it steals other people's resources, commits genocide against them and then lies like hell to cover its trail of evil. This third element is thoroughly exposed by the fake story of William Wilberforce.

Imperialism's lying 'historians' rewrote history to give Wilberforce the misleading image of a 'saint'. They deconstructed the truth and replaced it with their own misleadingly manufactured image. For centuries, these lies have been belched out through imperialism's lying machine and consumed by an unsuspecting public. The truth as expressed in this essay is that Wilberforce actively opposed the abolition of the so called 'slave trade' and slavery in general, doing all in his power to prolong both long after their demise loomed. It was Afrikan people that abolished both the so called 'slave trade' and slavery. That is the true history, the true message to be passed on the future generations.

List of mentioned Sources

1. Black. Clinton , (1999), *History of Jamaica* , Longman
2. Du Bois. William, (1996), *The World and Africa: An inquiry into the part which Africa has played in world history*, International Publishers, New York
3. Ferguson. James, (1998), *The Story of the Caribbean People*, Ian Randle Publishers, Kingston, Jamaica
4. Foot. M.R.D., (2002), *Secret Lives: Lifting the Lid on the Worlds of Secret Intelligence*, Oxford University Press
5. Foot. Paul, (1991), *Man's Unconquerable Mind*, Socialist Worker Review, No.144, July/August 1991, pp.16-19

6. Fryer. Peter, (1984), *Staying Power: The History of Black People in Britain*, Pluto Press
7. Greenwood. R., & Hamber. S., (1980), *Emancipation to Emigration*, Macmillan Caribbean
8. Hart. Richard, (1998), *From Occupation to Independence: A Short History of the Peoples of the English Speaking Caribbean Region*, Pluto Press
9. Hart. Richard, (2006), *A talk on the subject of: The Slaves Who Abolished Slavery*, Centerprise Bookshop, Dalston, London, 11th October 2006
10. Hochschild. Adam, (2005), *Bury the Chains: Prophets and Rebels in the Fight to Free an Empire's Slaves*, Mariner Books
11. Howarth. David, (1973), *The British Empire; Volume 2*, BBCTV Time Life Books
12. James. C.L.R., (1963), *The Black Jacobins*, Vintage Books
13. Martin. Steve, (1999), *Britain's Slave Trade*, Channel 4 Books
14. Milwood. Robinson, (2010), *Dis-empowerment and Engagement: Raising Consciousness*, TamaRe House Publications
15. Schama. Simon, (2006), *Rough Crossings: Britain, the Slaves and the*
16. Walwin. James, (1993), *Black Ivory: A History of British Slavery*, Fontana Press
17. Williams. Eric, (1944), *Capitalism and Slavery*, Andre Deutsch

Internet References
1. A Web of English History, http://dspace.dial.pipex.com/town/terrace/adw03/c-eight/people/wilberf.htm
2. Agnes Bronte 1813 - 1892, http://freespace.virgin.net/pr.og/agnes.html
3. John Jay: An American Wilberforce, http://www.johnjayinstitute.org/index.cfm?get=get.johnjaypaper
4. Ligali, (Monday 6th November 2006), Set All Free Deny Wilberforce Film Endorsement, http://www.ligali.org/article.php?id=563
5. Man's Unconquerable Mind, http://www.marxists.org/archive/foot-paul/1991/07/toussaint.htm
6. The Amazing Change, http://www.theamazingchange.com/timeline.html
7. William Wilberforce 1759-1833, Biography, http://www.brycchancarey.com/abolition/wilberforce.htm

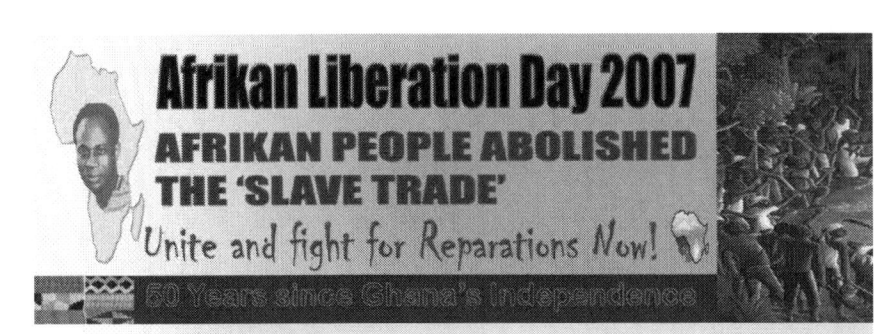

Afrikan Liberation Day 2007
AFRIKAN PEOPLE ABOLISHED THE 'SLAVE TRADE'
Unite and fight for Reparations Now!
50 Years since Ghana's Independence

Afrikan People Abolished
the
'Slave Trade'

Ukombozii
Education for Liberation
Afrikan Freedom Means Defeating Neo-Colonialism
www.ukombozii.org

Chapter 5

5 Afrikan People Abolished the 'Slave trade'

5.1 Introduction
5.1.1 British imperialism: Unrepentant for its crimes against humanity
On 25th March 1807 British imperialists claim to have abolished one of their own institutions. It was an institution that brought with it such a level of human misery that it amounted to an unremitting act of genocide against Afrikan people. The imperialists refer to that genocide as the 'slave trade'. It is more appropriately referred to as a part of the anti-Afrikan *Maangamizi*. The first point this raises is evident: British imperialism is so obscenely and profoundly barbarous that it required an act of Parliament to get it to stop kidnapping Afrikan people, chaining us and deporting us from our homeland in conditions worse than those suffered by cattle. The British establishment has totally failed and continue to fail to acknowledge this and its other acts of genocide against Afrikan people as a crime against humanity. Its actions were and are completely and utterly wrong and morally indefensible. In its attempts to mislead Afrikan, British and other peoples of the world, they are trying to claim the credit for bringing the shameful genocide that it perpetrated to an end. The arrogance of it intentionally misleading propaganda strategy is exposed by the fact that it took British imperialism over 200 years of profiting from its chattel slavery

system before it even began to publicly debate the possibility that this anti-human evil practice might be wrong.

An important part of British imperialism's propaganda strategy of misdirecting and disorientating the public has been to thrust a character called William Wilberforce on to the centre stage of its interpretation of the history of the 'abolition of slavery'. If Britain's modern imperialists can get away with it, they intend to give Wilberforce the entire historical stage and use him to smother and hide the real history. British imperialism's intention is to use Wilberforce's inflated image as a tactic to claim the moral high ground in a debate where its proven disgraceful and disgusting track record leaves its evil practices thoroughly exposed. It is therefore vital that Afrikan people approach this area of history with the objective of exposing the truth about British imperialism's evil motivation and conduct throughout the entire *Maangamizi*. A thorough historical analysis will, amongst other things, prove that British imperialism did not stop kidnapping and deporting our people because it suddenly realised just how evil and wrong those behaviours were. The analysis will also prove that these genocidal habits ceased because British imperialism was actually forced to halt that element of the *Maangamizi*; the unstoppable forces emanating from Afrikan people determined to liberate themselves from bondage left imperialism with no other choice.

5.1.2 Wherever there were Afrikan people there was resistance to imperialism's chattel slavery system

Afrikan people defended themselves against imperialism's chattel enslavement system at home in Afrika, on the high seas, in the Americas and some activity also took place in Britain. As Afrikan people rose up on Afrikan soil to defend themselves against the European imposed genocide of chattel enslavement, thousands of Britain's kidnapper sons were killed. On the high seas, Afrikan heroine and hero warriors released themselves from their chains, rose up and killed countless thousands of Britain's kidnapper son's as part of the process of commandeering ships and freeing themselves. In the America's, particularly in the Caribbean - where Afrikan people formed the physical majority, tens of thousands of Britain's invader and occupier sons were killed by Afrikan people determined to free themselves from British imperialism's, evil chattel enslavement bondage.

The British working class paid a heavy price for supporting their imperialist masters in the process of kidnapping, deporting and enslaving innocent Afrikan people. When the price in blood proved to be too high, they turned against their upper classes and campaigned for the abolition of imperialism's grotesque anti-human genocidal chattel enslavement system. With their mass support base in their homeland seriously eroded, British imperialists were forced to capitulate – they transferred from chattel slavery to colonial slavery. However, at the base of Britain's working class people's discontent was the resolute and often violent defense of Afrikan people's liberty by Afrikan people themselves. Afrikan people's defenses which occurred in Afrika, on the Atlantic and in the America's, supported by diplomatic activity led by Afrikan people in Britain, forced the British working class to confront their imperialist masters. Ultimately, the confrontation contributed to British imperialism abandoning its so called 'slave trade' and later its chattel slavery economy in favour of colonial enslavement.

On Afrikan soil – the kidnapping part of the *Maangamizi* - Afrikan people organised resistance to imperialism's evil anti-Afrikan chattel enslavement process on at least 3 different levels: firstly, Afrikan nations that were sufficiently well organised simply abolished the process of aliens coming from foreign lands to kidnap and deport Afrikan people from their homes; secondly, Afrikan nations that were less powerful, organised systematic processes of national resistance designed to thwart the enslavement practices of the imperialists and their local allies; thirdly, there were countless smaller scale acts of heroism from Afrikan battalions that bravely attacked imperialism's human trafficking ships on the coastline in organised forays designed to free their sisters and brothers held prisoner on board.

On the brutal Atlantic crossings – one of the most grotesque parts of the *Maangamizi* - Afrikan people were no less brave. The emergence of even the slightest of opportunities would result in them rising up to kill their evil kidnappers in order to commandeer the human trafficking ships upon which they were imprisoned. In some cases the seaboard uprisings were unsuccessful and kidnapped Afrikan people would be made to suffer the most hideous forms of punishments. These punishments were usually specifically designed to kill Afrikan heroines and heroes in a way that was so gruesome, that they would operate as a deterrent to other would be Afrikan insurgents. In other cases, kidnapped Afrikan people would take control of the human trafficking (in reality *pirate*) ships, only to be overpowered later by heavily armed naval ships and kidnapped for enslavement a second time. Some of the seaboard uprisings had victorious outcomes so it is vitally important that we remember and highlight the fact that there were a number of triumphant cases. These were cases where kidnapped Afrikan people released themselves from their chains, rose up on the human trafficking ships, subdued the kidnappers, took control and then successfully sailed the vessels back to Afrika and their well earned freedom.

Afrikan people's resistance in the Americas – the forced labour part of the *Maangamizi* - also took a range of different forms. Three of the most significant forms were: (i) Maroonage - mostly in the mountains of the Caribbean; (ii) uprisings on the forced labour camps (plantations); and (iii) conspiracies where the very threat of an Afrikan uprising would engender fear in the hearts of the wicked enslavers. There were literally hundreds of Maroon campaigns, plantation uprisings and conspiracies throughout the Americas. There were so many that to do justice to each of them in one document would require the creation of an Afrikan anti-slavery resistance encyclopedia. Therefore, for the purpose of countering the 2007 bi-centenary of the alleged British Parliamentary 'abolition' of the so called 'slave trade', reference will be made primarily to islands in the Caribbean that were and continue to be directly undermined by British colonial practices. Two colonies that suffered under French imperialism [Haiti & Guadeloupe] are also included because of their strategic and tactical importance to Afrikan people's resistance in the Caribbean islands stolen by Britain. The focus has been on resistance from the late 1770s to the 1810s as a basis for clarifying and identifying some of the forces impacting on what British imperialism mischievously and misleadingly describes as the 1807 'abolition' of the 'slave trade'.

5.2 Narrow perspectives on abolition and resistance
5.2.1 Wilberforce: The bogus 'king of abolition'
In its determination to lie to the British public by generally distorting the history of chattel enslavement, British imperialism has constructed a false saintly image around one of its own cadre. William Wilberforce has been presented to the world as an iconic figure, a super hero, who single-handedly 'abolished' the chattel slavery system and its associated evils. It has used its army of apologists, sometimes referred to as

'historians' or 'journalists' to lie to the public. Their role is to distort the truth by presenting selected pieces of factual evidence in a manner that defies their appropriate context so that the history becomes distorted. Their con trick is designed to make us think about William Wilberforce and nothing else when ever our attention is drawn to the 'abolition of slavery'. In this way, Wilberforce is used by British imperialism as a decoy to contain our thinking – to keep us thinking 'inside the box' created by imperialism's 'historians' for us. Wilberforce's bogus image as an emancipator operates as an anchor that chains our thinking inside an ideological space specifically designed and constructed by British imperialism to give the false impression that imperialism is an asset to humanity.

Bogus Anti-Slavery Resistance

William Wilberforce

Brother Omowale

Some onlookers may be surprised to find that scrutiny of Wilberforce's actual behaviour reveals that he had very little to do with the real underlying processes involved in the 'abolition of slavery'. He is really British imperialism's man – a symbolic figure head put forward by British imperialism to falsely claim the credit for bringing slavery and the so called 'slave trade' to an end. Furthermore, when examined closely, his track record is extremely damning because the picture that emerges is one of a figure who was worse than useless to Afrikan people struggling for freedom. It would have been bad enough if he had merely failed to take positive actions towards the achievement of 'abolition', but his behaviour exposes him as a British imperialist agent whose actions appear to have been specifically designed to damage and delay the Parliamentary 'abolition' of the so called 'slave trade' and the inhumane system of chattel slavery.

Even if, for arguments sake, the assessment of Wilberforce presented here turned out to be incorrect and Wilberforce was not the objective enemy of Afrikan people in the form of a subversive British imperialist agent, his elevation to the status of 'anti-slavery super hero' is still very unhelpful to the Afrikan liberation struggle. This is because his fictitious 'heroic' status is used by imperialism to distort the historical truth about how chattel slavery and the process of kidnapping and deporting Afrikan people across the Atlantic came to be 'abolished'. All of this means that the fundamentally important contributions of Afrikan people and others to the 'abolition' process have been deliberately disregarded and sidelined. This has given the misleading impression that Afrikan people were impotent in the process of their liberation.

Furthermore, the false impression is given that Afrikan people should be especially grateful to a 'saint' by the name of Wilberforce for freeing them from chattel slavery bondage. The idea that Afrikan people could have had something to do with the 'abolition' of the chattel system which was used to enslave them is ejected from all discussion and discourse by the out and out lie that Wilberforce 'saved us'. One of the consequences of these processes has been the disempowerment of those Afrikan people who have accepted the need for a non-Afrikan saviour. These Afrikan people have been conditioned to accept the ludicrous idea that a non-Afrikan 'hero' from the imperialist enemy camp will solve their problems for them and save them. The elimination of the contributions made by Afrikan warriors to the 'abolition' process is a method specifically designed to ensure that our thinking is held firmly 'inside the box'.

5.2.2 Imperialism's other contenders for the bogus 'abolition crown'
When the idea of Wilberforce being some kind of hero is challenged, those people whose thinking has been chained into imperialism's pre-ordained ideological space then look for other British 'abolitionists' and quibble about whether nor not they did more than Wilberforce to effect the 'abolition of slavery' and the so called 'slave trade'. Within this limited frame of thinking, some of these others may even have a realistic claim to Wilberforce's bogus crown as the supposed 'king of the abolition movement'. For instance, Thomas Clarkson conducted copious research designed to prove to Parliament and the public at large just how gruesome and shamefully evil the human trafficking part

of the *Maangamizi* was (Fryer, 1984, p. 57/8; Greenwood, 1980, p. 63; Martin, 1999, p. 74). Granville Sharpe played a significant supportive role in the case of an Afrikan man called **James Somerset** in 1772. This was a landmark court case that paved the way for Afrikan people to claim a 'non-enslaved' status when on British soil (Fryer, 1984, p. 68; Greenwood, 1980, p. 63; Martin, 1999, p. 75). Furthermore, it was Thomas Buxton that led the Parliamentary process right through to the so called 'abolition of slavery' which was enacted in 1833 (Greenwood, 1980, p. 68/9; Ferguson, 1998, p. 157).

> **Bogus Anti-Slavery Resistance**
>
> **William Wilberforce**
> **Thomas Buxton**
> **Granville Sharpe**
> **Thomas Clarkson**
> **Mass petitions**
>
> *Brother Omowale*

In the greater scheme of things this level of analysis fares only marginally better than focusing entirely on Wilberforce. All that is really happening is a debate about which of British imperialism's professed 'do gooders' should be crowned king of the 'abolition' movement. The illusion created is one of slavery being 'abolished' by the good graces and charity of the British upper classes. To the extent that this con trick succeeds in removing the contributions of Afrikan freedom fighters from public vision, the public's thinking remains hijacked by imperialism's predetermined mirage and virtually everybody's thinking remains firmly entrenched 'inside the box'.

5.2.3 'Abolition' and the British working classes

It is also vital to a full understanding of the history that we acknowledge how the British working classes and women's groups in particular played an important part in the 'abolition' process. For instance, millions of working class people in Britain signed petitions in support of the 'abolition of slavery' and its associated evils (Martin, 1999, p. 109);

thousands more engaged in mass demonstrations (Martin, 1999, p. 72); and women's groups campaigned for and organised the boycott of sugar produced by West Indian enslavers in favour of Asian sugar grown by 'non-enslaved' people in India (Williams, 1998, p. 184). This was all done in an attempt to undermine the 'slave economy' and to destroy the credibility of chattel slavery practitioners. This calibre of evidence seriously undermines imperialism's ideological mirage of upper class Britain freeing Afrikan people from slavery and the so called 'slave trade'. However, even when this level of challenge is mounted, our thinking is still confined to initiatives that were conducted by European 'do gooders' in Britain. This vantage point also leaves the critical contributions made by Afrikan people to the 'abolition' process completely sidelined. Therefore, from this perspective our thinking still remains contained 'inside the box'.

5.2.4 Afrikan people in Britain drove the diplomatic front for 'abolition'

The first group of kidnapped Afrikan people forcibly deported to Britain, arrived in 1555 (Martin, 1999, p. 134). By the last quarter of the 18th century, British imperialism's kidnapping and compulsory deportation of Afrikan people resulted in 10-15k of London's 800k population being Afrikan people (Martin, 1999, p. 88). The total population of Afrikan people throughout the whole of Britain was estimated at 20k (Martin, 1999, p. 136). The majority of the Afrikan people in Britain were held captive and enslaved by British citizens. However by employing a variety of ingenious strategies and methods, a small percentage of them managed to procure their personal 'freedom'.

It is obvious that of all of the groups of people in Britain, Afrikan people had the most to gain from the 'abolition of slavery' and the so called 'slave trade'. For this reason it is likely that they had a tendency to be amongst the most sympathetic advocates of the anti-slavery cause as well as amongst the most active groups of people fighting for the 'abolition of slavery'. The evidence of their involvement whether enslaved or 'free' is scant, but it is possible to trace some of the names of Afrikan people involved in the broad anti-slavery movement in Britain.

There is documented evidence of the involvement of Afrikan people such as: **Mary Prince, Olaudah Equiano, Ottobah Cuguano, Jonathan**

Strong, James Somerset, Joseph Knight, Ayuba Diallo, George Bridgewater, Ignatus Sancho, Francis Barber, William Davison, *Robert Wedderburn, Ukawsaw Gronniosaw, John Ystumllyn, William Cuffay* and **Julius Soubise**. However, this list of names cannot do justice to either the volume or quality of activity that would have been forthcoming from the 20k strong Afrikan community based in Britain. It is obvious that their role has been played down by imperialist 'historians'.

Afrikan people in Britain provided leadership to the campaigns aimed at their own people's liberation in a number of different ways. Firstly, Afrikan people consciously joined or associated with groups sympathetic to the abolitionist cause. For example during the 1780's & 1790's **Olaudah Equiano** was a member of the London Correspondence Society (Fryer, 1984, p. 107 & 210). Similarly in 1819, **William Davison** was a member of the Marylebone Union Reading Society (Fryer, 1984, p. 216). **Mary Prince**, was a member of the Anti-Slavery Society during the 1820's and 30's (History of Mary Prince). In the 1830's, **Robert Wedderburn** was a member of the Owenite Movement (Fryer, 1984, p. 227) and throughout the 1830's, **William Cuffey** was a member of a range of different organisations including: the Grand National Consolidated Trade Union 1834; the Metropolitan Taylor's Association 1839 and the Chartist Movement 1839 (Fryer, 1984, p. 238).

Anti-Slavery Resistance

> **Granville Sharpe, Thomas Clarkson, William Wilberforce, Mass petitions Ottobah Cuguano, Oluadah Equiano, Mary Prince, Jonathan Strong, James Somerset, Ayuba Diallo, George Bridgewater, Ignatius Sancho, Julius Soubise**

Brother Omowale

Secondly, Afrikan people actively participated in public meetings, including the petitioning of parliament. For instance **Mary Prince** directly petitioned parliament 24th June 1829. Even though this was after the so called abolition of the 'slave trade', her action was to have a profound impact on the parliamentary processes which in 1834 claimed to abolish slavery in the British Empire. Prince's petition represented the mere tip of the iceberg, since the main medium used for convincing the population of Britain about the wicked nature of slavery was mass open meetings. **Olaudah Equiano** (Fryer, 1984, p. 109-111), **Robert Wedderburn** (Fryer, 1984, p. 222) and **William Cuffey** (Fryer, 1984, p. 238) all spoke regularly in public meetings as part of a series of campaigns designed to raise the consciousness of the masses of working people in Britain about the evils of slavery and the unjust impact that it was having on the lives of Afrikan people.

Thirdly, Afrikan people wrote and narrated their biographies telling of the brutality they suffered and experienced. In 1789 **Olaudah Equinao** wrote *The Interesting Narrative of the Life of Olaudah Equiano, or Gustava, the Afrikan* (Shepard, 2000, p. 822; Gates, 1987, p. 1) and in 1831 **Mary Prince** narrated her biography *The History of Mary Prince: A West Indian Slave Related by Herself* (Shepard, 2000, p. 843; Gates, 1987, p. 183; History of Mary Prince). In 1824, **Robert Wedderburn** whose mother was enslaved on the island of Jamaica wrote about the explicit cruelty of slavery in his book *The Horrors of Slavery* (Fryer, 1984, p. 227). All of this formed part of the diplomatic effort, led by Afrikan people to rid the world of the vile imperialist practice of enslaving Afrikan people.

Fourthly, Afrikan people were involved in important anti-slavery court cases. For instance in 1765 **Jonathan Strong** (Fryer, 1984, p. 115) and in 1772 **James Somerset** (Fryer, 1984, p. 121; Shepard, 2000, p. 584) fought cases that significantly impacted on the state of laws relating to slavery in England and Wales. **Jonathan Strong** successfully used the courts to avoid being resold by his former wicked enslaver, on the grounds that his wicked enslaver had previously ill-treated him. **James Somerset**, on the other hand, managed to strike close to the heart of slavery as practiced in England and Wales. Though the decision in his case did not abolish slavery in Britain as is sometimes claimed, James Somerset's case actually won a landmark ruling that, at least theoretically, outlawed the involuntary enslavement of Afrikan people in England and Wales.

Fifthly, Afrikan people engaged in militant action designed to promote justice and end the enslavement of Afrikan people. Afrikan warriors such as **William Davison**, **Robert Wedderburn** and **William Cuffay** engaged in revolutionary political activity against the imperialist perpetrators of slavery (Fryer, 1984, p. 213). **William Davison** was executed as a direct result of the subversive activities of a government sponsored undercover agent provocateur (Fryer, 1984, p. 213). He was tricked into participating in a plot to kill a cabinet minister, a plot which was hatched by government agents and was always doomed to fail. **Robert Wedderburn** was similarly feared by the British state; his name appeared alongside that of **William Davison** on a secret government list (Fryer, 1984, p. 213). After a long anti-slavery career in Britain, **William Cuffay** found himself convicted for 'levying war on the queen' (Fryer, 1984, p. 243). He was then deported. All three of these Afrikan anti-slavery warriors were revolutionary Socialists.

The pattern that emerges from this survey is one of Afrikan political activists tending to ally themselves with groups of British people who established organisations with a progressive attitude towards the abolition of slavery. The fight was the fight of the Afrikan activists and the British people who took up that struggle were their supporters. The truth is that it was the Afrikan activists who brought their European comrades into the struggle to rid the world of slavery and European women seemed to be more receptive to their anti-slavery message than European men. In order to facilitate this process, the stories and experiences of the Afrikan activists were fed into the organised groupings that they were a part of and then through those groupings cascaded to the British public at large via meetings and the press. Some of the highpoints in this anti-slavery resistance process involved petitions to parliament with signatories in the millions and boycotts of products created through the exploitation of enslaved Afrikan labour.

Afrikan people's stories, court cases and other political activities had a massive impact on the British public, most of whom were ignorant about the evils and injustices of slavery. The evidence provided by Afrikan people in Britain was *the* crucial spark that ignited mass movements for justice among the working classes. The release of their information raised consciousness amongst the masses of Britons to a point where they began to seriously challenge the British establishment about both the plights of the working classes and the suffering of enslaved Afrikan people. It was therefore the political and diplomatic work of Afrikan people, working in an extremely hostile British environment, which led the national processes that brought about the abolition of slavery and the so called 'slave trade'. It most certainly was not some character called Wilberforce as is misleadingly portrayed by some.

One of the methods of lying used by imperialism to distort history is simply to omit from or prevent the emergence of relevant facts in historical discourse i.e. failing to tell the whole truth. In the case of Afrikan enslavement, an army of imperialist liars presented to us as 'historians' have insulted the memory of our Afrikan ancestors who fought for Afrikan liberation in Britain during the chattel enslavement period. They have done this by under reporting the contributions of Afrikan people and presenting William Wilberforce as some kind of leader in the Afrikan liberation process. Some of these 'historians' have taken the lies to even higher levels of distortion by attempting to present Wilberforce as the saviour of enslaved Afrikan people.

The contributions made by Afrikan people in Britain to killing off the process of kidnapping and deporting Afrikan people into chattel slavery is critical to understanding the truth about how that phase of the *Maangamizi* ended. However, if we limit ourselves to even this slightly fuller and more honest level of analysis, our thinking remains hijacked. We are left with the impression that all that was required to end the kidnapping and deporting process was the diplomatic activities of a few people (both Afrikan and European) operating in Britain. This level of analysis is also bound to fall short of revealing the whole truth. It creates a scenario where the efforts of people in Britain are dominant and therefore not put into their proper context. The critically important efforts of people outside Britain, particularly Afrikan people, continue to be ignored. Again, this fairly narrow level of analysis continues to hold our thinking quite rigidly 'inside the box' falsely constructed for us by European imperialism.

5.3 Broadening the scope
5.3.1 Thinking outside of imperialism's ideological box – The Abolition Matrix

Only by thinking 'outside the box' can we reconstruct a fuller, more accurate and more honest account of the history of 'abolition'. It obviously took much more than the diplomatic activities of Afrikan people and non-Afrikans in Britain to 'abolish' the imperialist system of kidnapping and deporting Afrikan people across the Atlantic. There were a range of vitally significant activities and forces that contributed to abolishing the human trafficking part of the *Maangamizi*. These activities took place in different locations around the world. Some of them took place in the Afrikan continent, others happened on the Atlantic Ocean, yet others occurred in the Americas and some activity also took place in Britain. The activities took a variety of different forms which can be broadly categorised as being primarily: military, diplomatic or economic in their essence. By mapping out the range of activities in a strategic framework, we begin to get a truer idea of the magnitude of forces that brought down the process of kidnapping and deporting Afrikan people from their homeland into imperialism's system of chattel slavery. That map is the ***Abolition Matrix analytical tool***.

The Abolition Matrix I

Location of Action

Type of Action	Afrika	Atlantic	Americas	Britain
Military				
Economic				
Diplomatic				Granville Sharpe, Thomas Clarkson, William Wilberforce, Mass petitions Ottobah Cuguano, Olaudah Equiano, Mary Prince, Jonathan Strong, James Somerset, Ayuba Diallo, George Bridgewater, Ignatius Sancho, Julius Soubise

Brother Omowale

Whilst the geographical categories are fairly obvious, some explanation is necessary as to what is meant by the categories: Politics, Economics and Military in the anti-slavery resistance process. It is important to note that these disciplines have a lot in common. They all have human activity at their core. It is therefore unreasonable to expect to be able to draw a hard and fast distinction between each of the categories; there is bound to be some degree of overlap. In addition, all human activities operate on one of two levels i.e. survival and developmental (or instinctive and conscious). It follows that some aspects of economic, political and military activity operate at the animalistic or instinctive level, while others operate at potentially higher and higher levels of consciousness.

The Afrikan revolutionary **Amilcar Cabral** lays an initial benchmark by explaining that politics is fundamentally the relationship between people. Economics, on the other hand, is the relationship between people and nature (McCulloch, 1983, p. 84). Human beings have consciousness and free will, they are a special aspect of nature, the strongest force in nature (Cabral, 1974, p. 71). It follows that since people are an integral part of nature and are wholly contained in nature then politics must be contained within Economics. Since nature is bigger than people, even all of the people put together, we can conclude that economics is bigger than politics. Another way of interpreting their relationship is to say that all politics is economics, but not all economics is politics.

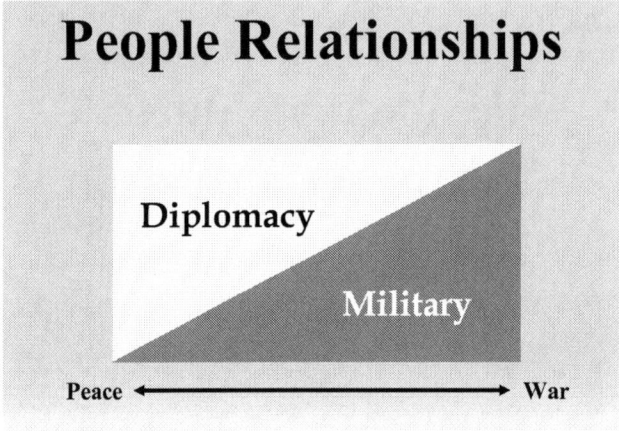

People Relationships

Diplomacy

Military

Peace ←――――――――――――→ War

Brother Omowale

The relationship between the two disciplines has parallels with the relationship between thinking and doing in human beings. Thinking broadly equates to politics and doing broadly related to economics. It is impossible for a human being to do something without some level of thinking. In a similar way it is impossible for a group of human beings to engage in economic activity without engaging in politics. It follows that politics drives the economic activities of groups in a similar manner to the way in which thinking drives actions in human behaviour. In a manner of speaking, politics is the thinking part of economics and what we usually refer to as economics is the part of economics that results from what human beings actually do or tangibly produce.

With the help of ***Cabral's*** formula, the relationship between politics and economics can be understood from another angle also. We can reason that if nature did not exist, people could not exist. Nature provides the context within which humanity exists, survives and thrives. It follows that nature (or the environment) is fundamental to all human activity. We can therefore deduce that if economics did not exist, then politics could not exist. Economics is therefore the foundation of politics as well as its container.

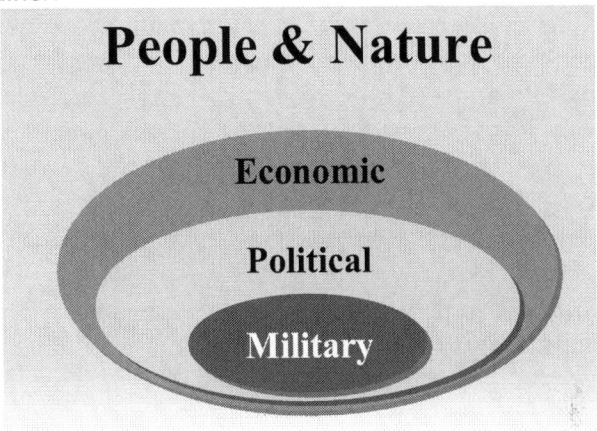

People & Nature

Economic
Political
Military

Brother Omowale

In much the same way that economics is comprised of different elements, so too is politics. Politics is fundamentally the relationship between people and political relationships can take a variety of forms. For instance, they can be either friendly or hostile; they can, at the same time, also be either physical or non-physical. The form that group relationships take influences the nature and calibre of the political relationship. Where groups have hostile relationships and decide to settle their disputes by physical means, this leads automatically to military activity. All other political relationships, whether good or bad, are diplomatic in essence. Diplomacy then is the process of building relationships and settling disputes between groups on a non-physical basis. It is now clear that politics comprises both diplomatic and military activity. It is also important to note that diplomatic activity is always present in relationships between groups, even during times of war.

Politics is essentially about relationships; this means that if politics did not exist, it would not be possible for any form of inter-human relationship to exist. Since military relationships are also a form of inter-human relationship, this also means that if politics did not exist, then military relations cold not exist. Politics is therefore the foundation and the container of all military activity. Chairman Mao expresses this truth in a number of ways. He says:

> "War is a continuation of politics. In this sense war is politics and war itself a political action; since ancient times there has never been a war that did not have a political character ... war cannot for a single moment be separated from politics ... War is a continuation of politics by other means. When politics develops to a certain stage beyond which it cannot proceed by usual means, war breaks out to sweep the obstacles from the way ... politics is war without bloodshed while war is politics with bloodshed." (Mao, 1975, p. 152/3).

Kwame Nkrumah expresses the relationship between military, political and economic activity in the following terms:

> "Military strategy presupposes political aims. All military problems are political, and all political problems are economic." (Nkrumah, 1980, p. 15/16).

In other words, politics is a part of economics; it is wholly contained inside economics and also has economics as its foundation. Similarly, military activity is part of politics, is contained inside politics and has politics as its foundation. This means that economics is the container of politics and politics is the container of military activity. Furthermore, politics, which equates to the thinking part of economics, gives purpose to economics; politics also gives purpose to military activity. It follows that politics is the master of the other disciplines because it drives both economic and military activity. At the same time, it must also be recognised that politics responds to existing economic and military situations. In other words, political and thought processes are influenced and guided by reality.

For the purpose of the anti-slavery resistance framework, **economics** is the relationship between people and nature. **Politics** – the relationship between people and people, can be divided into its constituent elements of diplomatic and military activity. **Diplomacy** is the process of building relationships and settling disputes between groups on a non-physical basis. **Military** activity refers to situations where groups have a hostile relationship and decide to settle their disputes by physical means.

5.3.2 The value of the Abolition Matrix framework and beyond

This ***Abolition Matrix*** framework exposes the method that British imperialism is using to 'box our thinking' in order to distort history and distract our attention away from the multiplicity of factors that led to 'abolition'. The framework places Wilberforce's activities in a fuller context, thereby exposing his virtual irrelevance to the overall process of 'abolition'. Secondly, it exposes the way in which Wilberforce is falsely given the credit for the 'the abolition of slavery' and its associated evils. Thirdly, it exposes the way in which British imperialism's deliberate misrepresentation of history has led to Wilberforce becoming the beneficiary of the efforts of the many Afrikan and other warriors who dedicated and in many cases sacrificed their lives in order to destroy the chattel enslavement system.

Furthermore, it guides, encourages and promotes an honest overview of the relevant historical period. For this reason the expanded framework or something similar should be at the heart of the curriculum for the teaching of 'slavery'. Afrikan people can use this framework for teaching their children the truth about how chattel slavery was brought to an end. This can be done regardless of whether or not the British state gives its alleged 'support' or 'approval'. In addition, Afrikan people can build alliances with other oppressed groups with a vested interest in seeing the truly rounded analysis of the history brought to the public's attention. They can lobby the imperialist British government with the agenda of forcing them to make this approach to 'teaching slavery', the one that is used by schools, colleges and universities across the whole country.

The honest analysis of history promoted by this framework proves beyond a shadow of a doubt that it was Afrikan people's actions that led to the abolition of the so called 'slave trade' as part of a process of abolishing the whole system of chattel slavery. However, even the efforts of Afrikan freedom fighters must be put into their proper context in order to make sense of the forces that brought down chattel slavery. It is vital that this fuller picture of the history of anti-slavery resistance emerges and is popularised amongst Afrikan people and all other oppressed groups. It will help to raise the self-esteem of Afrikan people who have for a long time been disempowered through being indoctrinated by imperialism's version of events. It will also teach non-Afrikans to have a healthy respect for Afrikan people who, against all odds, managed to overcome the most oppressive system of exploitation ever known to humanity. This will also contribute to Afrikan and other oppressed people in Britain beginning to appreciate and understand the importance of their roles in achieving complete constructive change both in this society and around the world.

Finally, it should be remembered that even with this new expanded vision, it is wise that we retain the ability to think 'outside this bigger box'. It is still vital that we remember that there were significant forces operating beyond even this broader framework. For instance, the very fact that Britain was involved in imperialist military campaigns against the Chinese, Indian and Aboriginal people in these peoples' own lands meant that they had fewer troops available to attempt to subdue Afrikan people fighting for freedom in the Americas. In this way, the struggles of other oppressed peoples indirectly contributed to an environment that was more favourable for Afrikan freedom fighters. We therefore received indirect help from other peoples fighting against imperialism even though they were fighting specifically for their own freedom and not ours. Their struggles helped to divide the political, economic and military might of British imperialism by forcing it to fight wars in disparate locations around the world all at the same time. It is this overstretching of imperialism's power that helped Afrikan people destroy chattel slavery and it is this same overstretching of its power base that will ultimately lead to imperialism's final down fall.

5.4 Sources of Afrikan people's abolition on Afrikan soil
5.4.1 Levels of Afrikan abolition of the so called 'slave trade'
There is a body of important information that remains largely concealed relating to the history of how Afrikan people on the continent courageously fought against those that kidnapped and deported their sisters and brothers during the chattel enslavement era. Some home based Afrikan people were particularly courageous in opposing the kidnappings because they were operating, in dangerous circumstances, against a tide of human theft and associated misery orchestrated and controlled by imperialist cartels in their regions of the continent. Afrikan defenders of liberty on the Afrikan motherland were constantly obliged to defend themselves from becoming captives of imperialism's

kidnapping cartels. They were therefore forced to employ a diverse range of methods and tactics to fight against the organised forces of the kidnappers [both Afrikan and European] operating in their lands.

The various forms of Afrikan people's resistance on the motherland to imperialism's kidnappers can be categorised under three broad headings: Firstly, those Afrikan states that, for a time at least, abolished imperialism's practice of kidnapping and compulsorily deporting their sisters and brothers from their homes; secondly, those Afrikan people that offered national level resistance to imperialism's kidnapping incursions, but did not necessarily have sufficient force to put a full scale abolition in place; and thirdly, those Afrikan people that entered into relatively small scale sporadic coastal battles with the imperialist kidnappers aimed at preventing the theft of their sisters and brothers, or at rescuing them after capture.

5.4.2 Afrikan people in Afrika were the first to abolish the 'slave trade'
Unlike the British, Afrikan people did not wait two to three hundred years to be persuaded that slavery was wrong; they abolished it immediately. There were a number of Afrikan nations in Afrika that abolished imperialism's system of kidnapping and enslaving Afrikan people long before Britain or any of its European allies. One example comes from the Bini people of what today is called Nigeria, who abolished the 'slave trade' in their area from the early 1500's until the late 1600's. Given the intense pressure placed on Afrikan people by the imperialists to support their kidnapping enterprise, an abolition lasting some 150 years was a remarkable achievement. Unfortunately for Afrikan people, the Bini people's abolition of the 'slave trade' was eventually abolished by the clandestine tactics of European imperialism. Justice explains that:

> "Eventually, there was a foreign inspired civil war, at the end of which Oba Akensua won and reintroduced slavery" (Justice, 2005, p. 132).

A later example comes from **Agaja Trudo** who became the chief of Dahomey in 1708. He inherited a kingdom with an economy based on the kidnapping of Afrikan people, but came to the realisation that it was against the best interests of Afrikan people for the kidnapping and deportation to continue. In 1724 he declared the abolition of the 'slave trade', burned down European camps and deportation centres and blocked all so called 'slave routes' to the interior. It was a very successful abolition with the kidnapping and deportation of Afrikan people being ground to a virtual halt (Rodney, 1981, p. 81).

Agaja Trudo also realised that it would be necessary to put systems in place to ensure that there was no underhand or secret kidnapping taking place. The vigorous enforcement of the Afrikan abolitions meant that those imperialists agents who were hell bent on re-introducing slavery had to be dealt with. Many European kidnappers were killed as a result of their obstinate refusal to cease kidnapping Afrikan people. Others were killed when they dared to undermine Afrikan sovereignty by instigating wars against progressive Afrikan societies that had abolished the so called 'slave trade'.

In 1725 *Agaja Trudo* attempted to consolidate his abolition by sending an ambassador to Britain. The ambassador's remit was to inform the British authorities that Dahomey was willing to trade with them in goods and services, but the trafficking of Afrikan people would not be tolerated. His ambassador was ignored by the British establishment throughout the entirety of his time in London. No one would agree to see him or talk to him and his attempts at securing diplomatic consolidation of the abolition was not completed as a result of Britain's destructive anti-human intransigence.

Instead of co-operating with *Agaja Trudo*'s missionaries, British imperialism embarked on its own secret underhand 'diplomatic' mission. The British knew that there was a history of animosity between the Dahomey Empire and that of Oyo to the east. These differences were exploited by the British with the express intention of instigating wars between them so as to reintroduce the system of kidnapping and deporting Afrikan people into British enslavement – a process which was so lucrative for them. The British were eventually successful in abolishing this Afrikan abolition of the 'slave trade' and achieved this by instigating what were to become decade long wars between the two Afrikan nations. By 1730 the Dahomey abolition had been completely broken down by the secret British intrigues and a kidnapping spree ensued.

Agaja Trudo's diplomatic initiative is extremely important in that it highlights the underlying political character of the abolition. This is because whilst much of the violent resistance to imperialism's kidnappings has the potential to be (incorrectly) interpreted as spontaneous, ill-thought through reactions to injustice, international diplomacy cannot be belittled or dismissed in that way. This diplomatic initiative is clear evidence that the political will to end the process of kidnapping, deporting and enslaving Afrikan people was clearly institutionalised in the societies of at least some Afrikan people in the motherland. Furthermore, this political will was sufficiently well organised to seriously seek the abolition of chattel slavery in the international arena. Abolition was therefore an official policy in Afrika well over 100 years before Britain came around to practicing or even appreciating that level of civilisation and humanism. Indeed, the indictment against British imperialism is even more damning because of the way in which it passively and actively opposed this anti-slavery initiative.

5.4.3 British imperialism abolished Afrikan abolitions of the 'slave trade'

It is important to understand the destabilising processes that were used to destroy the types of Afrikan abolitions of 'slave trading' mentioned above. In fact the destabilising processes were so devastating that they effectively ended up disempowering and destroying the Afrikan nations involved; reducing them to a shadow of their former power. British imperialism specifically employed divide and rule tactics designed to compel Afrikan nations to supply fellow Afrikan people for compulsory deportation into enslavement. It used Afrikan people to capture other Afrikan people, both within and beyond their own nation, and then cunningly blamed the capturers for the whole act of enslavement.

The first part of the destabilising process was to create an environment of fear amongst Afrikan nations by promoting total mutual mistrust. They did this by lying to each of the two or more Afrikan nations or sub-groups that they intended to trick and subvert. They simultaneously presented themselves as the friends of the Afrikan nations that they intended should war with each other. They secretly 'advised' each of the nations that the other was well armed and intended to attack them to take their lands and enslave them. They secretly 'offered to help' each of the nations by supplying them with the guns that they would need to fend off their supposed 'aggressors'. The catch was that guns could only be bought if Afrikan people were used as currency (Fryer, 1989, p. 10).

Once the Afrikan nations had been tricked, the choice that confronted them was to either: (i) give up a few of their people for the guns necessary for the survival of their nation, or (ii) refuse to sell anybody and be overwhelmed by their supposedly armed 'aggressor' nation, with the consequence that of all their own people would be defeated and sold into slavery. Inevitably, the Afrikan nations chose the latter option in a desperate attempt to ensure their own survival. Some sold their own people, then organised raids on weaker neighbours to kidnap Afrikan people for whom the British would provide them with 'desperately needed' guns. When they felt that they had secured enough guns they would attack their supposed 'aggressor'. They would justify their own attack on the grounds that, in their view, it was a defensive tactic, designed to ensure that they themselves were not attacked and enslaved.

In addition to those Afrikan nations that were tricked into: (i) internal wars and (ii) warring against their neighbours to produce Afrikan kidnap victims for European enslavers, the imperialists used another devastating method. British and other imperialists set up their own proxy states. They were established for the specific purpose of destabilising Afrikan nations opposed to the kidnapping and deportation of Afrikan people. Again they armed them on the basis of guns being received in return for Afrikan people.

It is important to acknowledge that these proxy states which terrorised the Afrikan nations around them are guilty as charged for their part in the process of kidnapping Afrikan people. Their motives were purely and simply to make profits for themselves and they did this at the expense of the liberty of their own sisters and brothers. Their existence destabilised whole regions of Afrika and bred mistrust between hitherto peaceful neighbours. Formed in 1712, the Bambara state of Segu is said to have fulfilled this type of role (Breaking the silence).

Once the wars and raids had started some Afrikan nations became trapped in a vicious cycle where they felt forced to capture other Afrikan people in order to make themselves militarily strong enough to avoid being captured. The more they captured fellow Afrikan people to obtain guns for their own protection, the more their fellow Afrikan people captured them in an attempt to protect themselves. The continuous escalation of this cut throat environment, where all other Afrikan nations were perceived as enemies, eventually meant that it was beyond the capacity of any single group of Afrikan people to stop the kidnapping. All of the Afrikan nations in the affected regions were caught in a downward spiral whether they wanted to be in it or not.

To get an idea of how successful these vicious underhand activities were, we must understand that British imperialism alone dumped 394,000 guns in West Afrika annually as a stimulus to inter and intra-tribal war and the general political destabilisation of the region (Justice, 2005, p. 142). Another 50,000 guns were dumped in the Loango-Congo area every year (Justice, 2005, p. 143). Other European imperialist nations assisted Britain in this process. For instance, in the case of the Gold Coast, guns were supplied to the Ashante by the Dutch, while the British armed their southern cousins the Fante (Justice, 2005, p. 127).

Another part of imperialism's strategy for kidnapping Afrikan people was to flood Afrikan nations with drugs. The drug used for this purpose was alcohol. There is little doubt that alcohol was sold to Afrikan nations (Rodney, 1981, p. 77), but its undermining and destabilising effects seem to have gone largely unrecorded by 'historians'. A speciality of the imperialists was to shower Afrikan people with alcohol and entre into 'agreements' and even 'treaties' with Afrikan leaders when they were drunk. It did not escape the imperialist's attention that it was easier to kidnap a drunken person that it was to kidnap a sober one and they used that knowledge with deadly effect (Williams, 1997, p. 78-81). For addicted Afrikan people Alcohol became a motivating force for kidnapping their sisters and brothers (Anderson, 1995, p. 60 & 78). Reduced to the mindset of a junkie, their personal 'fix' became more important to them than the welfare of their and their neighbours national welfare.

Afrikan groups and individuals who actively participated in the kidnapping and deportation of their sisters and brothers cannot be absorbed of their personal responsibility for their part in undermining the future development of Afrika. However, history demonstrates that Afrikan complicity in the theft and compulsory deportation of fellow

Afrikan people eventually became a matter of survival for participating Afrikan nations rather than a desire. All Afrikan peoples in the affected regions were, in fact, unwitting victims of a system of internal kidnapping that had been externally stimulated by British imperialism and its allies. Once they had set up the system, all the British had to do was stand back, with their supply of guns and alcohol and wait for the captured Afrikan people to be brought to them.

The fundamental truth is that the majority of Afrikan people were against the kidnapping and deportation of their people. There were many attempts by Afrikan people to abolish the kidnapping because it so undermined Afrikan nations, Afrikan development and Afrikan culture. Every time Afrikan people abolished the kidnapping and deportation, the imperialists used secret underhand methods to abolish the Afrikan abolitions. It was the imperialists that started the whole kidnapping process and did everything in their power to ensure that it continued, because their interests were intimately bound up with it. Up until the birth of industrial capitalism, when their interests changed, they constantly supported, practiced and profited from kidnapping, deporting and enslaving Afrikan people.

5.4.4 Afrikan national resistance to the so called 'slave trade'

Even where full abolition of the kidnapping and deportation process was not instituted, there were still striking examples of organised Afrikan national resistance. Afrikan defenders of liberty employed a range of methods to fight against the kidnappers [both Afrikan and European] operating in their lands. One such example is warrior sister **Nzinga**, a leader of the Ndongo and Matamba peoples in Angola (Shepard & Beckles, 2000, p. 5; Rodney, 1981, p. 80) who fought against European imperialism's enslavement of Afrikan people.

For **Nzinga**, anti-slavery resistance developed into a lifetime pursuit. She fought against imperialist kidnappers continuously over a 40 year period ranging from 1623 until her passing at the age of 80 in 1663. On a number of occasions she was reported to have been killed, only to later re-emerge as a warrior carrying out precision military attacks against the anti-Afrikan kidnappers on her soil. Her army's persistent guerrilla campaigns struck fear into the hearts of Dutch and Portuguese kidnapping cartels. **Nzinga's** determination to defeat European imperialist attempts to enslave her people was so great that when she learned that her own biological brother had turned traitor and collaborated with the enslaver enemy, she had him executed.

Another example came in around 1720 when **Tomba**, one of the leaders of the Baga people in the Guinea-Conakry area of West Afrika, tried to build alliances amongst Afrikan people in the region with a view to bringing an end to the kidnapping and deportation of Afrikan people. This was a clear attempt to organise national level resistance to imperialism's kidnapping and theft of Afrikan people in the region. **Tomba's** idea provoked the development of an unprincipled alliance between European kidnappers, mixed descendents of Afrikan people and Europeans and Afrikan people directly 'profiting' from the kidnappings. Their purpose was to destroy **Tomba's** anti-slavery initiative (Rodney, 1981, p. 80).

This wicked anti-Afrikan, pro-slavery alliance was not content with simply destroying **Tomba**'s Afrikan self-help initiative. It seems to have set **Tomba** up to be captured and transported into forced labour bondage on a human trafficking ship called *The Robert*. However in 1721, Afrikan people imprisoned on *The Robert* escaped their chains and under **Tomba's** leadership, bravely fought for their freedom. They managed to kill three kidnappers before they were recaptured by their oppressors. As punishment for fighting for their freedom, they were made to eat body parts of the kidnappers that they killed in their incredibly brave bid for liberty and freedom (Anderson, 1995, p. 116). It would be totally absurd to suggest that Afrikan heroes and heroines such as **Tomba**, **Nzinga** and their descendents are, in some way, responsible for the enslavement of Afrikan people currently living in the Afrikan Diaspora. On the contrary their actions provide clear evidence of their enforcement of Afrikan laws forbidding slavery.

5.4.5 Coastal battles to defeat the so called 'slave trade'
In addition to the abolitions and nationally organised forms of resistance, the Afrikan motherland experienced a host of smaller scale coastal battles. Many of these battles were between Afrikan people fighting to preserve their people's liberty and their British imperialist enslaver enemy.

> "... many Afrikans repeatedly attacked [human trafficking] ships in the pre-middle passage effort ... Afrikans, attacked

several [human trafficking] ships, freed captives and [confiscated] the cargo." (Bly, 1988).

The Afrikan hero warriors experienced differing degrees of success in warding off the alien pirate and privateer invaders. For instance, Afrikan people in the motherland are known to have refused to supply fellow Afrikan people to the European imperialism's pirate enslavers. Captain Samuel Stribling was captain of *The Afrikan Queen* a human trafficking ship which left Bristol in 1792. The ship docked at Old Calabar (now Nigeria) to deport kidnapped Afrikan people. He found little in the way of co-operation from Afrikan people who simply refused to support his enterprise by kidnapping and selling fellow Afrikan people.

This left Stribling's ship waiting for a long time because it needed to be filled with kidnapped Afrikan people in order to make its prospective journey to the Caribbean sufficiently profitable. We are informed that:

> "At least 21 of the ship's crew died during the 7 or 8 months spent at Old Calabar waiting whilst the captain purchased [kidnapped Afrikan people]" (Portcities Bristol).

This was just one of a number of incidents of this kind that caused James Rogers, the ships owner to go bankrupt. This example clearly demonstrates that Afrikan people were not habitually falling over themselves to kidnap and sell their sisters and brothers. Even this calibre of 'passive resistance' through non-cooperation with the kidnappers contributed significantly to the destruction of the so called 'slave trade'.

Afrikan people in the motherland are also known to have physically battled with the imperialist kidnappers, sometimes losing their lives in the process, to preventing the kidnapping of their sister and brothers. For instance in:

> "... 1767, when seven English ships - five from Liverpool, one from Bristol and one from London - were waiting [to receive kidnapped Afrikan people] on the Old Calabar River. A group of armed [Afrikan warriors] from Old Calabar attacked the English [kidnappers], but they were

unsuccessful because the King's soldiers helped the English [kidnappers]. The leader of the Old Calabar warriors was then beheaded, and the survivors were sold into slavery in the West Indies." (Breaking the silence).

Despite their brave policing efforts which involved killing several British kidnappers, many of these Afrikan heroes were themselves kidnapped or killed.

There are many other examples of this kind of bravery amongst Afrikan people policing the motherland's shores. For instance in 1733 a human trafficking ship was menacing the Afrikan continent by kidnapping Afrikan people in the area of the Gambia River. One night at midnight, Afrikan freedom fighters baring fire arms raided the vessel and forced it ashore in an attempt to rescue their captured sisters and brothers. This was clearly an organised rescue effort because the chief kidnapper is on record as having admitted that the Afrikan freedom fighters rushed the vessel 'in great numbers'. In another example in 1764, all but two kidnappers on a human trafficking ship from New London died whilst roaming the coast in an attempt to steal Afrikan people; Afrikan freedom fighters, outraged by the calibre of their behaviour and conscious of the need to defend their people, captured and killed the remaining kidnappers (Karenga, 1993, p. 138; Bly, 1998). It would be ridiculous to accuse these Afrikan warrior heroes, some of whom gave up their lives and liberty, of selling other Afrikan people into slavery. It would be equally ridiculous to accuse other Afrikan people of selling those heroes that were captured into slavery.

There is also evidence confirming that Afrikan people in the motherland risked their lives in raids to release kidnapped fellow Afrikan people from the bondage of imperialism's enslavers. For instance in 1740, Afrikan freedom fighters in Sierra Leone released 23 kidnapped Afrikan people from the human trafficking ship *The Jolly Bachelor* and in the course of policing the coast and defending Afrikan liberty killed all of the kidnappers. The Afrikan heroes then went on to more fully restored justice. They exacted reparations from the imperialist enslaver enemy by confiscating the ship and all goods on board (Karenga, 1993, p. 138; Bly, 1998). Similarly in 1758, Afrikan people in Gambia were so horrified when they witnessed their sisters and brothers being sold to William Potter, captain of the human trafficking ship *The Perfect*, that they attacked it. In the process of restoring justice, they put the whole crew to death. These Afrikan heroes saved over 300 of their people from being deported into enslavement (Breaking the silence).

If it is true that some Afrikan people from home were involved in the kidnapping and deportation of their own people, then it is equally true that many Afrikan people from home were actively involved in fighting against the same process. An honest refection reveals that not all Afrikan people were involved in the theft and compulsory deportation of their fellow Afrikan people into slavery; in fact a substantial proportion were most definitely not. It is true that some Afrikan chiefs consistently and unrepentantly participated (Martin, 1999, p. 30; Rodney, 1981, p. 119). It is also true that other Afrikan chiefs participated in it at one point and then bravely fought against it, even achieving its abolition at another point (Shepard & Beckles, 2000, p. 5; Barkindo, 1989, p. 92; Rodney, 1981, p. 81). Yet others (Shepard & Beckles, 2000, p. 5; Rodney, 1981, p. 80; Women in power, 1700-1740) continuously fought against it, in some cases defeating the imperialist kidnappers and sending them packing. Also, in some parts of Afrika such as Zimbabwe, there does not appear to be a history of Afrikan people participating as agents of the trans-Atlantic kidnapping and deportation process at all.

It therefore does a great disservice to the millions of Afrikan people at home who were tricked into participating in the chaotic kidnapping situation orchestrated by European imperialism, together with those that actively fought against human trafficking to blame them for the plight of those Afrikan people who were unfortunate enough to be deported into enslavement. Perhaps there is a case for posthumously identifying, honouring and thanking our home based Afrikan anti-slavery hero warriors for their role in ensuring that the gruesome kidnapping and deportation situation was not made even worse.

5.4.6 Consequence of Afrikan people's homeland resistance to the 'slave trade'
The Afrikan abolitions of slavery, the national wars of resistance and the coastal battles that took place on Afrikan soil resulted in the deaths of many Afrikan people. On a daily basis hundreds and possibly thousands of Afrikan people were giving their lives as part of the process of destroying imperialism's genocidal system of anti-Afrikan slavery. At

the same time, many European kidnappers were also killed. It was the deaths of the British warmongers and kidnappers in particular, that had a profound affect on the British public. The loss of their warmonger and kidnapper sons, husbands, brothers and fathers led to consternation amongst the working class people of Britain. They then demanded that the whole process of kidnapping Afrikan people from their homeland be brought to an end. Wilberforce had absolutely no influence on the freedom fighters pursuing their legitimate right to liberty. Indeed, a substantial proportion of these acts of resistance took place even before he was born. He was simply an imperialist appointed opportunist who falsely claimed the credit for 'abolition'. The truth is that on a daily basis hundreds and possibly thousands of Afrikan people were giving their lives as part of the process of destroying imperialism's genocidal system of anti-Afrikan slavery.

In today's terms the situation was much like the response of the British public to the loss of British soldiers unjustifiably invading Iraq, Syria and Afghanistan. Ordinary Britons are largely unconcerned with the deaths of thousands upon thousands of Iraqi, Syrian and Afghanistani women and children. The main impetus for the 'Stop the War' campaign is the deaths of a few hundred of their British invader sons. The parallel holds true for British imperialism's kidnapping, deporting and enslaving of Afrikan people also. The British public's consternation was not primarily concerned with the deaths of millions of innocent Afrikan children, women and men that were murdered and raped by British imperialism's kidnappers and enslavers; instead, they were distressed by the deaths of their own kidnapper sons. Ending the so called 'slave trade' and later the whole chattel slavery institution was a by-product of their desire to save their own sons from the lethal consequences of raiding unsuspecting Afrikan villages and stealing Afrikan people. It was these forces of Afrikan resistance, both violent and non-violent in form, which pressured the British public and consequently forced British imperialism to abandon its so called 'slave trade' as an initial stage to abandoning the whole genocidal chattel enslavement process. To pretend that it was Wilberforce is to distort history.

5.5 Sources of Afrikan people's abolition in the Atlantic
5.5.1 Kidnapped Afrikan people commandeered the human trafficking ships
Afrikan people kidnapped and held in bondage on the Atlantic crossing

did not sit idly by waiting to be transported into oblivion. On many occasions they commandeered their floating prison in determined bids to liberate themselves from their obscenely cruel bondage. Despite having all of the odds stacked against them, being held in chains for up to a year and attempting to survive in spaces providing them with 'less room than a man in a coffin' (Williams, 1997, p. 35), Afrikan prisoners of war bravely rose up to challenge and sometimes even subdued their evil oppressors. They proved time and time again that they were brave enough to rise up in militant fashion to take their freedom. According to one historian a total of:

> "382 [seaboard] revolts have been recorded ..." (Breaking the silence).

These revolts happened in spite of the fact that most human trafficking ships were floating armouries equipped with pistols, muskets, cutlasses, cannons and around the clock guards.

The courageous Afrikan prisoners of war who rose up to seize control of the floating prisons had varying degrees of success. It may come as a surprise to some, but many prison vessels were commandeered by courageous kidnapped Afrikan freedom fighters in their bids to liberate themselves from their obscenely cruel bondage. The uprisings had varying degrees of success: in some cases such as *the Robert* in 1721 they did not manage to gain control of the vessel; in others they gained control, but were eventually overpowered by imperialist warships and sold into slavery as happened with *the Thomas* in 1797 (Beckles, 1993, p. 37); others such as *the Neptunius* in 1795 were blown out of the water by a British warship as it attempted to return to Afrika (Breaking the silence); or they were released after court cases as was the fate of **Senghay Pieh** and the other Afrikan people who overpowered the crew on *the Amistad* in 1839 (Anderson, 1995, p. 86); in other cases such as *the Marlborough* in 1752 (Martin, 1999, p. 79), they eventually turned the ship around and triumphed over piracy by sailing back to Afrika.

5.5.2 Uprisings that did not take control of the ship

There are many cases of Afrikan people's uprisings on the human trafficking ships which did not manage to gain control of the vessels. For instance on 26th March 1789 on board *the Felicity*, Afrikan freedom fighters managed to get hold of fire arms, an axe, a cutlass and other weapons. They released some of the other Afrikan freedom fighters and attempted to take over the vessel. They managed to kill the chief kidnapper and some members of his pirate crew, with a loss of two of their own lives; a further three Afrikan freedom fighters were killed in the battle before they were subdued and forced below deck. This was a brave but 'unsuccessful' attempt to take over the floating prison and free themselves. (Karenga, 1993, p. 138; Bly, 1998).

Another example came in 1721 when eight kidnapped Afrikan freedom fighters on a human trafficking ship called *the Henry of London* managed to free themselves of their chains. They set about attempting to subdue the ship and its fifty man crew. However, after being driven back by cutlasses and firearms, these brave freedom fighters jumped overboard rather than surrender to the enemy. Ten years after this, on a Massachusetts registered human trafficking ship called *The William* the chief kidnapper, along with the majority of his lower ranking pirate kidnappers, were killed when Afrikan freedom fighters imprisoned on board rose up to regain their liberty. This happened whilst they were just off the coast of Afrika, but frustratingly there is no evidence to confirm that the warriors were able to make it back home (Breaking the silence).

In 1751, approximately 260 Afrikan people kidnapped on *the Middelburgs Welvaren* escaped from below deck and revolted against their kidnappers. The kidnappers were completely reckless in putting down the revolt. Apparently unconcerned that they might sink their own ship and drown themselves, they pointed the ship's cannons at the Afrikan freedom fighters and fired. This act of genocide resulted in the deaths of 230 innocent Afrikan people.

On a similar note, in 1765 a human trafficking ship called *the Sally* arrived on the island of Antigua in the Caribbean. The kidnappers described a revolt that had taken place on board their vessel just four hours after leaving Calabar in Nigeria. A number of the Afrikan freedom fighters were said to be vomiting as a result of seasickness. They had been allowed on deck to be tended to by their healthier sisters and brothers. The Afrikan freedom fighters then seized the opportunity and managed to free their entire group. This was followed by an intense battle with the kidnappers which resulted in 80 Afrikan warriors being forced overboard to their deaths (Breaking the silence).

On another occasion, Afrikan freedom fighters on board the *Vigilantie* in 1780 overpowered the kidnappers and took control of the vessel. Rather than kill the kidnappers, as often happened in these situations, they were humane enough to allow the kidnappers to leave in the vessel's lifeboats. However, the Afrikan freedom fighters were eventually intercepted and captured by a British warship (Breaking the silence). A similar story emerged in 1795 where in the course of defending Afrikan liberty, kidnapped Afrikan freedom fighters killed the three most senior kidnappers (the captain, first and second mate) on the human trafficking ship *the Brig-Rachell, Leetch of Boston* (Bly, 1998).

5.5.3 Ships successfully taken and later recaptured

It may at first seem ironic, but some of the female prisoners of war were spared the indignity and sheer misery of being bound and chained below deck. They were 'fortunate' enough to be held on deck in the fresh air, kept clean, sometimes not even chained and allowed to 'exercise'. Theirs would have been an altogether more pleasant experience but for the fact that their 'exercise' included being rape fodder for their sexually depraved kidnappers. Many Afrikan women died as a result of their injuries due to rape. Those that did not die physically, died emotionally with some even committing suicide (Anderson, 1995, p. 52, 68 & 122).

Whilst it is correct to say that all of the Afrikan people kidnapped and imprisoned on the human trafficking ships suffered intensely, it must be acknowledged that Afrikan women were subjected to an extra degree of abuse and oppression. As the most oppressed group, Afrikan women often led the resistance against imperialism's seaboard atrocities. In between the episodes of rape that Afrikan women were forced to endure, they organised to liberate their children, their brothers and themselves.

For instance in 1797 on the human trafficking ship *the Thomas,* some of the Afrikan women on deck noticed that the musket chest was left unlocked. They monitored the kidnappers' shift patterns and identified a period when there were consistently only three kidnappers on watch. They identified which of the kidnappers held the keys and then struck. They managed to capture some guns, overpowered the crew, released their sisters and brothers below deck and took charge of the ship (Beckles, 1993, p. 37).

The uncontrollable rage of the Afrikan women who had been so mercilessly abused was such that the whole of the kidnapper crew were put to death. This left the victorious Afrikan warriors with a problem, since none of them knew how to manoeuvre the vessel. After floating around aimlessly for a period of time, they were intercepted by one of imperialism's pirate vessels and recaptured. Even though they were originally destined for Barbados, they were sent into forced labour bondage in the Bahamas.

Another important example came from the experience of the Afrikan people held captive on board a human trafficking ship called *the Neptunius*. In 1795, Afrikan freedom fighters bravely rose up, took control of *the Neptunius* and set about making their way home to Afrika. On route they met with the most violent of interventions from pirates (otherwise known as the British navy) which literally destroyed their hard won freedom in a brutal act of ruthless, unmitigated genocide. Since neither the human trafficking ship nor the Afrikan people on board were considered to be British 'property', the pirates took the encounter as an opportunity to point its cannons at the ship. Then without even a moment's hesitation or the slightest regard for the lives of the Afrikan people on board, then blew *the Neptunius* to smithereens (Breaking the silence).

The revolt of Afrikan freedom fighters on *the Amistad* is probably the most successful and the best known of its kind. On 30th June 1839, a group of Afrikan warriors led by **Senghay Pieh** rose up, captured the vessel and put all but two members of the kidnap gang to death. Sparing the lives of the two kidnappers was tactical. They were permitted to live so that they navigated the ship back to Afrika. However, despite having their lives spared the kidnappers tricked them. The kidnappers steered *the Amistad* to the east by day giving the impression that they were sailing towards Afrika, but at night they headed west towards the Americas.

Eventually, *the Amistad* was intercepted by an American pirate/naval vessel called *the Washington*. This resulted in the heroic Afrikan freedom fighters being recaptured and imprisoned, taken to the

Americas and then brought to trial. During the trial, it was discovered that the fifty-two Afrikan freedom fighters on aboard *the Amistad* were neither born in the western hemisphere nor kidnapped prior to 1820. They were actually unlawfully smuggled directly from Afrika and this apparently gave them a legal status that was different from their enslaved Afrikan sisters and brothers held captive in the Americas. Surprisingly, the corrupt US Satan Supreme Court ruled that the Afrikan freedom fighters were free men and were therefore justified in rising up against their kidnappers. In 1841, after a number of fruitless attempts on the behalf of the Spanish to appeal the Supreme Court's decision, Senghay Pieh and the other freedom fighters of *the Amistad* were released from their false and unjustified imprisonment and successfully made their way back to Afrika (Anderson, 1995, p. 86; Bly, 1988).

5.5.4 Triumph: Conquered ships sailed back to Afrika
In 1752, 28 of the 400 kidnapped Afrikan people held captive on *the Marlborough* seized the muskets and in taking over the vessel initially killed all but 8 of the kidnappers on board. However, these Afrikan freedom fighters went a stage further than most revolts by not only commandeering the vessel, but also defeating another British ship sent to subdue them. After releasing their imprisoned sisters and brothers from below deck, they put another 6 kidnappers to death, bringing the total killed to 33 of the 35 kidnappers on board. They then subdued the 2 remaining kidnappers for use as navigators. They were then confronted and engaged in battle by the British ship *the Hawk*. Not only did the Afrikan warriors, who by then had mastered the use of fire arms, defeat *the Hawk*, but they actually chased it away.

However, there was a sad twist to the history because, after achieving this great triumph there developed a serious internal dispute. Afrikan warriors from Elmina in modern day Ghana and Bonny in modern day Nigeria began to argue over where the ship should dock first. The argument reached such proportions and developed into a battle of such intensity that it resulted in the deaths of 98 of the 400 Afrikan people on board. After this catastrophe, the survivors successfully sailed back to their respective parts of Afrika, with one navigator being assigned to each group (Martin, 1999, p. 79; Breaking the silence).

Another example of a successful return to Afrika came from the experience of the Afrikan warriors imprisoned on *the Little George*. In

June 1730, *the Little George* sailed from the Guinea Coast (on route to Rhode Island) trafficking a load of some ninety-six Afrikan prisoners of war. Several days into the voyage, at four-thirty in the morning, several Afrikan freedom fighters managed to break free from their chains and killed the three kidnappers on watch. They then forced the surviving kidnappers below deck where they were imprisoned pending justice. After having successfully taken control of the ship, the Afrikan freedom fighters set sail for Afrika. Meanwhile, below deck the surviving kidnappers created a bottle bomb and threatened to use it to sink the ship. Negotiations ensued and both parties agreed to grant the other their freedom. The Afrikan freedom fighters then successfully managed to sail back to the Sierra Leone River.

When they returned to the shore, there was nothing to prevent the Afrikan freedom fighters from reneging on the agreement. They could easily have set fire to the ship, with the kidnappers on board, after having made it to the shore. Nonetheless, they behaved in a principled way and kept to the agreement. They released the kidnappers, allowing them to go free and then set about leaving the ship. The kidnappers failed to reciprocate this principled response and after their release audaciously attempted to recapture and re-imprison the Afrikan warriors. Fortunately, this act of treachery failed and the Afrikan people who sailed home on the ship all managed to escape and returned home to enjoy their well earned freedom (Karenga, 1993, p. 138; Bly, 1998).

The rebellions on the pirate/human trafficking ships brought with them a high British death toll. These British deaths then set in motion the energies of the British working class - one of the most critical forces for abolition in the heartland of British imperialism itself. The British working class were involved in petitions against the kidnapping and deportation of Afrikan people because they were concerned about the mounting loss of British lives on the high seas and abroad. In order to kidnap and deport Afrikan people from their homes, it was necessary to have able kidnappers; British imperialism called these pirates, 'sailors'. In addition to being evil, theirs was a dangerous occupation, because out of a total of 12,263 kidnapper pirates 2,643 perished as a direct result of their 'work'. When the British public learned that almost a ¼ of their kidnapper sons were killed or lost (Williams, 1997, p. 166/7 & 190; Martin, 1999, p. 71), they engaged in the mass petitioning of Parliament and boycotts of Caribbean sugar. It was through this process that abolitionists perfected the modern party political tactics of lobbying Parliament and pressuring MP's (Walwin, 1993, p. 305).

5.6 Sources of Afrikan people's abolition in the Caribbean
5.6.1 Afrikan victories against great odds

Afrikan people's anti-slavery rebellions took place all across the Americas including North, South and Central America and the Caribbean. There are so many examples that it would need an encyclopedia comprising several volumes to attempt to cover them in a way that would do justice to them. For this reason, the focus in this section is on the major battles and wars of resistance conducted by enslaved Afrikan people in Caribbean islands that resulted in Afrikan people taking control of those islands. The analysis is also limited to the decades surrounding the so called 'Parliamentary abolition of the slave trade'. It highlights those rebellions and uprisings in the 1790's to 1810's that played a significant role by forcing the British state to reconsider its role as the Chief kidnapper of Afrikan people during the so called 'slave trade'. The analysis is also limited to those islands that were invaded and stolen by Britain or have had some level of colonial connection with Britain. These are obviously the encounters that would have most directly impacted on decisions in the British Parliament.

In the late 1790's and early 1800's enslaved Afrikan people revolted all over the Caribbean in a series of determined bids to take their freedom. Guerrilla warfare was used by these Afrikan freedom fighters to defeat the British colonial troops sent to the Caribbean to re-enslave them. Afrikan guerrilla warriors defeated British and other imperialists and took complete control of many islands including: Haiti (James, 1963, p. 370), Guadeloupe (Devaux, 1997, p. 15), St Lucia (Devaux, 1997, p. 17), St. Vincent (Devaux, 1997, p. 27) and Grenada (Fryer, 1989, p. 90); they occupied and took control of vast sections of other islands such as Jamaica (Hart, 1985, p. 148) and Dominica (Fryer, 1989, p. 90); they also put up strong military resistance to British colonial armies in those islands such as Barbados where they did not get a strong independent foothold.

5.6.2 Internal and external stimuli to Afrikan people's resistance

As has already been demonstrated, Afrikan people's resistance to imperialism's evil chattel enslavement system commenced long before their forced imprisonment on imperialism's hard labour camps in the

Caribbean. As early as 1502 an enslaved Afrikan freedom fighter jumped ship when his boat landed in Jamaica. He is believed by some to have been the first Afrikan Maroon in the America's following the arrival of Europeans (Sherlock, 1998, p. 57). This assertion must be regarded as inconclusive, since there is evidence that the first Afrikan Maroons in the region arrived before Europeans and mingled with the Caribs of St Vincent (Van Sertima, 1993, p. 190). However, regardless of which was first, both are examples illustrating early resistance by Afrikan people to enslavement in the Caribbean.

There was no opportunity to rest for the wicked imperialist enslavers, with uprisings and other forms of resistance happening constantly throughout the Americas. Prior to the 1790's there is documented evidence of varying degrees of Afrikan anti-slavery uprisings across the Caribbean. These included: 14 uprisings in Jamaica including Afrikan Maroon uprisings; 5 uprisings in Haiti; 5 uprisings in the Virgin Islands including 3 in St Croix, 1 in Tortola and 1 in St John. There are no documented uprisings in St Kitts, the birthplace of one of the leaders of the Haitian revolution – Henry Christophe, however the neighbouring island of Nevis experienced an uprising in 1761; Montserrat experienced uprisings in 1768 & 1776; there were 2 uprisings by enslaved Afrikan people in Antigua, including a major conspiracy led by Tackey and others in 1735/6; there were 2 uprisings in Guadeloupe; 1 in Martinique and 1 in Barbados (Honychurch, 1995a, p. 120).

Trinidad was a special case in that there are no documented up risings on the island. This appears to be because it was not occupied by Britain until 1797 (Hart, 1998, p. 12), which left little time for Britain to develop its evil brand of anti-Afrikan slavery as an institution on the island. Furthermore, it was dishonestly ceded to Britain by Spain in 1802 under imperialism's treaty of Amiens (Hart, 1998, p. 12). Nonetheless, there were at least 3 uprisings by enslaved Afrikan people on the neighbouring island of Tobago (Honychurch, 1995a, p. 120). There was a major uprising in Guyana in 1763, which had a profound affect upon British imperialism, although it should be pointed out that Guyana is neither an island nor is it in the Caribbean. All of the above are examples that serve to prove that Afrikan people fought for their freedom with distinction and a level of bravery that is sometimes underestimated.

It is obvious that Afrikan people rose up and destroyed imperialism's evil chattel enslavement system because of their innate human desire to be free from oppression. However, it is also important to recognise the political, economic and military context within which Afrikan people rose up, revolted and rebelled against imperialism in order to take their freedom. In addition to the innate desire of Afrikan people for freedom, there were a number of global forces that had a significant impact on Afrikan people in the America's which helped to stimulate them into action for liberation. One of the most important of those external forces was the French revolution.

The French revolution which took place in 1789 divided the French nation. It brought about a civil war that forced the military machine of French imperialism to concentrate primarily on matters in France. This had the simultaneous effect of weakening the hold of French imperialism on its stolen colonies overseas. For instance, later in 1789, there were uprisings in both Martinique and Guadeloupe (James, 1963, p. 81) - islands that were colonially linked to France. Two years after the French revolution, the Haitian revolution erupted with devastating consequences for French imperialism. By the mid-1790's the anti-imperialist forces in France were so strong that they abolished slavery and this ignited Afrikan people to fight for their own liberation in several islands in the Eastern Caribbean.

Whilst all of this was going on the war between Britain and France and the American war of Independence all weakened France and Britain and had a corresponding impact on the capacity of Afrikan people to resist enslavement throughout the Caribbean. These global scale forces together provided the backdrop against which enslaved Afrikan people rose up and fought against imperialist forces in order to secure their freedom.

5.7 Haiti: Epicentre of revolutionary upsurge
5.7.1 The magnitude of the Haitian Revolutionary victory

Haiti was by far the richest colony in the world during the enslavement era. It produced more wealth for its coloniser France that North America, in its entirety, produced for Britain. The imperialist nations of the time were fully aware that whichever of them controlled Haiti would be the richest and most powerful imperialists in the world. This is precisely the reason why France, Britain and Spain – the leading imperialist nations of the period spent so much time and effort fighting its Afrikan inhabitants and each other for possession of it.

The revolution carried out in Haiti by enslaved Afrikan women and men working in concert, was a world shattering event. It represented the all time single most important symbol of Afrikan people's resistance to imperialism's genocidal chattel slavery form of exploitation. The victorious Haitian revolution lasted from 1791 – 1804 and during that time Afrikan revolutionaries defeated British imperialism twice, French imperialism twice, Spanish imperialism twice and on top of that they defeated the class of lighter skinned Afrikans in Haiti when they made the error of trying to re-impose slavery on the island (Man's Unconquerable Mind).

The 3 external attackers were literally the world's superpowers of that time and Toussaint was the leader of the Haitian revolution for all but the last defeat of France. It is this series of gigantic feats that stakes his claim to be being the greatest military strategist in the history of humanity. To get a sense of the magnitude of these victories in the modern day, it would be like the Island of Jamaica whilst being completely out gunned and out resourced militarily defeating US Satan, Russia and China twice each in rapid succession.

5.7.2 The Haitian revolution ignites
The Haitian revolution began on or about the night of the 22nd August 1791 in the Caiman Woods under the leadership of an Afrikan warrior priest and hero of the revolution named **Boukman Dutty**. The war started in the aftermath of 2 weeks of intense nocturnal Afrikan rituals. However, in many parts of Afrikan culture men cannot go to war without first securing the approval of the women. This is often given in the form of consent from a 'queen mother' figure. **Cecile Fatiman** (aka **Castere Bazile**) was the mambo or priestess who led the ceremony at the side of **Boukman** for those 2 weeks.

As 'queen mother' Afrikan heroine **Cecile** was a key figure at the meeting where the sons of Afrika gathered to form a strategy to take Haiti out of slavery. During the rituals she is said to have become possessed by warrior spirit Ogun, made the critical sacrifice of a black pig and called on all those present to drink its blood as part of inviting the spirit of the Afrikan ancestors to come to assist in defeating the enslavers.

Speaking in the voice of the spirit, she named those who were to lead Afrikan people in Haiti to freedom, appointing Afrikan heroes **Boukman, Jean-Francois, Biassou** and **Jeannot**. It was some time later that other Afrikan heroes such as **Toussaint L'Ouverture, Henry Christophe, Jean-Jacques Dessalines, Moise, Andre Rigaud** and her future husband **Louis Michel Pierrot** became the leading generals in the 12 and ½ years it took to achieve the Haitian Revolution's final victory.

5.7.3 The beginning phase of the revolution

The early phases of the revolution saw the formerly enslaved Afrikan people overrunning and destroying the majority of the forced labour camps and towns in the north of the island (Carruthers, 1985, p. 9). The fighting was ferocious, with Afrikan people determined to give their lives, if need be, in pursuit of Afrikan freedom. They employed all available means and advanced under slogans such as: 'Vengeance! Vengeance!' (James, 1963, p. 88), 'Kill the whites!' (Carruthers, 1985, p. 11) and most profoundly, 'Liberty or death!' (Carruthers, 1985, p. 27) This was no idle chant, because in the first two months of fighting, the death toll was extremely high with 10,000 Afrikan people and 2,000 Europeans losing their lives (Ferguson, 1998, p. 135).

Impression of the Caiman Woods Ceremony:
The Start of the Haitian Revolution in 1791

The controlling power of France on the island had effectively been destroyed early in the revolution (Sheppard, 2000, p. 976). On 28th September 1791, in a vain attempt to retain some semblance of power, the French national assembly made a proclamation granting an amnesty to all persons charged with 'acts of revolution'. It made little difference, the fighting proved too contagious and insurgency was now erupting everywhere on the island. Amidst the chaos, the French enslavers lost control, scrambled to any European imperialist nation (including France's enemies Britain and Spain) that might help them keep power and then busily ran for their lives.

The Afrikan freedom fighters did not have it all their own way; they were forced to make great sacrifices. For instance, just 3 months into the revolution in November 1791, whilst fighting bravely for the freedom of enslaved Afrikan people, **Boukman** was killed (Shepard, 2000, p. 974; James, 1963, p. 96). He was the first of the original leaders to lose his life. It caused great mourning amongst the Afrikan revolutionary warriors, but it did not dampen their resolve for freedom, nor did it prevent them from dispossessing the French of their control of the island. **Boukman's** death served as confirmation that the Afrikan freedom fighters would rather give their lives than settle for anything less than self-determination.

5.7.4 Afrikan revolutionaries defeat multiple enemies

This first defeat of the French was so substantial that it set in trail a series of events that eventually destroyed French imperialism's resolve to continue enslaving Afrikan people; it contributed to the abolition of slavery in all French colonies. The new French Commissioner who was sent to the island in September 1792 in an attempt to salvage something from the situation, was forced to unilaterally 'abolish' slavery in Haiti on 29th August 1793 (Sherlock, 1998, p. 185; James, 1963, p. 128/9). This decision was later formally backed up by the French revolutionary government on 4th February 1794 (Devaux, 1997, p. 13). The latter decision claimed to have abolished slavery in all French colonies – at least temporarily.

Following the initial French defeats, both Britain and Spain sent troops to St Dominigue in 1793 (Sherlock, 1998, p. 186) hoping to cash in on French imperialism's misery. Despite the fact that British troops were able to claim that they had captured the island's capital in June 1794 (Ferguson, 1998, p. 17), by 1795 they were sufficiently subdued to be desperately calling to their Caribbean colonies (Sherlock, 1998, p. 187) and the British Parliament (Ferguson, 1998, p. 141) for reinforcements.

Likewise, on 22nd July 1795 **Toussaint** and his Afrikan army, fighting in alliance with the French forced the surrender of his former allies, the Spanish. It was the first emphatic defeat of the Spanish and it had driven them into confinement in what had become the Spanish part of the island (Carruthers, 1985, p. 42).

Despite receiving some 40,000 additional soldiers in 1795 (Ferguson, 1998, p. 141) to assist their second great attempted assault, the British army was no match for the Afrikan revolutionaries led by **Toussaint L'Ouverture**. **Toussaint's** armies defeated the British on seven separate occasions in as many days (James, 1963, p. 201). Humiliated, completely outgunned and out manoeuvred, the British were resoundingly defeated by the Afrikan revolutionaries. **Toussaint** accepted the surrender of British General Thomas Maitland and expelled them from the island on 30th April 1798 (James, 1963, p. 204 & 213/4; Sherlock, 1998, p. 186/7).

In their haste to get away, the British army abandoned many troops including Afrikan soldiers. These Afrikan troops were now extremely dangerous to the British, because they had witnessed first hand, how easy it was for European soldiers to be defeated in battle. This presented the obvious danger that should they return, they would relay this news the enslaved Afrikan people in the other British colonies. On receiving this news, enslaved Afrikan people in those colonies might then be sufficiently inspired to rise up and in the process of taking their freedom, wipe out the wicked British enslavers. It was therefore tactically safer to leave these Afrikan troops to join the armies of **Toussaint L'Ouverture**.

5.7.5 Settling internal disputes

In the midst of successive wars against a range of foreign invaders, there had been a somewhat fragile alliance between the dark skinned and light skinned Afrikan people on the island (Carruthers, p. 43). The alliance eventually erupted into an Afrikan civil war based on the misconceived desire of some of the lighter skinned Afrikans to enslave their darker skinned Afrikan sisters and brothers.

The 'War of knives' between light and dark skinned Afrikan people began in 1799, with **Andre Rigaud** and **Toussaint L'Ouverture** as respective leaders and **Dessalines** commanding **Toussaint's** assault. In early 1800, the deciding battle culminated in the siege of Jacmal – **Rigaud's** stronghold. During the siege, revolutionary Afrikan heroine, nurse, healer and pacifist **Marie Clair Heureuse Felicite Bonheur** played an active role saving lives in the battle.

On their first meeting, she persuaded **Dessalines** (they would later marry) to allow her entry to the town to administer medical care. Her infirmary was the first in modern history (approximately a century before Mary Seacole or Florence Nightingale). In addition to saving soldiers, she saved women, children and elders. Hers was a constructive contribution that lessened the loss of Afrikan lives in a battle eventually won by **Toussaint** and the dark skinned Afrikan revolutionaries.

She became a woman of considerable influence. Other than **Toussaint**, she was the only person able to persuade **Dessalines** for refrain from killing Europeans and is reputed to have saved many of their lives. Her influence was so strong that she insisted that no weapons be brought into their home and **Dessalines 'the ferocious'** complied.

Another Afrikan revolutionary heroine active during the siege was **Marissante Dede Bazile** aka **Defile**. She is said to have joined **Dessalines'** army after being raped by her wicked European enslaver. Operating as a cook by day, she is also said to have been part of the revolutionary Afrikan heroines active in the unofficial 'prostitute corps' – they gave their bodies in service of the revolution by night. **Defile** was intensely loyal to **Dessalines** and deeply in love with him. Her place in Haitian history is assured as the woman who gave **Dessalines** - the first president of Haiti - a fitting burial following his assassination in 1806.

In early 1800, the civil war was firmly brought to an end by Toussaint and his armies at the heavy cost of 10,000 light skinned Afrikan lives (Sherlock, p. 188; Ferguson, 1998, p. 141/2). His opposing general would flee to France only to return later as part of the French invasion force (Bob Corbett, Part III).

5.7.6 Toussaint takes firm control
Having overcome this devastating internal dispute, the task of subduing powerful foreign invaders was still not complete. **Toussaint** gave his most feared and respected general – his adopted nephew Moise - the

task of subduing the Spanish for the second time. **Moise** seemed to enjoy slaughtering Europeans and it did not take long for his forces to completely wrought the Spanish. The task of taking control of the island was thoroughly completed in 1800 (Carruthers, 1985, p. xv). Spanish were completely defeated and formally handed over the island to the Afrikan revolutionaries on 21st January 1800 (James, 1963, p. 239; Sherlock, 1998, p. 186).

By mid-1801 **Toussaint** was the leading figure in Saint Domingue. His next logical step appeared to be a declaration of independence. He had defeated the Spanish and British, ousted the French Commissioners, defeated **Andre Rigaud** and his light skinned Afrikan army in the civil war, taken possession of the eastern section of Hispaniola (the name for the whole island) and put in place a constitution granting him a life time term as its governor general (Bob Corbett). **Toussaint** was now firmly and unquestionably in charge of the island.

On 21st November 1801, **Toussaint** took the drastic step of executing his own nephew (James, 1963, p. 285) apparently for his open defiance on the issue of how Europeans should be treated. It appears that he was displeased with **Moise**'s enthusiasm for exterminating Europeans,. **Toussaints** had guaranteed the safety of a group of Europeans, whom **Moise** had wiped out. This was the reason given for his execution, though it is not impossible that Toussaint was fearful of **Moise's** rapid rise in popularity which could potentially have challenged his leadership (James, 1963, p. 278). Ironically, the execution took place on the same date that the French military invasion force, comprising 68 shiploads of soldiers, was dispatched from France (Ferguson, 1998, p. 142).

5.7.7 The arrival and impact of the French invasion force
The French arrived in Haiti on 2nd February 1802 (James, 1963, p. 295) and offered **Toussaint's** Afrikan generals the option of keeping their rank if they submitted to the authority of France (Carruthers, 1985, p. 64). Internal divisions developed under the pressures exerted by the French and most of Toussaint's generals were seduced and submitted. In fact, only **Toussaint**, **Dessalines** and **Christophe** refused to submit (Carruthers, 1985, p. 64). The situation was impossible, not only did they have to face the French invading force (including old adversary **Rigaud**), but they had to fight the rest of their own army as well. Hopelessly, outgunned and outnumbered, it wasn't long until they were

in pitch battles with their foes.

Marie Jeanne Lamartiniere

The scene for one of the most important battles of the whole war was Crete a Perrot a fortified garrison containing 1,200 Afrikan revolutionaries including **Dessalines** and his commanders: **Magny, Lamartiniere, Monpoint** and **Larose**. They were surrounded by 12,000 French troops, under canon fire, had run out of supplies and were facing certain death. Outnumbered 10 to 1, after nightfall on 24th March 1802 they came out fighting. The Afrikan heroine **Marie Jeanne Lamartiniere** stood out above all others, fearlessly charging across the battlefield distributing cartridges and loading guns. Whilst firing her own rifle amidst the hail of enemy bullets she repeadly shouted her famous words of encouragement:

> "To arms! We will not be defeated my brothers! I will fight with you! I will die with you!"

Marie Jeanne Lamartiniere entered the battle a nurse and wife of **Brigadier Commander Lamartiniere**. He too was one of the 600 surviving revolutionaries, but soon after fell sick and died, whilst she emerged as Haiti's greatest ever warrior. They left 3 French generals dead and a whole host of their troops either dead or wounded. Her bravery was pivotal, saving the lives of **Dessalines** and the other entrapped revolutionary commanders. **Dessalines** who described her as Haiti's bravest warrior, bestowed her the nation's highest military honour. Had that critical battle not been won, the future first president of Haiti would almost certainly have perished.

The weight of opposing such a formidable invasion force was great and it seems to have affected discipline in the Afrikan revolutionary armies because, some of the Afrikan warriors are known to have rebelled against **Toussaint** (Carruthers, 1985, p. 70). It is not clear whether these rebellions were, in any way, inspired by the actions of **Dessalines** and **Christophe**, but it was in that environment that a secret meeting took place between the three generals. The outcome remains secret to this very day, but there is speculation that they agreed a secret pact resulting in **Toussaint** offering himself as a sacrifice for the greater goal of Afrikan revolutionary victory in Haiti.

However, it is clear that after the initial fighting **Christophe** and later **Dessalines** joined the side of the French enemy invaders (Carruthers, p. 70; Sherlock, 1998, p. 188) and the French used them to attack and pacify the stalwart Afrikan revolutionary resistance forces (Carruthers, 1985, p. 70). They would inflict devastating losses on the revolutionary forces, but despite this their loyalty was always questioned by the French.

In May 1802, **Toussaint** who was now hopelessly isolated, retreated to his stronghold (Ferguson, 1998, p. 143). The French then invited **Toussaint** to come to a negotiating meeting with full safe conduct. During the meeting they arrested him and eventually placed him aboard a frigate called *the Creole* before transferring him to another warship - *the Hero* (Toussaint L'Ouverture).

It was during the Atlantic journey that **Toussaint** warned his captures that overthrowing him was merely the cutting down of the trunk of the tree of liberty – the roots were deep and would rise up and secure Haiti's liberation. It was under these circumstances that **Toussaint** (arguably the greatest general of all time) fell for the French leader's trick, was kidnapped and transported to France (Ferguson, 1998, p. 143).

Having been captured in June 1802, **Suzanne Simone Baptiste L'Ouverture**, wife of **Toussaint L'Ouverture** and her children were transported to meet her husband. The ship holding **Toussaint, Suzanne** and their children arrived on 2nd July 1802 and on 25th August 1802 Toussaint was imprisoned in Joux castle in the Lower Pyrenees, while his family was held captive in Bayonne under the supervision of General Ducos (Toussaint L'Ouverture). **Toussaint** was now an old man who had lived all of his life in the tropics and had little resistance to the freezing conditions, a starvation diet, neglect and general ill-treatment. After ten horrendous months in jail on 7th April 1803 his murder was complete (Ferguson, 1998, p. 143). Meanwhile, like her husband **Suzanne** refused to reveal names of his companions and was tortured. One indicator of the level of ill-treatment is Afrikan revolutionary heroine **Suzanne L'Ouverture** was 250 pounds at capture and a mere ninety when eventually released.

After **Toussaint's** capture there was turmoil. The situation was complex with fighters constantly switching allegiances in a rapidly shifting political environment. On 20th May 1802 (Shepard, 2000, p. 924) the French added further to the complexity by declaring their intention for Afrikan people when they reintroduced slavery on the island of Guadeloupe (James, 1963, p. 340). The decree was declared in Guadeloupe on 16th July 1802 (Shepard, 2000, p. 926) and news of the decree reached St Dominigue before the end of that month (James, 1963, p. 431).

Amidst the ongoinng confusion, the Afrikan revolutionary heroine and army officer **Suzanne Bele** aka **Sanite Belair** and her husband (and **Toussaint's** other adopted nephew) Commander **Charles Belair** remained consistently loyal to the revolutionary cause. **Charles**, **Toussaint L'Ouverture's** favourite to succeed him disliked Europeans with a passion. He had an unfortunate habit of inviting European women to his quarters, where refusal to oblige would result in their deaths. Acceptance on the other hand, would arouse the jealousy of his wife who would personally kill them. **Sanite** is reputed to have killed her husband's secretary – a European male – by tying him and repeatedly stabbing him.

Sanite, **Charles** and their forces were widely respected as heroes of the revolution for their unflinching loyalty to **Toussaint** and the liberation cause. On the pretext of holding talks designed to combine their forces against the French, **Dessalines** invited the **Belairs** to see him, arrested them and sent them to the French. They were tried in a kangaroo court and on 2nd October 1802 and executed on the 5th. They died bravely, both of them, with **Sanite** unflinchingly watching the execution of her husband, then facing her own firing squad and refusing to have her eyes bound. **Dessalines**, who conducted the executions, betrayed and murdered two of the nation's most popular revolutionaries on behalf of the French. His actions may have been inspired by a desire to remove potential opponents that might pip him to the post to becoming the republics emperor in the future.

Despite the magnitude of his revolutionary betrayal, **Dessalines** still wasn't trusted by the French and unbeknown to him, the order had been issued for his arrest. On 11th October 1802, he was invited to breakfast by a priest – it was a trap – the location was surrounded. However, the priest's Afrikan servant – Afrikan revolutionary heroine **Madam Pageot** warned him by pressing her elbows to her side and moving backwards as though bound. Recognising the signal, he immediately made good his escape. Had he been captured and no doubt killed, the outcome of the revolution might well have been different. Not only did Madam **Pageot's** initiative save **Dessaline's** life, but it was the catalyst for his rejoining revolutionary ranks.

Determined that they would not under any circumstances be re-enslaved and inspired by the desire to retake the island, **Dessalines**, **Christophe** and their followers turned on the French (Sherlock, 1998, p. 188). Again, it is a matter of speculation as to whether this tactic was agreed in the earlier secret meeting between **Toussaint**, **Dessalines** and **Christophe**. They inflicted massive defeats on the French, who by now were also being rendered impotent by disease.

The impact of **Dessaline's** escape was immediate. On 13th October 1802 generals **Petion** and **Clairvaux** turned on the French also. Having defected from France *en masse*, the Afrikan revolutionary generals convened a joint meeting to coordinate their efforts on 2nd November 1802 at Archahaye near St Marc. It was at this meeting that they swore an oath to the ancestors of 'liberty or death' and **Dessalines** ripped out the white part of the French tricolour. Some months later on 18th May 1803, the bicolour – the new Haitian flag was sewn by another of the Afrikan revolutionary heroines **Cathrine Flon** - his goddaughter.

5.7.8 The French lust for Afrikan women
Whereas under British imperialism's systems of anti-Afrikan slavery miscegenation was frowned upon, the French equivalent actively

encouraged it to the point of openly permitting Afrikan people and Europeans to marry. This arrangement produced many light skinned Afrikan women who eventually came to represent the highest image of beauty in the French colonial elite's psyche.

Men in French imperialism's elite were so taken by the idea of their epic beauty that they actively sought marriage with light skinned Afrikan women as their first option. These women's beauty was recognised as so outstanding that they were stereotypically deemed to add to French imperialism's elite men's social status. This is exemplified by the fact that their 'top man' i.e. genocidal maniac murdering emperor Napoleon was married to his empress, the light skinned Afrikan woman Josephine who was born in French imperialism's enslavement colony Martinique.

Afrikan women in Haiti naturally participated in a wide variety of forms of resistance including bravely fighting on the battle field alongside Afrikan men. However, Haiti also brought French men face to face with their greatest desire - an abundance of beautiful light skinned Afrikan women. Understanding the lust of French imperialism's invading troops, it was recognised that these Afrikan women could make a critical contribution to the liberation effort through espionage or spying. The Haitian revolutionaries therefore hit the French imperialists at their weak point by providing corps of 'prostitutes', many of whom had the fundamental mission of spying for the revolution.

5.7.9 Satisfying the Frenchman's lust for a higher cause
It is a sad fact that where there is war there is rape and in the context of slavery Afrikan women had no substantive protection from rapists. Against this background, a number of Afrikan women came forward and 'opted' or 'volunteered' for 'prostitution', often as an alternative to becoming rape fodder in the war zone. Some of those women had the dual role of being Afrikan freedom fighters of the most secret and intimate kind.

Theirs was perhaps the greatest of sacrifices in a revolution where, for Afrikan people, intense suffering was the norm. In addition to the clear violations of their bodies, their spying role bore the certainty of execution if caught. They bravely gave their bodies, their very dignity humanity and being to French imperialism's invading troops for the higher goal of the liberation of Afrikan people from slavery.

5.7.10 Henriette St Marc – heroic self-sacrifice

Henriette St Marc, an outstandingly beautiful Afrikan woman and heroine of the Haitian revolution was one such freedom fighter. Like the majority of Afrikan women in Haiti, **Henriette** came from modest origins. On the face of it she was engaged in prostitution for the money and lacked moral standing. In reality however she was a heroine who gave all for her people's freedom and never lost sight of her morally principled revolutionary objectives. Hers is the story of hundreds possibly thousands of Afrikan heroines of the revolution whose names have been excluded from the historical record.

Her mission consisted of seducing French soldiers in exchange for information and ammunition. Her strategy rested mainly on utilising her outstanding beauty and irresistable charm which she used to glean information from French imperialism's soldiers. She was so successful that she manged to persuade some of them to part with ammunition – in one action weakening the enemy militarily and strengthening the revolution. The fact that she had so many admirers amongst French imperialism's soldiers testifies to her sucess rate. If we multiply her efforts in the bedroom by hundreds, even thousands of times we begin to sense the massive shift that she and the many unknown Afrikan heroines were able to achieve in the balance of forces on the battle field.

Very little is known about the circumstances of her arrest, only that she was caught in Cap Francais as she was leaving for a rebel camp. The French imperialists accused her of spying for the revolutionaries and supplying them with arms and ammunition procured through her liaisons with French imperialism's invader troops. Afrikan heroine **Henriette** was sentenced to death and was executed by hanging in the market place in front of the church Croix-des-Bouquets in the town of St Marc where there is an image depicting her murder to this day.

Noone knows the exact day and time of her murder because the French colonial murderers had a conveyor belt system for murdering Afrikan freedom fighters. They would start the murders at 10am and carry on that grusome racist slaying process throughout the day. They would stop at nightfall and recommence at 10am the next morning. All we can say with certainty was that heroine Henriette was murdered during the third week of December 1802 as part of French imperialism's conveyor belt system of cold blooded Anti-Afrikan murder.

5.7.11 Afrikan Revolutionaries triumph in Haiti

On 18th May 1803 Britain pounced and declared war on France weakened by the Afrikan revolutionaries of Haiti. This meant the end of reinforcements and supplies for the already floundering French troops on the island. The conditions were set for the Afrikan revolutionaries to dispense with French imperialism once and for all, a process carried out over the course of the following 6 months. The final major defeat of the French at the hands of Afrikan revolutionaries came at the Battle of Vertierres on 18th November 1803. The Afrikan revolutionaries were led by General Francois Capois and this finale was the summation of Afrikan people's emphatic victory over the French in particular and imperialism in general.

Afrikan heroine and warrior priestess **Cecile Fatiman** was married to **Louis Michel Pierrot**, who in tandem with **Francois Capois** 'Death', led battalions of Afrikan warriors at Vertierres. She appears to have been a leading figure in both the opening and final battles of the Haitian revolution. She lived in the Cape until the age of 112 in full possession of her mental faculties. She holds a very special place in the history of the revolution as the heroine who appointed Afrikan hero **Boukman** to lead the opening phase of the military struggle and was married to **Pierrot** the hero who fought in the final military battle, marking was 'Liberty or death!', but her epic contribution resulted for her in the deserved outcome of liberty and long life.

Out of the 34,000 troops sent to the island by France 24,000, including their leader, were dead and a further 8,000 hospitalised (Ferguson, 1998, p. 144). After this second catastrophic defeat at the hands of Afrikan people in Haiti, the French were in such a hurry to get away from the island that they neglected to take all of their soldiers with them. Their total humiliation was complete when they left their abandoned colleagues to face the full consequences of upsetting the Afrikan revolutionaries whose hard won freedom they tried to take away (Sherlock, 1998, p. 188).

Monument to the Battle of Vertières

Dessalines was ruthless in clearing all guilty Europeans from the island (Carruthers, 1985, p. 92 & 130/1) as a prelude to the total abolition of slavery. After this final victory, processes were put in place for the formal declaration of the independence of Haiti. The name St Dominigue was cast aside and the original Carib name of the island was reinstated. Haiti – the land of many mountains – was declared independent under the leadership of President Jean Jacques Dessalines on 1st January 1804 (James, 1963, p. 370; Sherlock, 1998, p. 189).

This moment could not have been achieved without the earlier contribution of another Afrikan revolutionary heroine. **Victoria Mantou**, affectionately known as **Toya** who was a military commander in the Haitian revolutionary army. Her battalion fought the French in the Artibonite region. She was the adopted aunt of general Dessalines, his mentor and personal combat coach. She guided him in his youth, instructing him on face to face combat and knife throwing. Hers is one of the substantial, but partially hidden contributions to the successful Haitian revolution.

What happened in Haiti was one of the most remarkable military feats in the history of humanity. The relatively poorly armed Afrikan revolutionaries on the island defeated the world's three greatest superpowers of that period of history. This was a feat that would have been regarded as totally impossible had it not actually happened. These massive victories provided concrete proof that enslaved Afrikan people determined to take their freedom could repeatedly defeat all of the most highly trained and heavily armed European imperialist armies in the world. They represented such an exceptionally outstanding series of victories that enslaved Afrikan people across the whole of the Americas were inspired to resist their own enslavement. Enslaved Afrikan people began to truly realise that their enslavers were not invincible. It was an important catalyst for Afrikan revolutionary momentum in the America's aimed at destroying slavery and it provided a foundation for the achievement of enslaved Afrikan people's liberation throughout the region. This realisation also sent a clear emphatic message to the evil European enslavers in the Caribbean who began to realise that their period of domination was rapidly coming to an end.

Afrikan Revolutionary Warriors Toussaint, Flon & Dessalines

5.8 Caribbean-wide revolution and the Haitian connection
5.8.1 Jamaica
The neighbouring island of Jamaica was a land of sporadic Afrikan rebellion; there are at least 17 document anti-slavery uprisings recorded in its history (Honychurch, 1995a, p. 120). In 1795 Jamaica experienced the second major uprising of the Afrikan Maroons (Robinson, 1993, p.

154/5). The British had reneged on their treaty obligations resulting from the first Maroon war which ended in 1739 and then harassed the Afrikan Maroon community in Trelawney (Robinson, 1993, p. 98; Hart, 1985, p. 105). The Afrikan Maroon community then responded by rising up to defend their rights and prepared themselves for war. On 30th July 1795 the character calling himself 'governor of Jamaica' blamed the revolutionary activities on the island on Afrikan people inspired by the French revolution. He was clearly worried about the Haitian Revolution which he saw as an important factor contributing to the cause of the second Afrikan Maroon war (Sherlock, 1998, p. 187).

In the build up to the war, **Afrikan Maroon captains Johnson** and **Smith** were called back from their new homes in Westmoreland by the Afrikan Maroon community (Hart, 1985, p. 146; Robinson, 1993, p. 165). They were called back specifically to lead the Afrikan Maroons in the impending war. Meanwhile, fearful that the Afrikan Maroons were determine to defend themselves by military means, **Afrikan Maroon captains Palmer** and **Parkinson** were asked to come from Montego Bay by the British in an attempt to persuade the Afrikan Maroon community to surrender (Hart, 1985, p. 146). However, instead of acquiescing to the desires of the British, **Palmer** and **Parkinson** used their influence to persuade the Afrikan Maroon community to fight the British to the end (Hart, 1985, p. 146). The Afrikan Maroon community now had four of their warrior leaders at the helm rather than the planned two – they were ready for war. On 12th August 1795 fighting broke out (Robinson, 1993, p. 154/5).

With a force of 300 Afrikan Maroon warriors fighting against a combined force of 1500 hand picked soldiers, supplemented with more than 3,000 supporting militia, the British suffered very heavy losses, but ultimately neither side was able to subdue the other (Black, 1991, p. 96). The tactical superiority of the Afrikan Maroon guerrilla warriors meant that they were able to hold their own. To prevent a humiliating defeat, the British imperialists pulled out all the stops and brought in man eating killer dogs to boost their forces. However, this move provided little compensation since the British had already suffered an extremely high death toll and a substantial proportion of their number had effectively disserted (Robinson, 1993, p. 225).

The British had by this time already suffered their first major thrashing at the hands of the Afrikan revolutionaries in the adjacent island of Haiti. In fact, the British forces in Jamaica had even refused to send troops to reinforce their defeated colleagues (Sherlock, 1998, p. 187). They therefore knew what it was to suffer defeat at the hands of enslaved Afrikan people determined to take their freedom. They also realised that they were unable to defeat the Afrikan Maroon warriors in combat and were fearful that the second Afrikan Maroon war might ignite further insurrections on the island which they would be unable to put down. Continuation of the war could possibly have caused British imperialism to lose control of the island. Jamaica was ripe for revolution and if the British imperialists were not careful, Afrikan people on the island would humiliate them in much the same way that Afrikan people in Haiti humiliated French imperialism.

Rather than risk losing the whole island to a mass uprising of enslaved Afrikan people, on 12th December 1795 the British, realising that they could become boxed into a corner, asked the Afrikan Maroons for a peace treaty. Under intense pressure from the killer hounds and cut off from world affairs in the hills of Jamaica, it is likely that the Afrikan Maroon warriors did not fully appreciate just how weak the position of the British military actually was. Eventually, the Afrikan Maroon community agreed to the British peace request and signed the treaty – much to the relief of British imperialism (Hart, 1985, p. 148).

The peace negotiations led to the relocating of the Afrikan Maroons. After the settlement the Afrikan Maroon community was transported from its stronghold in the hills of Trelawny to Nova Scotia in Canada (Sherlock, 1998, p. 148). This arrangement did not meet with the approval of the Afrikan Maroon community who renegotiated and through this achieved their successful return to Afrika. In 1800 the Afrikan Maroon community was transported from Canada back home to Sierra Leone on a ship called *The Asia* (Sherlock, 1998, p. 149).

There was another significant uprising in 1798 (Honychurch, 1995a, p. 120). This led to a new set of formerly enslaved Afrikan people taking to the hills of Trelawney under the leadership of an Afrikan warrior by the name of **Kofi** (Hart, 1985, p. 211). They effectively operated as a new set of Afrikan Maroons. This uprising was never of a magnitude that was going to lead to the overthrow of British imperialism in Jamaica. By building a clause into the treaty with the other Afrikan Maroons on the island requiring them to police uprisings on behalf of British imperialism, the British had built in an insurance policy against losing control of the island. Furthermore, by exiling the original Afrikan Maroons of Trelawney they ensured that they could not undermine this agreement by working with the enslaved Afrikan people on the island for their joint freedom.

Whilst it is true that Afrikan people never managed to gain complete control of the island of Jamaica, the Afrikan Maroons did nonetheless control significant areas of the island. Furthermore, the actions of the newer Afrikan Maroons provide evidence of the constant and continued resistance of Afrikan people to the unjust systems of enslavement. On top of that, the death toll of British soldiers was extremely high and this had an obvious impact on the capacity of the British military in the region. It is reasonable to conclude that the Afrikan Maroon community were powerful enough to ensure that their land rights were enshrined in the laws governing Jamaica. Indeed, they still exercise a degree of sovereignty on the island to this day.

5.8.2 Guadeloupe

As was the case in Haiti, the events in Guadeloupe, Dominica, St Lucia, St Vincent and Grenada were Afrikan revolutionary activities which had the French revolution coupled with the French abolition of slavery as a significant part of their motivating force. On 4th February, 1794, the Convention in Paris voted for the abolition of slavery (The Department of Guadeloupe; Ferguson, 1999, p. 138/9). The English ruling classes saw this as an opportunity to expand their stolen imperial territories and attempted to seize Guadeloupe, along with Martinique and St Lucia (Honychurch, 1995b, p. 105). The British managed to steal Guadeloupe from the French holding it from April 21st to June 2nd (Guadeloupe).

After Britain invaded Guadeloupe, the French sent a contingent of soldiers led by the Afrikan warrior **Victor Hughes**. At the same time they sent another set of warriors to Haiti under the leadership of French Jacobin Commissioner Legar Felicite Sonthonax (Honychurch, 1995b, p. 105). The difference between the two was that Sonthonax remained loyal to France and tried to regain Haiti in the interest of France, whilst **Hughes** did not follow suit in Guadeloupe. Sonthonax was eventually to make a fool of himself as he unsuccessfully tried to outwit the great Afrikan revolutionary leader of Haiti – **Toussaint L'Ouverture**. **Victor**

Hughes was to go on to distinguish himself as an Afrikan hero in his own right when he bravely rescued the island from the British occupation force, dismissed all French claims to Guadeloupe and retained the island in the interest of the enslaved Afrikan people who had hitherto been kidnapped there.

Hughes arrived in May 1794 operating in the role of a French Jacobin Commissioner (Ferguson, 1998, p. 139). He brought with him a portable guillotine:

> " ... shrouded in the bows of his ship and, as he approached the shore, he tore off the tarpaulin sheet and the sunlight glittered on its steel blade." (Harmsen, 2014, p. 60)

However, he was fundamentally a revolutionary Afrikan nationalist who then went on to successfully free, train and arm the enslaved Afrikan people in Guadeloupe. Within a month of arriving on the island, **Hughes** and his Afrikan army had successfully rid the island of all British and French enslavers. As part of the process of restoring justice on the island, twelve hundred European royalists, many of them wicked enslavers of Afrikan people, were executed using the guillotine (Harmsen, 2014, p. 67). **Victor Hughes** then abolished slavery on the island in accordance with the law voted by the French Convention (Troubled History of Guadeloupe; Guadeloupe: Culture and History). He then caused consternation in France as he threw off all shackles of French colonialism also and moved the formerly enslaved Afrikan people of Guadeloupe towards their total independence (Honychurch, 1995b, p. 110).

Guadeloupe then became a strategic centre for Afrikan people's resistance across the eastern chain of Caribbean islands. **Victor Hughes** became the chief co-ordinator and commander of Afrikan people's multi-island strategy of resistance against French and British imperial slavery systems (Devaux, 1997; p.15). After having led the movement that had successfully taken control of the island of Guadeloupe, **Hughes** used the island as a base for freeing the other islands. He sent warriors disguised as refugees to the neighbouring islands to fight and advise existing groups of Afrikan freedom fighters on military tactics (Honychurch, 1995b, p. 105). **Hughes** and his movement had a direct influence on military activities designed to achieve enslaved Afrikan people's liberation on the islands to the south of Guadeloupe. **Marin Pedre** was sent south by Victor Hughes which resulted in major steps forward for Afrikan liberation in the region. The islands that benefited from Hughes' intervention included: Dominica, St Lucia, St Vincent and Grenada – all of which came under the total or effective control of Afrikan warriors during the 1790's.

5.8.3 Dominica

The Afrikan Maroon community has existed in Dominica since the 6th June 1761 when the British attacked the then French colony and Afrikan people took to the hills (Fryer, 1989, p. 89; Timeline of Dominica's History). Afrikan Maroon warriors were provoked into war in 1785 when British soldiers pursued them into the hills. However, much to the surprise of the British, the Afrikan Maroons issued them with 'jolly good hiding'. The Afrikan Maroons were such a formidable set of warriors that by 1790, they had forced the imperialist enslavers to completely abandon 30 of the 80 forced labour camps on the island (Honychurch, 1995b, p. 100). They were effectively in control of the island as the terrified British and French enslavers, together with the British army gave up territory to them and literally ran away. All of this contributed to the reputation of Dominica as the 'almost ungovernable' land of the Caribbean (Fryer, 1989, p. 89).

This display of force by the Afrikan Maroons contributed the environment that led to the first ever documented strike by enslaved Afrikan people in the history of the Americas. Under the leadership of **Jean Louis Polinaire**, the enslaved Afrikan people simply downed tools, refused to run away and demanded that they be allowed to work for themselves for 3 days a week. The enslavers were essentially forced to agree to their demands, but when the British governor reneged on the agreement, the Afrikan strikers revolted and many of these strikers eventually ended up joining the existing Afrikan Maroon communities. Unable to defeat the Afrikan Maroons the British offered them terms to bring the war to an end. The terms were never accepted because the Afrikan Maroon warriors were resolute in the preservation of their hard won freedoms and the British too untrustworthy, but the war ended in 1790 when the British and French enslavers, recognised that they had been defeated and simply gave up pursuing the Afrikan Maroons.

One of the patterns of behaviour that developed on the island was for enslaved Afrikan people in Dominica to rise up against the wicked enslavers as a prelude to making good their escape. For instance, in 1791 there was an Afrikan uprising in the southern village of Grand Bay led by the Afrikan warrior woman **Angelique** (Honychurch, 1995b, p. 103); in 1794 there was another Afrikan uprising (Du Bois, 1996, p. 61); in 1802 the Afrikan soldiers of the 8th West India regiment revolted (Honychurch, 1995b, p. 111-114); and in 1812 Afrikan people rebelled on the Castle Bruce forced labour camp and took to the hills (Honychurch, 1995b, p. 116). On all of these occasions the Afrikan warriors took to the hills and strengthened the Afrikan Maroon communities (Hart, 1998, p. 35).

The Afrikan Maroon community was also bolstered by a constant stream of enslaved Afrikan people running away from the forced labour camps into the hills. It is arguable that over the course of two wars and umpteen skirmishes, the Afrikan Maroons effectively controlled the island of Dominica during the late 1790s and early 1800s. Their system of shifting bases co-ordinated and dispersed all over the island gave British forces virtually no chance of effectively combating them as they raided the forced labour camps at will. They also developed a dispersed but collective system of leadership, so that the capture of individual leaders did not undermine their continued existence as a community.

Balla was one of the most renowned leaders of the Afrikan Maroon warrior communities – so much so that songs about this heroic leader are sung on the island to the present day. The Afrikan Maroon community also produced women leaders who distinguished themselves on the battle front as well as in other areas of the organised resistance to British imperialism. Both **Angelique** and **Chantelle** are remembered as heroines of the Afrikan Maroon communities of Dominica. They were just two of the many Afrikan women leader heroines of the Afrikan Maroons in Dominica. Others included: **Martian, Calypso, Marie-Rose, Tranquille** and **Victorie**. These Afrikan heroine leaders and Afrikan women in general were a formidable force in the defense of Afrikan freedom both in Dominica and throughout the Americas.

There is also evidence of collaboration between the Afrikan Maroon warriors of Dominica and the Afrikan revolutionary forces under the leadership of **Victor Hughes** (Honychurch, 1995b, p. 104). The renowned Afrikan Maroon leader **Pharcelle** had made provisional plans to launch a rebellion to coincide with the planned invasion of Hughes' Afrikan revolutionaries. That planned joint initiative was thwarted when **Pharcelle** was compromised into negotiating a deal with the British. He did nonetheless assist when the invasion eventually took place in May 1795, but was in no position to launch the agreed uprising (Gott, 2012, p. 106).

Victor Hughes was therefore unable to mobilise the enslaved Afrikan people of Dominica to join with him in rising up against the island's wicked enslavers (Ferguson, 1998, p. 140). It is clear that the wicked enslavers would have been no match for the combined forces of the Afrikan Maroon warriors, the Afrikan people held captive on the forced labour camps and Victor Hughes' Afrikan revolutionary forces. Had this joint initiative occurred, there is little doubt that Dominica would have come under the total control of Afrikan people. Nonetheless, the heroic resistance of the Afrikan Maroon warriors is still a source of tremendous pride and typifies the calibre of militant resistance to slavery that existed on the island.

The names of many of the Afrikan Maroon leaders from the two Afrikan Maroon wars in Dominica have been remembered and it is only appropriate that they should be named here. These Afrikan heroes include – from the first war (1785-1790): **Congo Ray, Jupiter, Zombie, Juba, Cicero, Hall, Mabouya, Goree Greg, Sandie** and **Pharcelle** (Honychurch, 1995b, p. 94-95). In the second war (1809-1814) the heroic leaders included: **Elephant, Soliel, Battre Bois, Hill, Nicholas, Diano, Noel, Robin, Quashie, Apollo, Jean Zumbi, Lewis, Maco, Clemence and Nico** (Honychurch, 1995b, p. 116 & 118). Yet another renowned Afrikan hero warrior was **Jacko**, a veteran leader of the Afrikan Maroons in Dominica who made Maroonage his lifetime pursuit. This Afrikan hero spent most of his adult life i.e. over 40 years fighting for Afrikan liberation from the hills of Dominica. His heroic career spanned both Afrikan Maroon wars. He eventually fell in battle on 12th July 1814, preferring to die fighting rather than surrender to the British imperialist enemy (Honychurch, 1995b, p. 116; Fryer, 1989, p. 90).

The end of the second Afrikan Maroon war again failed to bring about the end of Afrikan Maroonage on the island. Whilst the British army was unable to defeat the Afrikan Maroons, there was no such restriction on the forces of nature. In 1813 the island was struck by a freak of nature; there were two hurricanes in quick succession (Fryer, 1989, p. 91). By destroying the terrain, the hurricanes destroyed the Afrikan Maroon's tactical advantage over the much better equipped British forces. Despite the assistance of nature, it still took the British army another year to inflict heavy casualties on the relatively unarmed Afrikan Maroons. Even this would not have been achieved but for the duplicity of Afrikan traitors (Honychurch, 1995b, p. 118), coupled with the most ruthless and draconian of colonial genocidal measures (Honychurch, 1995b, p. 118). To their great credit, no formal peace treaty was ever signed by the Afrikan Maroon community in Dominica despite the repeated attempts of the British to encourage them to do so (Honychurch, 1995b, p. 117/8).

Although they suffered heavy casualties, the Afrikan Maroon warriors of Dominica were never defeated. One of the last remaining Maroon leaders - **Apollo** reached a negotiated settlement (in his own time) and was co-opted into the West India Rangers (Pattullo, 2015, p. 155). Others simply remained at liberty in the hills right up until the 1840's – when they were satisfied that slavery was abolished (Honychurch, 2014, p. 245).

When the unwavering resolve of the Afrikan Maroon Community of Dominica is put into context, what is revealed is one of the most remarkable acts of military resistance of Afrikan people in the Caribbean and like the battle of Crete a Pierrot in Haiti, possibly even worthy of note at the world level of history. To put their feat into perspective, by the early 1800's all of the other uprisings and island takeovers in Jamaica, Guadeloupe, St Lucia, St Vincent and Grenada, which had so damaged, split and weakened the imperialists had been settled or had subsided.

The Afrikan Maroons of Dominica were, more or less the only remaining organised local adversary, fighting British imperialism single handed and in isolation. This meant that there were no other substantive wars in the region to split and spread the enemy's forces – leaving them to take on its full undiluted might. In addition, Britain had abolished its anti-Afrikan kidnapping and deportation racket in 1807, drying up the supply of revolutionary reinforcements that Afrikan Maroonage had previously so relied on for its strengthening.

Furthermore by 1812 and with the ongoing decline of weakening France, British imperialism – their operational enemy - was edging its way to becoming the world's number one superpower. With all of these cards operating in British imperialism's favour, it was almost as if God too had turned against the Afrikan Maroon warriors when two hurricanes struck Dominica in quick succession in 1813.

That exposure made them sitting targets and they were pounced on by the British maniac given charge of the colony. It was under these intensely adverse circumstances that a sizable number of Afrikan Maroon heroes and heroines were murdered by British imperialism. It was under these same circumstances that some remained concealed in the hills of Dominica never to surrender or be captured. It was the resolute resistance of those who died as well as those who survived that ensured that Afrikan Maroonage on the island was never defeated.

5.8.4 Saint Lucia

St Lucia's first recorded Afrikan rebellion took place in 1748 and Afrikan Maroonage took permanent root on the island in 1777 (Devaux, 1997, p. 2). Afrikan Maroonage intensified on the island on 1st April 1794 when Britain invaded St Lucia to steal from the French the land that the French had already stolen from the indigenous American Indians. Some of the 1800 enslaved Afrikan people on the island used the confusion caused by the invasion to take to the woods and formed the original nucleus of the Afrikan Brigands (Devaux, 1997, p. 13).

Those enslaved Afrikan people in St Lucia who took to the hills in an act of collective self-defense, refused to call themselves Maroons. They resented this title which in their Creole language meant 'runaways'. They refused to see themselves as 'runaways' and asserted the fact that they were warriors. They chose the title 'Brigands' because it was a much more accurate description of their warrior status. As the British gained a footing on the island, they tried to use it to re-establish the slavery system that had been abolished by the French Jacobins. This resulted in more Afrikan people (most of the island's population) running away to the hills to join the Afrikan Brigands in order to fight for their 'freedom'. A four year war ensued in which soldiers and arms were supplied to the Afrikan Brigands from **Victor Hughes'** victorious Afrikan army in Guadeloupe (Devaux, 1997, p. 32).

Derek Walcott Square 2017

Later in 1794 against overwhelming odds, **Marin Pedre**, a Brigand leader sent from **Victor Hughes'** Afrikan army in Guadeloupe, inflicted a serious defeat on the British (Devaux, 1997, p. 73). The fighting continued to intensify with the height of the Afrikan Brigand rebellion coming in 1796/7 (Fryer, 1989, p. 90). After suffering several defeats, the British were forced to withdraw from St Lucia along with virtually all other Europeans (mostly British and French). Their scarpering meant that the Brigands were in full control of the island (Devaux, 1997, p. 17). Justice was delivered when the guillotine was put into action in what today is Derek Walcott square, the main square of St Lucia's capital Castries (Ferguson, 1998, p. 138). These were in addition to the beheading of a smaller number of wicked enslavers, who some time earlier had received their justice in the southern town of Soufriere (Harmsen, 2014, p. 68).

Once the island was fully secured, St Lucia became a supply depot for the islands to the south: Afrikan warriors; arms; ammunition and stores were supplied to the other islands from Guadeloupe via St Lucia (Devaux, 1997, p. 29). This was a remarkable victory for enslaved Afrikan people, who against all the odds defeated one of the most powerful imperialist nations of that time. Despite British imperialism's best efforts, the Brigands were never defeated. Nonetheless, after a protracted guerrilla war lasting until 1799, there was eventually a negotiated settlement (Fryer, 1989, p. 90) and one of the outcomes of the settlement was the incorporation of the Afrikan Brigands into the British army's West India Regiment. Sadly, their heroism ended in confusion because they were later sent to Sierra Leone to kill and subdue their fellow Afrikan people at home (Devaux, 1997, p. 38 & 55).

5.8.5 Barbados

Barbados has a number of unique characteristics among the Caribbean islands. Firstly, it always suffered its colonial oppression from the British and was never fully colonised by other imperialist nations such as Spain and France. Secondly, Afrikan people enslaved on the island were mostly women (Beckles, 1993, p. 14). There was a ratio of 3 women to 1 man which was the opposite of all of the other islands in the region – where Afrikan men formed the majority. Thirdly it is a very flat island; the terrain was not conducive to the kind of Guerrilla warfare conducted by Afrikan people on some of the other islands housing forced labour camps.

Enslaved Afrikan people on the island were amongst the first to put up organised collective resistance to enslavement in the Caribbean. They conducted two conspiracies in 1649 (along with European indentured labourers) and 1701. There were also two out and out rebellions in 1675 and 1692 (Beckles, 1993, p. 71). These uprisings brought crushing defeats for Afrikan warriors, who against all odds fought bravely for their liberation. In 1794, an attempted uprising possibly secretly inspired by **Victor Hughes'** undercover agents was similarly crushed (Du Bois, 1996, p. 61).

With few hiding places, an uninterrupted form of colonial domination and predominantly female resistors, struggle took a different form in Barbados. Afrikan Maroons on the island resorted to concealing themselves in the fields of sugar cane where they were easily caught. There is no doubting the bravery of the Afrikan Maroons in Barbados, many of whom repeatedly ran away in the full knowledge that they would certainly be captured and mercilessly punished. An Afrikan Maroon warrior and heroine that falls into this category of anti-slavery resistance is **Queshebah**, who was held in bondage on the Codrington forced labour camp (Beckles, 1993, p. 64/65).

The futility of Maroonage on the island meant that Afrikan warriors in Barbados had to be more creative and more adventurous in the defence of their communities. The peculiarity of their circumstances forced Afrikan Maroon warriors to notice that if they created a raft and set sail from the west coast of the island, the tide would carry them to either St Lucia or St Vincent. The journey was perilous and many Afrikan Maroons lost their lives in the process. However, those warriors that were successful would be met by the Brigands of St Lucia or the 'Black Caribs' of St Vincent and would continue the fight for the liberation of Barbados on those islands (Beckles, 1993, p. 60 & 66).

When this route to resistance was blocked, the energy for liberation amongst enslaved Afrikan people fermented on the island and finally erupted in 1816. The **Bussa** rebellion of 1816 is named after the Afrikan man who was one of the leaders of the uprising (Beckles, 1993, p. 72). However, what is not always revealed is the fact that the real leader was his key advisor an Afrikan warrior and elder woman by the name of **Nanny Grig** (Beckles, 1993, p. 73). She operated in a similar capacity to another Afrikan leader mother figure of the Caribbean - her namesake the great **Nanny of the Afrikan Maroons** in Jamaica.

The role of Afrikan women in this and other anti-slavery rebellions in the Caribbean cannot be overstated. As Hilary Beckles explains:

> "Women ... were not only to be found in the vanguard of the [Afrikans'] anti-slavery movement, but were central to the production of anti-slavery ideologies. As non-violent protestors, as Maroons, as protectors of social values, and as armed rebels, [Afrikan] women were critical to the forging of resistance strategies and an anti-slavery consciousness which rests at the core of the [enslaved Afrikan] communities' survivalist culture." (Beckles, 1993, p. 74).

5.8.6 Saint Vincent

Afrikan people were on St Vincent long before Columbus' bogus claim to discovery of the island (Van Sertima, 1993, p. 190). They had arrived from Afrika and mixed with the American Indians forming a group of people that came to be known as the 'Black Caribs'. In 1772 Black and indigenous Caribs successfully conducted a guerrilla warfare campaign against the British with the result that they were granted land and freedom (Understanding slavery). In 1773 as part of the settlement of the guerrilla war they agreed to police the island on behalf of the British (Understanding slavery). However, when the French abolished slavery in 1794 (Devaux, 1997, p. 13) the scene was set for enslaved Afrikan people to favour France over Britain - which still formally and unapologetically maintained the evil system of chattel slavery.

Furthermore, the British reneged on their agreement with the Black Caribs and the Black Caribs responded by rising up under the leadership of **Young Chatoyer** (Devaux, 1997, p. 29). This resulted in a major rebellion taking place in St Vincent (Understanding slavery). In 1795, five hundred Brigands were sent to St Vincent from St Lucia in order to assist and support the Black Caribs in the rebellion. **Marin Pedre**, the seasoned Afrikan anti-slavery warrior, was sent south by **Victor Hughes** the victorious Afrikan conqueror of colonial Guadeloupe. **Marin Pedre** who had already distinguished himself in St Lucia by defeating British and French enslavers on that island arrived on St Vincent. **Marine Pedre** worked together with Young Chatoyer to liberate St Vincent.

However, following the untimely death of **Chatoyer**, **Pedre's** roles were to operate as the military leaders in order to co-ordinate and strengthen the ongoing, island wide rebellion (Devaux, 1997, p. 29). With the support of Pedre's Afrikan warriors from St Lucia who were fighting in the capacity of French Jacobin soldiers, the 'Black Caribs' overran the island of St Vincent (Ferguson, 1998, p. 139). Heavy fighting continued for another year, until negotiations were conducted which resulted in some 5,000 'Black Carib' warriors being relocated to the island of Roatan just off the coast of Honduras in 1797 (Understanding slavery).

5.8.7 Grenada

When the French declared the abolition of slavery on 4th March 1794 (Devaux, 1997, p. 13) it set the scene for enslaved Afrikan people throughout the Americas seeking their 'freedom' to favour France over

Britain. The revolutionary leader in Grenada at that time was *Julien Fedon* who organised and led a major revolt against the British on 2nd March 1795 (Marable, 1987, p. 7). There was an intense level of solidarity amongst the people with the majority of enslaved Afrikan people on the island joining the revolt (Fryer, 1989, p. 89). They were inspired by the tremendous successes of particularly the Haitian, but also the French revolution (Fryer, 1989, p. 89; Searle, 1984, p. 5). They also liaised very closely with *Victor Hughes* in Guadeloupe who was similarly inspired (Searle, 1984, p. 5). Enslaved Afrikan people in Grenada were promised emancipation together with the support of *Victor Hughes'* Afrikan army if they fought against British imperialism (Ferguson, 1998, p. 138).

After several bouts of serious struggle were won by enslaved Afrikan people in Grenada, the British governor and 50 of his criminal British enslaver colleagues were captured and executed (Marable, 1987, p. 7). The outcome was a tremendous success for human liberty and resulted in Afrikan people controlling the whole of Grenada, with the exception of the small British fortress in St George's the capital. Their control lasted for a period of almost 2 years (Marable, 1987, p. 7; Searle, 1984, p. Fryer, 1989, p. 90). *Fedon's* army was finally defeated by the combined and intensely concentrated forces of British and Spanish imperialism. The imperialists had learned from the humiliating defeats that they had suffered in Grenada, Haiti and other islands and responded by sending so many troops to the island that they outnumbered *Fedon's* Afrikan warriors 10 to 1 (Marable, 1987, p. 7; Fryer, 1989, p. 90). *Fedon* was never captured and remains a living legend on the island to this day (Marable, 1987, p. 7).

5.9 Reverberations of the Haitian revolution beyond the island of Hispaniola
5.9.1 The Haitian revolution brought Britain to its knees
The Haitian revolution should not be seen as an event confined to one island in the Caribbean, but rather as a focal point of inter-related military resistance dispersed across the entirety of the Caribbean. In the mid-1790's when the struggles in Haiti were and the other islands were at a height Haiti, Guadeloupe, St Lucia, St Vincent and Grenada were rescued and taken over by Afrikan people and Dominica was 2/3rd under Afrikan people's control, with the wicked enslavers confined to

the southern third of the island. Alongside this was the second Afrikan maroon war in Jamaica.

In total Britain lost 100k troops in the Caribbean. It received such a hiding at the hand of Afrikan warriors and lost so many troops, that it decided to completely abolish its anti-Afrikan kidnapping and deportation racket for good. A bill for what it called the Abolition of the 'Slave trade', passed its second reading in the British parliament on 23rd April 1792 and was due to become law on 1st January 1796. This was the bill jettisoned by the anti-Abolitionist subversive agent William Wilberforce and his cohorts.

The British needed to stave of military defeat in the region and ensure the survival of their empire. They therefore desperately needed to end the wars. This is why they cunningly embarked on a programme of surrender and negotiated settlements. The British surrendered to the great army of Toussaint L'Ouverture in Haiti and ran off with what they could. Additionally, they entered into a series of negotiated settlements with Afrikan Maroon warriors in Jamaica, St Lucia and St Vincent to prevent military collapse; and with a 10 to 1 advantage, managed to resteal Grenada from the resolute Afrikan revolutionaries. The Afrikan Maroons of Dominica would not entertain a negotiated settlement, nor could they be defeated. The strongest 'sanction' that 'defeated' Britain could muster in that case was to simply give up and leave them alone.

The British coffers were exhausted. If they devoted more troops to achieving victory in the Caribbean, they would have to come from elsewhere, making those places vulnerable to revolution. Their surrender to Toussaint, coupled with their scrambling around trying to tie Afrikan Maroon warriors into binding negotiated agreements designed to end the wars, was their veiled admission that the whole British Empire was on the brink of collapse.

Britain was in fact surrendering and negotiating its way out of the clutches of complete military defeat and the collapse of its empire. Following this successful series of manoeuvres which brought the wars to a halt, it was in a position to abandon the bill designed to stop Afrikan reinforcements from being sent into the former war zones to bolster the Afrikan revolutionary forces. This is what was really behind Wilberforce's duplicity and sabotage when he jettisoned the successful abolition bill. The Haitian revolution was on the brink of forcing Britain to abolish its so called 'Slave Trade'.

5.9.2 The language of a regional revolution

The language of the Afrikan people spoken in Haiti – Creole – is the same Afrikan language spoken in Guadeloupe, Dominica and St Lucia (Martinique too). During the revolution it was also spoken in St Vincent and Grenada. It cannot be a coincidence that virtually every island in the Caribbean where Afrikan people spoke it, militant revolutionary activity led to Afrikan people's outright control or virtual control of those islands. It was through the Afrikan Creole language that news of Afrikan military successes travelled between islands giving inspiration to Afrikan warriors.

This Yoruba and French based language is **the language of liberation of the Caribbean**. In almost every island where it was spoken the heads of wicked enslavers were chopped off in their tens, hundreds and even thousands. It was a force to be reckoned with in Afrikan people's struggle for liberation and freedom. The same language is spoken by Afrikan people on the other side of the world in Mauritius and the Chegos Islands. There are stories of the Haitian Revolution being the source of this development also. The root of the language may be in the Benin Republic (Dahomey) where modern day French speaking Yorubas understand the language upon hearing it, can translate, but do not speak it.

By contrast in Jamaica where the language wasn't spoken, Afrikan Maroon warriors fought the British to a standstill. This tremendous success therefore occurred in a language vacuum. Had the enslaved Afrikan people on the island spoken it, the likelihood is that they would have known of the defeats inflicted on Britain elsewhere therefore its weakened state. With this understanding, they might well have been inspired to join forces with their Maroon sisters and brothers, which would almost certainly have resulted in Afrikan people in Jamaica overturning British rule on the Island and chopping off some wicked enslaver heads there too.

A successful revolution in Jamaica would have meant the Free Afrikan people of Haiti and Jamaica would have been able to support each other against future imperialist intrigues. Instead the British, aware that neither the Afrikan Maroon warriors nor the enslaved Afrikan people of Jamaica knew of their defeats and correspondingly weakened military capacity, hurriedly offered the Afrikan Maroon warriors a negotiated agreement and removed them to Canada out of harm's way. It was a desperate, but cunningly deceptive manoeuvre to forestall military defeat, the collapse of empire and retain control of its richest colony. The language barrier which operated against effective fluid communications between Jamaica and the other islands most likely assisted Britain in carrying out this con trick.

This was all part of a broader communications problem confronting enslaved Afrikan people in the region. The imperialists knew the full extent of their empires. They could see the whole picture and knew where they were strong and weak. This allowed them to shift resources around to where they we most needed to forestall revolution. This was an important advantage, particularly in the Caribbean where the Afrikan revolution was dispersed across the region, with less than excellent communications.

The imperialists used the fact that the revolutionaries had little to no idea of the Asian and other parts of their empires; they had no idea of the upheavals and militant resistance that was occurring in those other parts. They did not therefore have a strategic level understanding of the impact of the efforts in destabilising their enemies grip on various parts of the world.

As a result they did not understand how overstretched, weak and fragile their enemy was. Had they developed appropriate international information gathering systems allowing them to know the extent of British and French imperialisms' weakness, they might well have fought on rather than negotiate. Alternatively they might have negotiated better outcomes for Afrikan people. In doing so there is the real possibility that their co-ordinated effort would have resulted in the collapse of the both British and French imperialisms, thereby freeing the world from their grip.

5.9.3 The French empire on the brink of collapse
The Haitian revolution was integrally linked to the wars between British and French imperialisms. Britain had taken its final hiding from the Afrikan revolutionaries in Haiti on 30th April 1798 with the surrender

and scarpering of General Maitland. By contrast French imperialism received its ultimate wroughting more than 5½ years later on 18th November 1803. This meant that British imperialism had more time to recover from its whipping than its French counterpart, putting it in a relatively stronger position in the early part of the nineteenth century.

Conscious of France's weakening military position brought about by the Afrikan revolutionaries on 20th May 1803 Britain broke with the peace treaty of Amiens, signed just a year earlier and declared war on France. This paved the way for the Afrikan revolutionaries in Haiti to wrought and dispense with the French. What's more in the background, the British were weakening France further by secretly supporting the Afrikan revolutionaries in Haiti in much the same way that US Satan supported the Afghans in their defeat of the Soviet Union in the 1980's/90's, eventually causing its collapse. The defeat at the hand of the Afrikan revolutionaries drained the coffers of the French treasury.

France had been the world's leading superpower. In the preceding 5 or so years, it had militarily taken on an alliance of Western European nations and defeated them – it was invincible. However, after hits hiding at the hands of Afrikan freedom fighters, it was reduced to an empty shell – a shadow of its former self – weakened beyond measure. With its heir of invincibility firmly dispatched, it became a sitting target. Hated and despised, it had so many embittered enemies all aware of its new military and economic vulnerability that attacks could come from anywhere. The whole French empire was tottering on the brink of collapse.

The loss of Haiti was an absolute body blow to the French empire – It was seismic. Losing the richest colony in the world was so profound that in many respects, it marked the beginning of the end of the entire French empire. It was a double blow: Firstly, there were the 10's of millions of Francs expended on the war to resteal Haiti from the Afrikan Revolutionaries, all of which was now lost. Then there was the ongoing loss of annual revenue from the richest colony in the world. France had not only been weakened, it was toppled, both militarily and economically. The massive loss of revenue meant a reduced ability to maintain the world's most powerful army, eventually bringing it down to, or even below the military capacity of its main imperialist rival - Britain.

France would later publicly admit the extent of its financial losses through a bogus claim of 150m Francs 'reparations' against the Afrikan people of Haiti for boldly and bravely freeing themselves from its tyranny. That ransom, imposed on Haiti in 1824, was in fact the cost of keeping the near fatally wounded French empire afloat. By extorting 150m Francs 20 years after the heroic victory of the Afrikan revolutionaries of Haiti, France was admitting losses at a rate of 7.5m Francs per annum. That 150m Franc ransom also marks the point at which European imperialism learnt and developed the stealing technique of imposing false, bogus debts on Afrika and her people in order to sustain itself.

5.9.4 French imperialism abandons the Americas

The French army would have been familiar with the classic military text *The Art of War* (written over two thousand years ago). In it Sun Tzu demonstrates one of the critical weaknesses of French imperialism's anti-Afrikan Haitian strategy. He explains that:

> "To go to war when there are insufficient funds in the treasury is a recipe for failure and the ultimate destruction of the state" (Tzu, 1998, p. 17)

The early victories of the Afrikan revolutionaries in Haiti had already insured that French imperialism received no revenues from the richest colony in the world. In fact its greatest problem was that it could no longer guarantee that former income. Sun Tzu then goes on to expose another folly implicit in its strategy when he points out that engaging in wars far away from home drain the treasury:

> "When a country is impoverished by military operations, it is due to distant transportation; carrying supplies for great distances renders people destitute. Where troops are gathered, prices go up. When prices rise, the wealth of the people is drained away. When wealth is drained away, the people will be afflicted with heavy and urgent extractions. With loss of wealth and exhaustion of strength the households in the country will be extremely poor and seven tenths of their wealth dissipated. As to government expenditures, those due to ... [replacing weaponry] ... will

amount to 60% of the total." (Tzu, 1998, p. 23)

This quote speaks precisely to the predicament French imperialism found itself in. It made a double error and this was in addition to its underestimation of the resolve Afrikan revolutionaries determined to preserve their freedom. Having made the error once, it wasn't going to do it again. It learnt its lesson, coming to the full realisation that it could not chance any further long distance wars in the Americas. The loss of the richest colony in the world, coupled with its weakened military power brought French imperialism face to face with the prospect of the imminent collapse of its empire. It was now reduced to grabbing at whatever straws it could to keep at least some of it alive.

Too weak to engage in any more long distant wars, French imperialism was forced to negotiate away territories which it had previously doggedly fought over with Britain. On 2nd May 1803 it sold Louisiana to Anglophone colonists in North America, relinquishing control of the Mississippi for a mere $15m. By doing so it saved itself the cost of another long distance war, which would most likely have resulted in the humiliation of having those same colonists simply move in and take it away by force. In any event the sales revenue was desperately needed to invest in its failing military venture in Haiti and against Britain and its other European foes. It was a last ditch attempt to forestall defeats. It also retrieved a portion of the revenues lost as a result of the earlier successes of the Afrikan revolutionaries in Haiti and was a kind of insurance policy against some anticipated future losses.

France effectively gave up claims to the Leeward and Windward Island chain, other than Martinique, Guadeloupe and St Martin and clung on to Cayenne on the South American coast, where the prospect of invasion was remote. To all intents and purposes, France retreated politically, militarily and economically from the Americas, whilst holding on to whatever crumbs its new disempowered status would permit. Not only was it an abandonment of the Americas, it was a virtual evacuation. The upshot of all of this is, had it not been for the heroic victory of the Afrikan revolutionaries in Haiti, there would be no US Satan as we know it today. US Satan owes its existence in its current form to the Afrikan revolutionary warriors of Haiti.

5.9.5 Trafalgar Square or Haitian Revolution square

The thrashing issued to French imperialism by the Afrikan revolutionaries in Haiti had yet another 'unexpected' consequence. Severely weakened both economically and militarily, France was now almost ready to be Britain's military pickings, but it had first to suffer a number of years of loss of its former massive revenues, stolen from Afrikan peopple to be punch drunk enough to be knocked out. It took until 1815 for that point to be reached. Their boxing ring was the Battle of Trafalgar. It was there that British imperialism KO'ed French imperialism – a feat which would have been impossible but for the fact that France had lost its former revenues, stolen from Afrikan people in Haiti.

Perhaps Britain should show its appreciation to these great Afrikan warriors by renaming Trafalgar Square, Haitian Revolution Square; and Nelson's Column, the Column of Marie-Jeanne Lamartinere, after Haiti's greatest ever Afrikan revolutionary warrior.

This unearthed historical connection may be of some assistance to sisters and brothers in Barbados, who in recent years have been involved in a live debate about what to do with their own 'Nelson's column'. They now have the option of renaming it in an historically correct and appropriate manner. Their decision could lead the way for British imperialism by renaming it after the greatest ever Haitian warrior – which by default translates to the greatest ever Afrikan hero in the Americas - Marie Jeanne Lamartinere.

Alternatively, they could make a more direct connection between the Haitian Revolution and Afrikan liberation activity in their own island. They may note for instance, that Britain's 'victory' at Trafalgar in 1815 came at a heavy price. Though 'victorious', it too was severely weakened militarily as well as economically. Recognising this important change, in 1816 Afrikan people in Barbados rose up and fought militarily for their freedom. Yes! The undercurrent of the Haitian revolution was behind the Bussa rebellion! There is already a monument to Bussa on the island, but perhaps it would be appropriate to rename the column after Nanny Rigg – the other great leader of that uprising.

5.9.6 Haiti and the Bolivarian revolution

Haitian president Alexandre Petion received Simon Bolivar on the 12th anniversary of Haitian independence - 1st January 1816. Petion was less than impressed with the former wicked enslaver and philanderer. Bolivar wanted to overturn Spanish colonialism in the Northern part of South America and areas of Central America. He wanted to create a republic, but had no plans for the Abolition of slavery. He had sought help from all over the Americas, but none were willing to support. He had only come to Haiti as a last resort.

Petion nonetheless agreed to offer Haiti's support, but only on the understanding that all enslaved Afrikan people in the liberated territories be released. The support provided was tangible: 250 military personnel supported by a small fleet; money, food and a printing press were made available; and finally, enough weapons to equip 6,000 soldiers (including 4,000 muskets and 15,000 pounds of gunpowder) were provided.

Some months later, Bolivar returned to Haiti and despite his poor showing was again supported with military personnel and materials. They returned and this time successfully defeated Spanish imperialism and in the process liberated great swaths of Central and South America. The beneficiaries included: Bolivia, Colombia, Costa Rica, Ecuador, Nicaragua, Northern Peru, North-west Brazil, Panama, the Guyanas and Venezuela.

Bolivar made good his promise to abolish slavery across these territories, but his betrayal of Haiti's freely given generous support sends out echoes of his racism. After all that Haiti had done for him and his people, he effectively assisted imperialism's anti-Afrikan Haitian blockade by refusing to officially recognise the Independent Republic of Haiti; he never traded with or even sent an ambassador to represent his republic on its shores; and as though that wasn't enough, in 1826 when he hosted the first gathering of the Independent States of America, he invited the wicked enslavers of US Satan and excluded the free Afrikan people of Haiti, the source of his own people's liberation. His racism amounted to betrayal.

5.10 Additional and broader level factors
5.10.1 Afrikan military victories: Impact on the 'abolition' of the 'slave trade'

The snapshot of military actions discussed above, represent only a small proportion of the skirmishes, battles, wars and corresponding deaths in the Americas that resulted from Afrikan people's anti-slavery resistance. The Haitian revolution alone was responsible for the deaths of 40,000 British invaders (Greenwood, 1980, p. 22). It is clear that many more troops were killed when British imperialism sent countless other military invaders into the islands in its attempts to quell the co-ordinated inter island resistance identified above. Similar deployments were made in what were often vain attempts to crush Afrikan Maroon resistance in the hills of the Caribbean. There were also a number of revolts by Afrikan troops in the West India regiment; plantation uprisings and other sporadic skirmishes.

In all of these cases, the loss of British lives was considerable. The humiliation and loss of lives were of such a magnitude that it took British imperialism over 100 years to grudgingly admit the scale of its defeat. Eventually, one of British imperialism's military historians openly admitted that Britain's warmongering in the Caribbean had cost the lives of 100,000 British soldiers (James, 1963, p. 212/213 & 227). However, as with the kidnapper sailor's death toll, the burden of the body count fell squarely on the shoulders of Britain's working class who were losing their sons, brothers, husbands and fathers.

These working class deaths were not for the primary benefit of their own class; instead the deaths served to further the aims of their imperialist masters – aims which were increasingly being frustrated and crushed by Afrikan people's resistance. When the British working class realised the full consequences for them of attempting to keep Afrikan people enslaved, they vehemently protested against slavery in order to protect themselves and reduce their losses. The British working class were looking after their own 'best interests' and the heroic struggles of enslaved Afrikan people meant that British working class self-interests now largely coincided with the best interests of the struggling Afrikan people.

The scale of the British military defeats at the hands of enslaved Afrikan people was a devastating blow to the British imperial state. The hiding that it received was arguably the greatest defeat ever inflicted on British imperialism up to that point in history. It is obvious that the main motivation for the anti-slavery rebellions came from Afrikan people's human desire to be free. Afrikan uprisings against imperialism's genocidal chattel slavery system triggered British working class discontent. That discontent forced the British establishment to re-evaluate its role in the so called 'slave trade'. The imperialists needed to prevent working class discontent fermenting into internal revolutionary activity. It had to abandon slavery in order to preserve its own hold on power in Britain. The Afrikan uprisings softened Britain up and paved the way for the so called 'British parliamentary abolition of the slave trade' in 1807.

Afrikan uprisings against imperialism's genocidal chattel slavery system triggered British working class discontent. It was the open expression of working class discontent that brought characters such as Wilberforce into the 'anti-slavery' framework. His real role was to appease the British working class on behalf of the British establishment and to prevent their discontent fermenting into internal revolutionary activity. The Chinese military strategist Sun Tzu explained that fighting wars far away from home was one of the most efficient methods for leading a nation to bankruptcy and destruction (Tzu, 1998, p. 23). British imperialism had fallen into this trap and was expending a lot of resources fire fighting far away from home in different parts of the Caribbean. At the same time, the British working class was becoming increasingly hostile towards its masters. In addition, the imperialists were burdened by the loss of revenues and the corresponding loss of profits resulting from their failed military adventures in the Americas. The possibility of bankruptcy and internal revolution proved to be critical problems for British imperialism.

The trump card leading to the Parliamentary 'abolition' of the so called 'slave trade' was the realisation that sending more kidnapped Afrikan people to work on the forced labour camps of the Caribbean simply served to reinforce the military might of the overpowering forces of the enslaved Afrikan people. Afrikan people had already defeated British imperialism in many islands across the Caribbean and sending reinforcements to them would render British imperialism even more impotent than already demonstrated. This forced the imperialists to come to terms with the fact that they had to let go of chattel slavery for the sake of their own survival. Whilst the imperialists may not have had much concern for the deaths amongst enslaved Afrikan people or the British working classes, they were terrified by the prospect of them losing control of Britain.

Afrikan people's violent resistance to imperialism's genocidal chattel slavery system was the source of the growing discontent amongst Britain's working class. Wilberforce had virtually nothing to do with the desire of Afrikan people in the Caribbean to violently overthrow their enslavement. Wilberforce was the government appointed opportunist who jumped on the back of the Afrikan liberation process in order help maintain imperialism by slowing the liberation process down. He was not the inspiration for enslaved Afrikan people, nor was he their champion. In fact, he was opposed to Afrikan people freeing themselves (Hart, 1998, p. 33). Rumours exaggerating the extent of Wilberforce's support for Afrikan people may have had a tertiary influence on enslaved Afrikan people, but the main motivation for the rebellions came from Afrikan people's human desire to be free. Modern day equivalents to Wilberforce are characters such as Scarman, who the British establishment brought in to tranquilise the Brixton uprisings in the early 1980's; or McPherson who was brought in as overseer of the inquiry into the racist murder of the Afrikan youth Stephen Lawrence. In years to come, these enemies of Afrikan people may be presented to those that know no better, as some kinds of 'Afrikan Hero[es]' (Gilroy, 1987, p. 104). Anybody with even an elementary understanding of the Brixton uprisings or the Lawrence murder would know how absurd it would be to hold Scarman and McPherson up as leaders of Afrikan liberation – just as absurd as holding Wilberforce up.

5.10.2 Afrikan People's resistance took every conceivable form

It is obvious that enslaved Afrikan people neither worked willingly nor offered their best endeavours to their enslavers. In fact they did everything that they could to sabotage imperialism's evil chattel slavery system which was the source of their oppression. In addition to violent rebellions and uprisings they resisted their oppressive situation in a variety of smaller, often underhand ways also. For instance, enslaved Afrikan people: often did as little work as possible; deliberately produced shoddy work; deliberately lost and damaged working tools; feigned illness; inflicted injuries on themselves; ran away from the forced labour camps; even committed suicide to deprive their enslavers of their labour and sometimes poisoned their enslavers (James, 1963, p. 16).

These and other forms of apparently 'passive resistance' served to undermine the whole 'slave economy'. They eroded both the quality and quantity of production on imperialism's forced labour camps and had a detrimental effect on the profits of the evil enslavers. By undermining and destroying the profits of the evil enslavers, Afrikan people's actions were attacking and destroying the very motivation for imperialism continuing its wicked chattel enslavement institution. Afrikan people were in fact making the whole evil system of chattel slavery completely unmanageable and unworkable. Official recognition of this fact came in 1789 when British imperialism commissioned an investigation and produced a Privy Council report which concluded that waged labour was three times more productive than enslaved labour (Ferguson, 1998, p. 132). Amongst other things, this finding proved that there was an economic advantage to the imperialist enslavers in disbanding, not only the process of kidnapping and deporting of Afrikan people, but also the whole of imperialism's genocidal chattel enslavement economy.

5.10.3 Afrika's abundant riches superseded Caribbean slavery

This was also the point in history where the imperialists in Britain and other parts of Europe were beginning to realise that Afrika was an abundant source of valuable resources. Indeed it was becoming clearer that Afrika was the wealthiest continent on earth. The Afrikan continent had been severely weakened by two serious historical incidents. Firstly, Arab imperialism had stolen land in the north and east of the continent. It enslaved millions of Afrikan people, taking many out of the continent into Arabia. Secondly, European imperialism critically wounded the continent by extracting countless millions of its people and transporting them to the Americas. In both cases the people taken were mainly from within the age groups most able to defend and lead the development of the continent. Afrika was therefore in a position where it could be conquered militarily and colonised.

With more wealth to exploit in Afrika than in the whole of the Americas put together, Afrikan labour was obviously more valuable in Afrika than it was in the Americas. Leaving Afrikan people to slave in Afrika would bring a greater net return on capital employed and correspondingly greater profits. Furthermore, leaving Afrikan labour in Afrika also brought the benefit that neither the kidnappers nor their innocent Afrikan victims needed to die in the process of transportation; the costs of enslaving Afrikan people in Afrika were also significantly reduced and this brought a double bonus in relation to profits. The imperialists sought to subdue Afrika as a future source of valuable mineral resources and labour.

This explains why slavery continued on the Afrikan continent for another hundred years after Britain claimed to have 'abolished' it in the Caribbean. We are informed that:

> "In 1924 Britain was forced to admit that slavery was still practiced in Sierra Leone, Northern Nigeria ... [and] ... Gambia ..." (The Democrat's Diary).

Legislation was not passed by the British colonial authority in Sierra Leone, a land with an abundance of diamonds, until 22nd September 1927 (League of Nations) and it did not come into effect until 1st January 1928 (The Democrat's Diary; Guardian Unlimited). Liberia waited even longer; the President and Vice President were forced to resigned on 3rd December 1930 when a League of Nations commission of inquiry proved that slavery was still in practice. The new administration took over on 23rd December 1930 meaning that slavery was still in existence at this point (The Perspective; Liberia 1912 to 1930). Not to be out done, Britain's colonial administration in Nigeria waited until 1936 before it finally 'abolished' slavery in its area of jurisdiction (Slavery).

5.10.4 World military, political and economic forces overwhelmed the institution of slavery

A few very important forces came via the British enslavers themselves. The older British colonies already had large numbers of enslaved Afrikan people who substantially outnumbered their enslavers (Ferguson, 1998, p. 131 & James, 1963, p. 53). Their numbers were in fact the real basis of their enslavers' prosperity. The existing large numbers was a double edged sword for their enslavers because it meant that it was too risky for them to import any more Afrikan people. The enslavers were living on a knife edge, in constant fear of the rebellions and raids mounted by enslaved and marooned Afrikan people. Rebellions whether successful or unsuccessful, could lead to their deaths, the loss of colonial lands and the loss of the stolen free labour of enslaved Afrikan people. Any further importation would simply reinforce the battalions of Afrikan maroon communities and rebel Afrikan people in the forced labour camps. Therefore, if they could prevent further imports to the colonies this would be a good method of preserving their own lives whilst at the same time allowing them to keep control.

They also feared being undercut by competitors from the newer British colonies as well as from other imperialist colonies in the Caribbean. British and French imperialists were constantly warring with each other over Caribbean lands that they each had stolen from the indigenous American Indians (Greenwood, 1980, p. 10-15). In the course of the warring Britain managed to steal two additional Caribbean colonies, Guiana and Trinidad. Both were underdeveloped and desperately needed the labour of enslaved Afrikan people in order to prosper. However, the longer established British colonials recognised that the two new colonies with their virgin soils would offer them stiff competition and they were willing to try any measure that might stave off financial disaster. If they could prevent the new colonies from importing Afrikan people, their position would be protected.

Furthermore, 50% of enslaved Afrikan people kidnapped and deported by Britain were sold to French enslavers and the French ran their sugar colonies more profitably than the British. The importation of more kidnapped Afrikan people meant that the French could undercut the British in the imperialist sugar markets (Ferguson, 1998, p. 149). This scenario had the added irony that the British trafficking of Afrikan people was helping the French to outperform them economically. If they could prevent the further importation of kidnapped Afrikan people, they could cut the supply of the much needed Afrikan labour to the French and gain the economic upper hand. In other words, the cutting of the supply of kidnapped Afrikan people would solve all of their major problems in one fell swoop. Therefore, in the spirit of self-preservation, the solution adopted by the older established British enslaver colonists was to join the growing demand to outlaw the process of kidnapping and deporting of Afrikan people to Caribbean colonies.

Another critical force came via the imperialists based in Britain. They were primarily concerned with immediate losses in their own profits and revenue that resulted from the uprisings of enslaved Afrikan people. Also the process of rapid industrialisation, which they were undergoing, would give them a longer term competitive advantage over the other imperialist nations. They therefore had an eye on the potential super profits that could be made from the pending transition from an agriculturally based economy relying on enslaved Afrikan people, to an industrially based one which needed low paid workers. They came to the realisation that giving Afrikan people the illusion of freedom through the paying of wages would make them much richer in the long run. With these changes, even some of the imperialists began to warm to the idea of abolition.

The imperialists were fully aware that Afrikan people's steadfast resistance made their genocidal chattel slavery system totally unmanageable. That resistance was one of the most pressing factors forcing them to recognise that change was inevitable. Since they could not maintain chattel slavery any longer, they needed a safe way out of their predicament. They needed to replace their wicked chattel slavery system with another, more subtle form of exploitation. Their exit strategy involved using new technology to promote the development of mass producing factories to catapult them towards capitalism.

As part of that process, they made the economic analysis that each human being is comprised of the person and the person's labour. Chattel slavery operated on the basis that the wicked enslavers 'owned' the person plus the person's labour. The evil aspiring capitalists noticed that it was human labour that was the wealth creating part of humanity. They wanted to own all the wealth created by each person's labour, but did not want the burden of paying for the maintenance and upkeep of the person. Since they did not need to 'own' the person, in order to 'own' the wealth produced by person's labour, they could give the person the illusion of 'freedom' by releasing the person from physical bondage. The new arrangement could work so long as they kept a firm grip on the person's labour. The advocates of capitalism therefore introduced wage slavery.

As enslaved Afrikan people were 'released' from chattel bondage, their enslavement was continued by other means. The new enslavers now 'released' the person and sought to keep ownership of only the person's labour. This gave the person the illusion of 'freedom', a trick which worked in the Caribbean where Afrikan people were no longer formally considered the physical property of the enslavers. Despite the illusion of 'freedom' that was presented, slavery still continued in a modified form. The person was now to be controlled in more subtle ways. The person was remotely controlled using external apparatus.

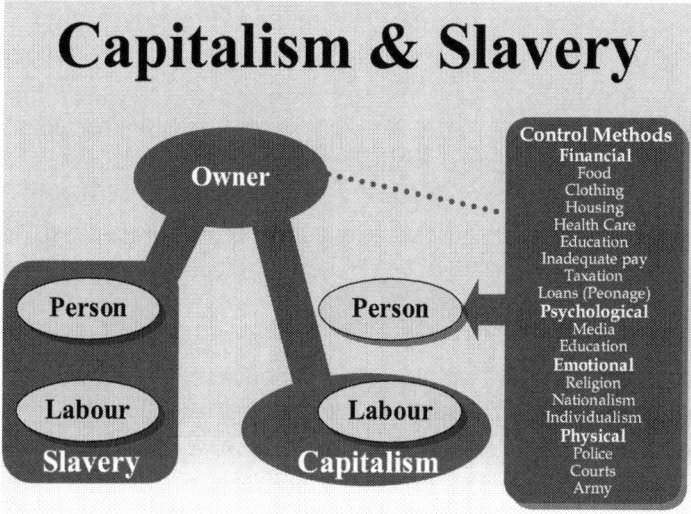

Capitalism & Slavery

Control Methods
Financial
Food
Clothing
Housing
Health Care
Education
Inadequate pay
Taxation
Loans (Peonage)
Psychological
Media
Education
Emotional
Religion
Nationalism
Individualism
Physical
Police
Courts
Army

Owner — Person — Labour — Slavery
Person — Labour — Capitalism

Brother Omowale

The new remote control system used money as a key resource to control and direct Afrikan people's labour power. The newly 'released' Afrikan people had no money to cover their living expenses. All they had was their labour which they could exchange for small payments or favours from the enslavers. They now had to cover the cost of their own food, clothing and shelter, costs which had been 'covered' by their wicked enslavers during the chattel enslavement period. Other important costs also lurking in the background included education and healthcare.

The remote control approach was a great system for the enslavers because they no longer had to worry about the maintenance costs associated with enslaved Afrikan people's 'welfare'; that burden was shifted to the Afrikan people themselves. The new arrangement further strengthened the enslaver's position because it meant that Afrikan people had to beg them for 'work' in order to cover the costs of their existence. Furthermore, imperialism awarded the enslavers a £20m subsidy or slush fund, which it called 'compensation' in order to ensure that the enslavers had the money to pay Afrikan wage earners (Williams, 1997, p. 43: Greenwood, 1980, p. 74). The subsidy also helped to ensure the enslaver's smooth and relatively painless transition from chattel slavery to the new peonage or wage slavery system.

The enslavers kept the upper hand by ensuring that Afrikan people were paid less than they required to meet all of their living expenses. As a result, most Afrikan people were forced to accept the patronage of the enslavers and this then put them in debt to the new remote control enslavement system. Their indebtedness simultaneously obliged them to work for the new remote enslavement system and denied them any realistic possibility of 'opting out'. The problem of Afrikan people's indebtedness was then compounded by the introduction of taxation which further reduced their income whilst simultaneously increasing their level of indebtedness.

The modern capitalist system has refined the process of remotely controlling 'the person' with even greater efficiency. It uses a range of methods specifically designed to keep potential 'objectors' and revolutionaries in 'order'. Political, psychological and emotional tools have been added to the kit and used to manipulate and control Afrikan people. For instance, the corrupt deployment of governors, embassy officials and Afrikan heads of state; formal education systems; mass media; religions; nationalism and individualism are all part of the control mechanism or tool kit. These are all examples of methods used by capitalism to control the ideas cascaded to Afrikan and other people. When a society's ideas are tightly controlled and manipulated, it has a profoundly distorting effect on the people's ability to think through and clarify their objective interests. The deliberately imposed barriers, designed by the world's elites to create confusion and prevent clear thinking, form one of the most important parts of capitalism's defense strategy.

Capitalism's new version of remote control slavery also relies on systems of physical coercion. Its police, courts and judicial system are used to criminalise and brutalise Afrikan people, in order to enforce their submission to capitalism's will. The army and its associated military intrigues is capitalism's ultimate sanction against resistors. Whether it is 'low intensity warfare' in the form of flooding a territory with agents, weapons and drugs as happened in Jamaica in the 1970's (Executive Intelligence Review, 1992, p. 317); or high intensity techniques such as the setting up of military bases, as is the case in Aruba and Curacao (U.S. Military Bases in Latin America and the Caribbean); or the actual invasion of territories, as experienced by the people of Grenada in 1983 (Searle, 1984, p. 1), the reason for these tactics is to keep Afrikan and other people's labour firmly under capitalism's control.

All of the factors mentioned above were far more important contributors to the abolition of the so called 'slave trade' than anything that Wilberforce ever did. They formed part of the range of forces that compelled the British government to change its approach to kidnapping and deporting Afrikan people from their homes. Wilberforce, who was unofficially appointed to his 'abolitionist leadership' role by the government, did little more than navigate his way through these forces. It is these forces that drove Wilberforce; not the other way round. Furthermore, an honest analysis reveals that all of these forces had the activity and resistance of Afrikan people as their fundamental cause.

5.10.5 Afrikan people abolished the 'slave trade'

It is important that this hidden history of Afrikan people's abolitions of slavery is brought to the fore. It reveals the truth that it was Afrikan people that abolished the so called 'slave trade'. The majority of these Afrikan abolitions were later abolished by imperialist kidnapping forces. This history is important because it corrects the false propaganda that British imperialism presents as history and proves that British imperialism was responsible for abolishing Afrikan abolitions of slavery and the so called 'slave trade'. In other words British imperialism and its allies have never, of their own volition, stopped enslaving Afrikan people. Instead, they moved from chattel enslavement to colonial enslavement, in the first instance, and then from colonial enslavement to modern day neo-colonial enslavement.

This history clearly demonstrates that every action that Afrikan people took to damage or undermine the system of chattel enslavement was doggedly fought against by British imperialism. Furthermore, every time Afrikan people took control of one of the human trafficking ships, they were abolishing (declaring it illegal) or attempting to abolish slavery. Every time that one of these ships was retaken by British imperialism's navy or its allies, imperialism was abolishing an Afrikan abolition of slavery and effectively re-introducing slavery.

Each and every Afrikan uprising that took place in an environment of anti-Afrikan slavery was a success as of itself. However, beyond that, every time an uprising successfully occurred on one of the forced labour camps (plantations) in the Americas, this represented an Afrikan abolition (a declaration of illegality) or attempted abolition of slavery. Whenever British imperialism's army and its allies attacked, reclaimed and re-instituted the forced labour camps, they were abolishing an Afrikan abolition of slavery and in fact re-introducing slavery. Judging by this standard, Afrikan people abolished slavery hundreds, possibly thousands of times – in each case asserting its illegality under Afrikan law. By contrast, whenever British imperialism reinstated slavery by abolishing the Afrikan abolitions hundreds possibly thousands of times.

Every time Afrikan Maroon warriors went into the hills of the Americas and created free spaces where the wicked enslavers would not dare tread, they were performing an Afrikan abolition of slavery and asserting its illegality. Every time British imperialism's army and its allies recaptured Afrikan Maroon warriors and brought them back into imperialism's sphere of influence they were abolishing an element of the Afrikan abolition of slavery and automatically declaring it illegal.

Every treaty agreed between Afrikan Maroon warriors and their European imperialist enemy betrays the acceptance on the part of Europeans that slavery was illegal on Afrikan Maroon territory. Every time Afrikan people took control of an island or a territory in the Caribbean or the Americas in general they were formally abolishing slavery. Every time British imperialism's army and its allies re-took these territories they were abolishing Afrikan abolitions of slavery. Every time European enslavers entered into treaties with the Afrikan maroon warriors that they were unable to defeat, they were accepting that slavery was illegal.

It was only when the pressure of repeated and constant Afrikan abolitions of slavery became too great to contain that the British and other European imperialists reluctantly and grudgingly turned to the tactic of appearing to favour abolition. Even at this point, the imperialists were dragged kicking and screaming into carrying out legislative actions aimed at 'abolition' by the Afrikan people resident on their soil. They even manipulated the good will of their Afrikan residents in their attempts to trick enslaved Afrikan people in particular and the world in general into believing that they were voluntarily 'abolishing slavery'. In reality, they used the idea of voluntary 'abolition' as a public relations exercise designed to assist them in keeping their hold on power.

All brands of European imperialism were forced to give up the chattel form of slavery whilst licking their wounds. In their typically misleading fashion, they all faked a philanthropic desire to abolish slavery as a moral action done for the good of Afrikan people. The truth is that they took these actions to stave off military defeat, financial ruin and political overthrow. For instance, under intense pressure from Afrikan warriors in St Croix the Dutch claimed to 'abolish' their 'slave trade' in 1803. The Dutch version of slavery was eventually sent packing after a revolt in St Croix ending on 2nd July 1848; slavery was 'abolished' on the same day. The Scandinavian branch of imperialism was dealt another couple of severe blows when Sweden was forced to 'abolish' its so called 'slave trade' in 1813 and its system of slavery in 1846.

The British were forced to 'abolish' the so called 'slave trade' on 25th March 1807 together with their version of slavery on 1st August 1833. The French were repeatedly dispatched by Afrikan freedom fighters. They were forced to 'abolish' slavery in Haiti on 29th August 1793 and throughout their empire on 4th February 1794. After stubbornly attempting to overturn the successes of Afrikan people's resistance, they were once again forced to 'abolish' the so called 'slave trade' on 29th March 1815 by international treaty which was reiterated in 1818 by domestic legislation; finally France's whole slavery institution was forced into 'abolition' on 27th April 1848. The Spanish were forced to 'abolish' their so called 'slave trade' in 1820.

European imperialism still busied itself abolishing the so called 'slave trade' during the notorious Berlin Conference held in 1884/5. Milwood explains how:

> "The French and Germans saw [Britain's] trick and deception at the Berlin Conference and declared and declared an immediate termination of the Trans-Atlantic slave trade." (Milwood, 2010, p. 222)

By making this declaration, they were in fact making a mockery of their claims to have 'legally' abolished their anti-Afrikan human trafficking, in some cases almost 80 years prior. The Portuguese were characteristically stubborn to the end and their brand of slavery was finally booted out of Brazil on 14th May 1888. The abolitions mentioned here represent only a sample of imperialism's bogus legislative propaganda campaign.

British and other brands of imperialism have dishonestly tried to focus our minds on their own legislative processes in their attempts to fool us into believing their false claims to 'abolishing slavery'. They have deliberately hidden or sidelined the hundreds of examples of real, physical and tangible examples of Afrikan people's abolitions of slavery. They have then falsely presented their consistent anti-human pattern of abolishing Afrikan people's abolition of slavery as a series of 'justifiable acts'.

Every time Afrikan people in Afrika retrieved or even attempted to retrieve their loved ones from the clutches of kidnapper pirates, they were policing their laws which forbade slavery. Every time they rose up against the pirates on their kidnapper ships, they were reaffirming Afrikan law's opposition to slavery. Every time an Afrikan maroon community was set up in the Americas, consistent with Afrikan law, there was no slavery. Every time Afrikan people rebelled against slavery in the Americas, they were asserting that it was against Afrikan law. Not only was it against Afrikan law, but in truth it was and has always been against natural law.

The real truth is that Afrikan people conducted hundreds of and most likely thousands of abolitions of slavery. The frontline of the Afrikan abolitions of slavery was obviously military activity aimed at overturning the evil chattel enslavement system, but as the **Abolition Matrix** demonstrates there were also economic and diplomatic dimensions which impacted positively. The pattern, volume and consistency of these Afrikan abolitions and the economic and diplomatic activities that supported them, were of such a magnitude that they forced British and other forms of imperialism to submit to the idea of the abolition of slavery.

In the case of British imperialism, the point had been reached when it had given its all in its repeated attempts to abolish slavery. British imperialism lost 100,000 soldiers, many thousands of its kidnapper sailors and many thousands of the anti-Afrikan enslavers who ran its forced labour camps in the Caribbean. Realising that British imperialism was now unable to protect them militarily, many of its anti-Afrikan enslavers cut their losses, packed up and ran away to India and other parts of empire (Fryer, 1989, p. 23). British imperialism was now thoroughly defeated militarily, stared economic ruin in the face and politically (James, 1963, p. 227), its domestic population was readying itself for revolution.

The Abolition Matrix II

Location of Action

Type of Action	Afrika	Atlantic	Americas	Britain
Military	Agaja Trudo Tomba, Glele, Nzinga, Kaipkaire, The Perfect Calabar River	The Robert, The Thomas The Malborough, The Little George British sailor's death rate	Boston Tea party Haitian Revolution Maroons Revolts Wars against France Carib Wars	War against France Chartist Movement William Davison
Economic	Afrika's Richness New Markets Capital Investments	Self Harm Ship Damage Ship Stripping Killing Kidnappers Injuring Kidnappers	Cost of Labourers Cost of Raids Disrupt production Cost of Sabotage Cost of sloppy work New Markets Capital Investments Old v New Islands	Development of Factories Capital/Labour intensity Imperialist Competition Old Money v New Money
Diplomatic	Agaja Trudo's Envoy	Amistad The Little George	Maroon Treaties Robert Wedderburn	Granville Sharpe, Thomas Clarkson, William Wilberforce, Mass petitions Ottobah Cugoano, Oluadah Equiano, Mary Prince, Jonathan Strong, James Somerset, Ayuba Diallo, George Bridgewater, Ignatius Sancho, Julius Soubise

Brother Omowale

If British imperialism had continued to kidnap and traffic Afrikan people into the Caribbean, it would have been adding reinforcements to the Afrikan Maroon armies in the region that had already so thoroughly defeated it. The trafficking of more Afrikan people would have led to more Afrikan Maroon armies inflicting more defeats on British imperialism. British imperialism would then have had to find the massive amounts of extra money needed to send more of its soldiers to their deaths. This in turn would have led to its political overthrow domestically. It was therefore left with no alternative but to give up trans-Atlantic slavery.

Its exit strategy was threefold: Firstly, it would focus on mastering the industrialisation process to launch capitalism and give itself an economic advantage over its imperialist competitors; secondly, it focused its attention on exploiting the wealth of the seriously weakened Afrikan continent, which was now emerging as the richest continent in the world; and thirdly, it would abandon kidnapping and sending Afrikan people across the Atlantic, leaving slavery in the Americas to die its natural death in due course. Instead it would enslave Afrikan people in their own land, where because of the abundant mineral wealth their labour was much more profitable.

British imperialism then embarked on a legislative programme designed to withdraw its piracy policy of kidnapping and deporting Afrikan people from Afrika. Enslaved Afrikan people in the Caribbean continued their military and other pressures through uprisings and forced imperialism to 'abolish' slavery. Nonetheless, the central contradiction remained clear throughout the entirety of these processes. Imperialism's parliamentary acts of 'abolition' were diplomatic efforts which represented a negotiated settlement designed to ensure that it did not completely lose the benefits of the labour of enslaved Afrikan people. It gave up chattel slavery as a means of saving face, saving money and switching to colonial and capitalist systems of slavery. Afrikan people forced all of these changes and their actions add to the body of evidence confirming that it was Afrikan people that abolished both slavery and the so called 'slave trade'.

List of mentioned Sources
1. Anderson. S.I., (1995), *The Black Holocaust for Beginners*, Writers and readers publishing incorporated
2. Beckles. Hilary, (1993), *Afro-Caribbean Women and Resistance to Slavery in Barbados*, Karnak House
3. Bly. Antonio, (1998), *Crossing the lake of fire: Slave resistance during the middle passage*, 1720-1842, Journal of Negro History, Washington, Summer 1998
4. Cabral. Amilcar, (1974), *Revolution in Guinea: An African People's Struggle*, Stage1
5. Carruthers. Jacob, (1985), *The irritated Gene: An Essay on the Haitian Revolution*, The Kemetic Institute
6. Devaux. Robert, (1997), *They Called Us Brigands: The Saga of St Lucia's Freedom Fighters*, SUNBILT Limited, St Lucia
7. Du Bois. WEB, (1996), *The World and Africa: Inquiry into the part which Africa played in World History*, International Publishers Company Incorporated

8. Editors of Executive Intelligence Review, (1992), *Dope Incorporated: The book that drove Kissinger crazy*, Executive Intelligence Review
9. Ferguson. James, (1998), *The Story of the Caribbean People*, Ian Randle Publishers, Kingston, Jamaica
10. Fryer. Peter, (1984), *Staying Power: The History of Black People in Britain*, Pluto Press
11. Fryer. Peter, (1989), *Black People in the British Empire: An Introduction*, Pluto Press
12. Gates. Henry Louis, (1987), *The Classic Slave Narratives*, Penguin Books
13. Gott, Richard. (2012), *Britain's Empire Resistance, Repression and Revolt*, Versobooks.com
14. Greenwood. R., & Hamber. S., (1980), *Emancipation to Emigration*, Macmillan Caribbean
15. Harmsen. Jolien et al, (2014), *A Short History of St Lucia*, Lighthouse Road, www.lighthouse-road.com
16. Hart. Richard, (1985), *The Slaves Who Abolished Slavery: Volume 2 – Blacks in Rebellion*, Institute of Social and Economic Research, University of the West Indies, Jamaica
17. Hart. Richard, (1998), *From Occupation to Independence: A Short History of the Peoples of the English Speaking Caribbean Region*, Pluto Press
18. Honychurch. Lennox, (1995a), *The Caribbean People*, Thomas Nelson and Sons Limited
19. Honychurch. Lennox, (1995b), *The Dominica Story*, Macmillan Education Limited
20. Honychurch. Lennox, (2014), *Negre Mawon: The Fighting Maroons of Dominica*, Island Heritage Initiatives
21. James. C.L.R., (1963), *The Black Jacobins*, Vintage Books
22. Justice. Prince, (2005), *The Blackworld: Evolution to Revolution*, AU Publishers
23. Karenga. Maulana, (1993), *Introduction to Black Studies*, University of Sankora Press
24. Marable. Manning, (1987), *African & Caribbean Politics: From Kwame Nkrumah to Maurice Bishop*, Verso, London
25. Mao. Tse Tung, (1975), *Selected Works: Volume II*, Foreign Languages Press
26. Martin. Steve, (1999), *Britain's Slave Trade*, Channel 4 Books
27. McCulluch. Joch, (1983), *In the Twilight of Revolution: The Political Theory of Amilcar Cabral*, Routledge and Kegan Paul
28. Milwood. Robinson, (2010), *Dis-empowerment and Engagement: Raising Consciousness*, TamaRe House Publications
29. Nkrumah. Kwame, (1980), *Handbook of Revolutionary Warfare*, PANAF Books

30. Pattullo. Polly, (2015), *Your Time is Done: Slavery, Resistance and Defeat: the Maroon Trials of Dominica (1813-1814)*, Pattullo Press
31. Robinson. Carey, (1993), *The Iron Thorn: The Defeat of the British by the Jamaican Maroons*, LMH Publishing Limited, Kingston, Jamaica
32. Rodney. Walter, (1981), *How Europe Underdeveloped Africa*, Bogle-L'Overture Publications
33. Searle. Chris, (1984), *Grenada: The Struggle against Destabilisation*, Writers and Readers Publishing Co-operative Society Limited
34. Shepard, Verene & Beckles Hilary, (2000), *Caribbean Slavery in the Atlantic World: A Student Reader*, Ian Randle Publishers, Kingston
35. Sherlock. Phillip & Bennett Hazel, (1998), *The Story of the Jamaican People*, Ian Randle Publishers, Kingston, Jamaica
36. Tzu. Sun, (1998), *The Art of War*, Wordsworth Editions Limited
37. Van Sertima. Ivan, (1993), *Afrikan Presence in the Early Americas*, Transaction Publishers
38. Walwin. James, (1993), *Black Ivory: A History of British Slavery*, Fontana Press
39. Williams. Eric, (1997), *Capitalism and Slavery*, Andre Deutsch

Internet References
1. A Timeline of Dominica's History, http://www.lennoxhonychurch.com/article.cfm?Id=394
2. Africa and Slavery 1500-1800 in *Middle East and Africa to 1875* by Sanderson Beck, http://san.beck.org/1-13-Africa1500-1800.html
3. Africa's Contribution to European Capitalist Development — the Pre-Colonial Period in *How Europe Underdeveloped Africa* by Walter Rodney, http://www.marxists.org/subject/africa/rodney-walter/how-europe/ch03.htm
4. Breaking the Silence – Learning about the Trans-Atlantic Slave Trade, www.antislavery.org/breakingthesilence
5. FReeper Canteen ~ Part IV of Women Warriors: Africa ~ February 10, www.freerepublic.com/focus/f-news/1075043/posts
6. Guardian Unlimited, The 1833 Abolition of Slavery Act didn't end the vile trade, http://www.guardian.co.uk/commentisfree/story/0,,1998227,00.html
7. Guadeloupe, http://ib.frath.net/w/Guadeloupe
8. Guadeloupe: Culture and History, http://www.caribbeanchoice.com/guadeloupe/culture.asp
9. Internet Puppet Theater, www.internetpuppets.org
10. League of Nations Photo Archive, Chronology of 1927, http://www.indiana.edu/~league/1927.htm
11. Liberia from 1912 to 1930, http://personal.denison.edu/~waite/liberia/history/ww1.htm

12. Man's Unconquerable Mind, http://www.marxists.org/archive/foot-paul/1991/07/toussaint.htm
40. MEMOIR OF GENERAL TOUSSAINT L'OUVERTURE. WRITTEN BY HIMSELF. http://thelouvertureproject.org/index.php?title=Memoir_of_Toussaint_Louverture%2C_Written_by_Himself

1. Portcities Bristol, http://www.discoveringbristol.org.uk/showNarrative.php?sit_id=1&narId=15&nacId=19
2. Resistance and Rebellion, Understanding slavery, www.understandingslavery.com
3. Slavery, British Council Magazine, http://www.learnenglish.org.uk/magazine/magazine_home_slavery.html
4. The Democrat's Diary, http://www.democratsdiary.co.uk/2007/01/celebrating-bicentennial-anniversary.html
5. The Department of Guadeloupe, http://www.asprs.org/resources/grids/03-2000-guadeloupe.pdf
41. The Haitian Revolution of 1971-1803, PART III; An Essay in Four Parts by Bob Corbett, http://www.uhhp.com/haiti/history/revolution/haitian_revolution_part_three.html
1. The History of Mary Prince, a West Indian Slave: Narrated by herself, http://www.english.ucsb.edu/faculty/rraley/research/Mary-Prince.html
2. The perspective, The Liberia's Culture of Unlawful Practices Continues Under New Officials, http://www.theperspective.org/articles/0624200602.html
3. The Troubled History of Guadeloupe, http://www.go2guadeloupe.com/travel-guide/discover/history/
4. Women in Power 1700 – 1740, www.guide2womenleaders.com/womeninpower/Womeninpower1700.htm

Afrikan People Abolished the 'Slave Trade'

Submission presented in
Parliament
Monday 26th March 2018

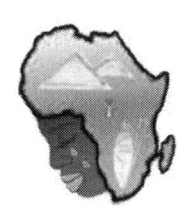

A Brief
Introduction
to
Afrikan Liberation:
The route to real
Reparations

Ukombozii
Education for Liberation
Afrikan Freedom Means Defeating Neo-Colonialism
www.ukombozii.org

Chapter 6

6 A brief Introduction to Afrikan Liberation

6.1 A snapshot of Afrikans in the world
6.1.1 The historical assault on Afrika and Afrikans

The central contradiction facing us as Afrikan people wherever we are in the world is that whilst Afrika is the richest continent in the world, Afrikan people are amongst the poorest. Far from being an act of nature, this contradiction is rooted in imperialist incursions into our Afrikan homeland and has been consolidated by the expansion of European imperialism which took place in Afrika and other parts of the world from the 15th century onwards.

It is the expansion of capitalism (imperialism), born in Europe during the 19th century, that has completely destroyed the connection between us as Afrikans and our wealth. The undermining effect has been so profound, that this brand of imperialism has effectively destroyed the hold on wealth that previous forms of imperialism (including Arab imperialism) commanded prior to its existence. The historical evidence to support this assertion is considerable. The detail is beyond the scope of this document, but we can attempt a simplistic appraisal aimed at demonstrating how Afrikans have come to be so impoverished.

In a nutshell, when European imperialism came to Afrika it engaged in a massive programme of theft. When it was confronted with the natural resistance of a people who saw their wealth being stolen, it engaged in the most horrendous genocidal maniac murdering spree ever conducted in the history of mankind. In order to disguise the full sadistic horror of its evil behaviour, it spun the most shameless web of lies known to humanity. It then had the audacity to attach labels such as 'history', 'education' and 'news' to its catalogue of obscene lies. It is this web of deceptive propaganda that gives true definition and full historical meaning to the deliberately misused term 'white lies'. The overall catalogue of barbaric evil, perpetrated by imperialism is of such magnitude, that it is beyond the capacity of humanity to fully document it. Despite this limitation, it is possible for us to make some observations regarding imperialism's savagery.

One of the results stemming from this calamity was that European imperialism succeeded in stealing virtually every Afrikan thing that it could get its hands on. It even managed to steal many a-material aspects of Afrikan culture which it was unable to get its hands on in any literal sense.

European imperialism stole Afrikan land, Afrikan people, Afrikan gold, Afrikan diamonds, Afrikan chocolate and a whole range of Afrikan valuables too numerous to mention. The fact that in some cases nominal payments may have been paid does not excuse or disguise the massive scale of the theft. At the a-material level it stole Afrikan names, Afrikan people's identities, Afrikan ideas, Afrikan languages, Afrikan religions, Afrikan customs, Afrikan rituals, Afrikan practices and so on.

The process of theft of the a-material was cunningly wicked. They simply prevented Afrikans, by methods of force or dissuasion from using those things that were from Afrikan culture and supplanted them with their equivalents from their own culture. Over a period of time, many Afrikans lost the use of a range of the a-material aspects of our culture because we simply forgot how to use them. In addition, the problem was compounded by the fact that Afrikans were then taught to resent anything that was Afrikan, based on the lying premise that Afrikans and Afrikan culture was inferior. This calibre of psychological torture was the seal designed to make the alienation of Afrikans from things Afrikan complete.

Some ignorant Europeans, inculcated with their own racism, may try to argue against this historical reality. These apologists for imperialism go to extraordinary lengths to deny the outrageously disgusting behaviour of their ruling elite. This contrasts starkly with the testimony of those perpetrators of evil who actually carried out the atrocities. Examples are given by Walter Rodney in his book *How Europe Underdeveloped Afrika*. For instance, one self confessed land grabbing thief colonel Grogan, infamous for his banditry, laid bare his motives for committing atrocities, of the most heinous kind, against the Kikuyu people in Kenya. He admitted:

> "We have stolen his land. Now we must steal his limbs. Compulsory labour is the corollary of our occupation of the country." (Rodney 1981, p. 165)

Since it is not our primary purpose to fully explore the outright arrogance, the inherently obnoxious character and the barefaced egotistical nature of Grogan's statement, we will simply note it and concentrate on the implications of his confession.

Clearly he was owning up to the grand theft (of Afrikan resources and labour) for more than just himself. The 'we' he refers to, is in fact a very big 'we': It includes colonel Grogan and his colleagues who actually perpetrated the theft; it includes those that subsequently came along and occupied the stolen land; it includes those that remained overseas but continued to receive the produce from the stolen land and labour; it includes those, who in the modern day continue to benefit from the historic and contemporary theft of Afrikan resources; it includes all of those people who deny Afrikans our just demands for reparations as a partial remedy for the hideous atrocities perpetrated against us. The whole of this European imperialist society is inculcated in the theft and must bare some responsibility for those atrocities and that includes the apologists.

For those apologists that persist in questioning the understanding of theft expressed above, the argument can be expanded still further. In his book *The Strategy and Tactics of the Revolution*, **Sekou Toure** illustrates a catalogue of diabolical behaviours implicit within imperialism that can be properly categorised as theft. He shows us that:

> "To steal is to seize others' property, either by force or by taking advantage of his absence to remove it. To steal is to subtract fraudulently others' property, to confiscate for oneself the property of a social group. To steal is to claim from somebody more than he owes you. To steal is to refuse to return what one owes. To steal is also to accept what one does not deserve. The exploitation of slaves is nothing but theft. Feudal exploitation is a theft.
>
> Capitalist and colonialist exploitation is a theft. Imperialist exploitation through unequal terms of exchange is a theft. Every form of human exploitation under any cover what so ever, is a theft. Treason, since it consists in defrauding others' trust, a trust which you have accepted and you do not deserve is a form of theft, undeniably the most violent and the most pernicious one." (Toure 1977, p. 340)

6.1.2 The contemporary assault on Afrika and Afrikans

Tragically for us as Afrikan people our losses are not merely historic. Imperialism imposed slavery, colonialism and currently neo-colonialism upon us, which means that our wealth is still being stolen with unrelenting vigour. We continue to suffer the legacy of our stolen wealth with the impact being felt right here in the present, in our day to day lives.

Imperialism has updated its programme of inhumane theft of Afrikan resources through a web of genocide promoting capitalist killer institutions. At the heart of this gangster mechanism we find institutions such as the International Monetary Fund (IMF), the International Bank for Reconstruction and Development (IBRD) otherwise known as the World Bank, the World Trade Organisation (WTO), the United Nations (UN) and the scoundrel multi-national thieving companies. The modern imperialist attack on Afrika is implemented, not through slavery or direct colonial governments as happened in the past, but through the continent's multiplicity of neo-colonial governments peopled by an Afrikan elite class dominated by traitors, that colludes with imperialism.

Collectively, these US Satan controlled imperialist institutional monstrosities are responsible for wholesale, unwarranted and unprovoked massacre of millions of innocent hard working and unsuspecting Afrikan people. These thieving capitalist killer institutions each have their particular role to play in battering the neo-colonial governments into submission. As a general pattern of operation, they bully the Afrikan elite class into submission to them and encourage their treacherous actions against their own people through a veiled system of intimidation, threats, extortion and bribes as well as pandering to their egos. The neo-colonial governments are used as a means for creating devastating mayhem and carnage in the lives of millions of ordinary Afrikan people who are simply fighting for mere survival.

Under the title of 'multi-lateral aid', Imperialism uses the World Bank and associated agencies to grant loans to neo-colonial governments at exorbitant rates designed to put Afrikan micro nations into an irretrievable situation of debilitating debt. History clearly demonstrates that it is imperialism that is in debt to Afrika, since it owes its very existence to its theft of the resources of Afrikans and other oppressed peoples. Nevertheless, this fictitious debt is designed to leave ordinary Afrikans and other oppressed peoples at the eternal and constant mercy of those who control imperialism's mechanisms.

Once the micro nation is tricked into believing that it is in 'debt', the IMF (or imperialism's murdering force) is employed to 'advise' the neo-colonial government on what to do next. The IMF invariably dictates to the neo-colonial governments the self crippling actions that they must take in order to create the best possible conditions for capitalist thieves. These thieves, otherwise known as investors, act through their savage multi-national companies, to come in and steal Afrikan people's wealth. This inevitably means dismantling the country's already poor infrastructure of hospitals, schools and other social amenities, with direct adverse consequences for the quality of life of ordinary Afrikan people.

The WTO was spewed into existence out of the notorious anti-Afrikan and anti humanity General Agreement on Tariffs and Trade (GATT) in 1995. It is there to ensure that Afrikans and other oppressed peoples do not have the option of trading their way out of the catastrophically crippling dilemma assigned to them by imperialism. Its purpose is to permanently maintain an unequal international trading situation in favour of countries at the imperialist centres (i.e. US Satan, Britain, France etc.) and against the interests of the countries at the imperialist periphery (in Afrika, Asia and South America).

On behalf of imperialism, it sets the biased prices at which Afrikan nations can buy from and sell to imperialism's multi-national resource grabbing monstrosities. The imposed unequal trading arrangement forces Afrikan nations to buy manufactured products at exorbitant prices, whilst selling Afrika's abundant resources for a pittance. This leaves the neo-colonial governments in a permanent and debilitating state of having a balance of payments deficit, created through spending substantially more money than they receive through trade.

By taking the emphasis away from resources and focusing instead on money, the illusion is created that Afrikan nations need more money to make ends meet. It is this illusion which creates the requirement, in the minds of the neo-colonial elite class, dominated by traitors, that they must go crawling on their knees to beg for further high interest loans from the IMF and World Bank, which only serve to make their peoples' situations even worse.

The ultimate purpose of the UN is to police the neo-colonial states on behalf of imperialism. It is a sad fact that the so called armies and police forces in the Afrikan neo-colonies have been trained by imperialism to fire their guns at innocent unarmed Afrikan civilians rather than to protect our people and our land from outside invaders. The UN operates as the external police force that smiles and fakes friendship as it invades the neo-colonial country when the internal policing institutions (i.e. the police and the army), through the people's resistance, have lost control of the neo-colonial state apparatus.

In this way, the UN supplies imperialism's rear guard or backup oppressive force that prevents the neo-colony from breaking away from its master's controlling clutches. Where necessary, it will arrange the physical execution of progressive leaders, as happened with Patrice Lumumba, because he dared to challenge imperialism's domination of his country. Prior to its ultimate role it provides a veil of political justification for a range of more subtle undermining interventions into the internal affairs of 'uppity' neo-colonial regimes. In any event, history allows us to safely conclude that:

> "... the UN is not an arena where small countries can moderate the ambitions and power of the larger ones." (Ovenden, 1992, p. 48)

In his book *Rogue State*, William Blum makes an analysis of US Satan imperialism, the current leader of world imperialism. He decodes the evil hidden agenda of US Satan imperialism along with its relationship to and deployment of the fore mentioned institutions of theft and genocide. Despite his emphasis on US Satan imperialism, his analysis provides a useful guide for analysing imperialism as a whole. Four critical objectives are identified as underpinning the brutality of international capitalism's thieving, killer institutions as follows:

> "1) making the world open and hospitable for - in current terminology - globalisation, particularly American based trans-national corporations
>
> 2) enhancing the financial statements of defence contractors at home ...
>
> 3) preventing the rise of any society that might serve as a successful example of an alternative to the capitalist model
>
> 4) extending political, economic, and military hegemony over as much of the globe as possible, to prevent the rise of any regional power that might challenge American supremacy, and to create a world order in America's image ..." (Blum, p 13, 2003)

On the Afrikan motherland there are many manifestations of the callous calculated extermination of innocent human beings. Imperialism uses its vicious instruments of exploitation and oppression: the World Bank, the IMF, the WTO and the UN to impose policies designed to facilitate a full frontal murderous assault on the already suffering (and often destitute) Afrikan masses. As a direct result of the cold blooded, premeditated activities of these institutions, in some parts of Afrika, life expectancy has fallen to below 40 years. Effectively, this means that some regions in Afrika are populated by children without parents or any adult supervision. This demographic catastrophe has far reaching implications for short, medium and long term planning in the particular regions themselves and for Afrika as a whole.

Whilst this is not the place to deal with the complex range of issues underlying this statistic, it must be clear to even the casual observer that leaving children to fend for themselves represents a situation of unprecedented abuse. The situation is made worse by the fact that Afrikan children have not simply been left alone to fend for themselves, but have through calculated genocidal practices been deliberately put into a situation of involuntary collective orphanage.

Imperialism has shamelessly planned and executed a reduction in overall Afrikan life expectancy, but not satisfied with that, it is slaughtering Afrikan children as well. The fascist British prime minister 'Anthony Liar Blair', during the World Summit on Sustainable Development held in South Afrika on 2/9/02, revealed that an Afrikan child is dying every 3 seconds. This means that every month, over 200,000 Afrikan babies lose their lives. This genocide is manifested in a variety of diabolical forms from deaths through Aids infection to the blowing up of innocent children by land mines.

What 'Anthony Liar Blair' failed to reveal was the part that he, as an agent of imperialism has played in this devastation heaped on Afrika, Afrikan people in general and Afrikan children in particular. There was no reference to the chemical warfare targeted against Afrikan people, of which Aids is just one aspect. Nor was any light shed on the shamelessly evil role that imperialism's arms industry plays in the organised assassination of our children.

In an attempt to camouflage its evil undertakings from those unfamiliar with its mode of operation, imperialism hides behind a number of coded names such as 'the west', 'globalisation' and 'the new world order'. In a similar manner, it uses the label 'privatisation' to disguise one of its main processes for looting Afrika's wealth. Privatisation is, in fact one of the modern day methods by which those at the heart of imperialism (i.e. institutional investors) steal the resources of other people. Using this technique, the local treacherous elite groups, prove their allegiance to our imperialist enemy by giving away the mineral, forestry and agricultural resources of their own people to imperialism's scavenging trans-national companies or conglomerates.

However, in addition to the theft role that the privatisation technique plays in relieving Afrikans of our wealth, there is also a privatising approach to ensuring instability on our continent. Imperialists deliberately promote wars in Afrika to assist them in their process of stealing our wealth. It is important to understand that at the centre of all modern imperialist wars is the idea of depriving indigenous peoples of the control and use of their own land. Alien control of their land, whether direct or indirect, creates the most fertile environment for imperialism to steal the resources contained in the land as well as commandeering the labour of the people on the land.

Wars give further protection to imperialism's anti-human interests by creating a chaotic environment for people that live in the affected area. Since the wars effectively divert local people's attention away from their wealth (some people become refugees and simply run away from their birth right to save their lives), imperialism uses the distraction caused by the chaos as a shield to facilitate the undercover theft of 'vacant' or unguarded resources.

US Satan and other imperialist nations' arms industries have embarked on a comprehensive campaign of privatising terrorism. They fund 'private' military operations in Afrika and other parts of the world. These include covering the costs of mercenaries, so called 'special forces' working under cover, treacherous forces indigenous to the region that is being attacked, military advisors and paramilitaries as well as the supply of weaponry and arms. In his book *Power and Terror: Post 9/11 Talks and Interviews* Noam Chomsky points out that US Satan military officers operate within private companies like DynCorp and MPRI (Military Professional Resources Incorporated). He exposes imperialism's despicable hidden agenda by explaining that:

> "The privatisation of international terrorism means that the advice and arms are free from congressional supervision."
> (Chomsky, 2003, p. 68)

These immoral outfits (based on the money orientated, bounty hunting, cowboy posse) are to war what the management consultant is to business. The tactic of employing them leaves the US Satan government free to present the lie, to the rest of the world that it has no hand in, nor knowledge of the atrocities the private military companies are committing on its behalf. In this way imperialism uses privatisation as a shield to mask the fact that it creates, stimulates and sponsors inter-Afrikan wars in Afrika itself and across the entire Afrikan Diaspora.

This type of devastation was exposed some 40 years earlier by **Kwame Nkrumah**. He identified the US Satan imperialist warmonger General Maxwell Taylor as the originator of a military technique known as 'special warfare'. In his book *Neo-Colonialism: The Last Stage of Imperialism*, Nkrumah explains that:

> "... the technique is for the foreign power to supply the money, aircraft, military equipment of all kinds, and the strategic and technical command from the general staff down to the officer 'advisors', while the troops of the puppet government bear the brunt of the fighting."
> (Nkrumah, 1980c, p. 252)

'Special Warfare' is a technique sponsored by governments, banks and trans-national companies based in the imperialist centres. It is the source of virtually all of the civil wars in Afrika as well as the wars between the Afrikan micro-nations which were themselves created by imperialism during the Berlin Conference of 1884/5.

As a direct result of these covert policies and practices of evil, Afrika is suffering externally imposed and internally implemented genocide against its people on a massive scale. This horrendous loss of human life, much of which is carried out by Afrika's contingent of child soldiers, is far in excess of anything currently being experienced in any other continent in the world. The result of this deliberate policy of orchestrated mayhem is that two thirds of the Afrikan continent is currently ravaged by war resulting in by far the highest death toll anywhere in the world today.

The appalling death toll has risen to levels which are beyond anything that the human mind is truly capable of comprehending: 5 million Afrikan people have been killed in war in the Congo in the last 5 years; 5

million Afrikan people have been killed in the war in Sudan in the last 20 years; 3 million Afrikan people have been killed in the war in Rwanda in the last 10 years; 1 million Afrikan people have been killed in the war in Uganda in the last year and this represents just a sample of our human losses.

The onslaught is relentless with the result that the death count continues to increase. It follows that the very existence of Afrikans as a part of humanity is seriously called into question since we see little sign or prospect of this tidal wave of evil activity abating. It must be remembered that this snapshot analysis merely serves to give some indication of the magnitude of the barbarous acts of carnage constantly organised by imperialism against the lives and interests of Afrikan people.

Whilst it may be a blessing of sorts for those who manage to escape the battle fields without losing lives, such 'fortune' should not be confused with the capacity of surviving Afrikans to live happy and unfettered lives. There are no reliable statistics available revealing the true number of Afrikans maimed and injured as a result of the wars in Afrika. However, one of the things that we can say for certain is that this figure is far greater than the number of Afrikans that have lost their lives.

Even those who do not suffer physical injury have their lives devastated by the wars. Afrika has a refugee crisis which physically displaces the Afrikan masses and undermines our capacity to build a successful, unified society. Of the estimated 33 million refugees in the world today, over half are to be found in our Afrikan motherland. At this point it should be remembered that we have not even attempted an assessment of the psychological damage caused to the Afrikans that have lived through imperialism's proxy wars on our continent.

The overall result is that Afrika is left to measure the continental scale bloodshed by the number of dead, injured, displaced and psychologically traumatised Afrikan men, women and children. On the other hand, imperialism's arms dealing trans-national conglomerates measure their Afrikan experience in profits amounting to hundreds of billions of US Satan dollars. Imperialism's arms industry is an unremorseful trade in blood money; its profits and money are drenched in the blood of millions of slaughtered and maimed Afrikan people who have no history of attacking the heartlands of the imperialists.

Another example of the conniving and underhand way in which imperialism destroys Afrikans physically, whilst simultaneously attacking our moral base is illustrated when we scrutinise the activities of its notorious 'foreign correspondents' or 'journalists'. It will come as no surprise to those Afrikans fighting against imperialism, that many of these 'journalists', in addition to their anti-liberation propaganda role, have a subversive role of spying on behalf of imperialism's intelligence agencies. Presenting their apparent desire for 'news stories' as a front, they use a variety of methods including note taking, photography, audio and video recording to gather intelligence information for their imperialist masters. Their mischievous and unscrupulous hidden activities continue to the present day and have resulted in the indirect loss of millions of Afrikan people's lives.

As if that kind of activity was not bad enough, these 'journalist' have stooped to new debts of sub-human and anti-human behaviour. In her book *We Did Nothing* Linda Polman inadvertently reveals one of the methods used by imperialism's journalists to fuel the atrocious genocide perpetrated and practiced across the entire Afrikan world. She explains how she was party to a negotiation process that resulted in a murderous money making scheme aimed at Afrikans in Haiti.

These Afrikans were paid for providing journalists with the corpses of fellow Afrikans that had been killed as a result of the uprisings and violent disturbances that were taking place on the island. For a fee of between one and two US Satan dollars, the bodies were presented and then photographed to create images designed to increase the sale of newspapers in the imperialist centres. The payments being offered, though small by the standards of Europe and US Satan, were substantial in terms of the local economy. They were far greater than anything that local people could otherwise hope to earn. Unsurprisingly, this led to a keenness amongst local Afrikans to bring the dead bodies of their brothers and sisters to the journalists offering the rewards.

Eventually, Afrikans resorted to killing other Afrikans in order to create the corpses for which they would receive the bounty payments. In other words, new corpses were being produced, which were not people who were killed as a result of local conflicts, but were a direct result of the economic inducement offered by the so called journalists. So many Afrikan dead bodies were brought to them that they altered their conditions of payment: they began paying for only the most horrifically mutilated of the dead bodies produced. Following the same economic process, they became inundated with the bodies of Afrikans who had been murdered in a variety of cruel and sadistic ways.

The number of Afrikans murdered proliferated further, since every economic murder brought with it a spate of revenge murders – each with its own economic bonus. The scale of the horror was intensified by the fact that the severity of the economic executions and mutilations would then be superseded by the revenge executions and mutilations. The situation then degenerated to proportions of genocidal cruelty on a national scale. This represents a horrific contemporary scenario created and stimulated by imperialism's 'foreign correspondent'.

This journalistic barbarism is executed across many parts of the Afrikan world. A press bureau photographer whom Polman calls John was the person that she witnessed making use of this ruthless and atrocious practice in Haiti in 1994. This was part of a calculated process that led to thousands of Afrikan people being robbed of their lives as a direct result. The same technique was employed to ensure the demolition of millions of Afrikan people's lives in the war in Rwanda in the same year.

Putting this 'technique' into its proper context, it becomes clear that this is just one of the many methods that imperialism uses to deliberately manipulate, what on the surface appears to the world as self inflicted genocide amongst Afrikans. On closer examination however, we discover the 'hidden hand' of imperialism planning, manipulating and implementing the most appalling crimes against humanity. Such practices raise the genuine question of whether there are any limits to the calculated savagery of western imperialism.

We might expect that the consciences of the imperialist 'foreign correspondents' might compel them to own up to the obscene role that they play in sponsoring the carnage amongst Afrikans worldwide. Instead, they use their position as the story teller to disguise, distort and discount their own evil doings. At the same time, they have the audacity to present a misleading picture to the world, of mindless Afrikans thoughtlessly roaming around killing other Afrikans for no apparent reason. The calculated evil of the lies that they propagate, is only superseded by the callous nature of the worldwide genocide casually inflicted upon Afrikans by the ruthless imperialist system.

6.1.3 The contemporary assault on Afrikans in Britain

The genocide and general deprivation suffered by Afrikans worldwide is also suffered by Afrikans here, in Britain. British capitalism uses neo-colonialism as its mechanism for stealing the wealth of Afrikans in Afrika. At the same time, it mimics this process within Britain and organises Afrikans into internal neo-colonies from which it can steal labour and resources on an as and when required basis. A deliberately anti-democratic and inhumane policy of containment (within these colonies) is then put in place, designed to ensure that we as Afrikans cannot improve our collective situation so that we remain ripe for exploitation.

There may be those that attempt to deny the reality that Afrikans are contained as a colony within the belly of the British imperialist beast. They may argue that colonial status automatically requires geographical remoteness. However, the falseness of this argument is most aptly crystallised by an analysis of the settler colonies imposed on Afrika by imperialism. South Afrika, Rhodesia, Kenya and Algeria provide just a few examples. **Franz Fanon** in his book *The Wretched of the Earth* identifies the following patterns:

> "The colonial world is a world cut in two ... The zone where the natives live is not complementary to the zone inhabited by settlers. The two zones both follow the principle of reciprocal exclusivity ... The settler's zone is strongly built ... brightly lit ... an easy going town ... always full of good things ... The settlers town is a town of white people ...
>
> The town belonging to the colonial people, or at least the native town, the Negro village ... the reservation, is a place of ill fame, peopled by men of ill repute ... The native town is a hungry town ... starved of meat, of shoes, of coal, of lights ... a town wallowing in the mire." (Fanon, 1990, p. 29-30)

The contrast described here is clearly visible in Britain and this confirms that geographical remoteness is not a critical factor in determining colonialism. **Fanon** is describing a divided world where imperialism has the power to colonise indigenous people, even in their own land. It follows that it is only a minor task for British imperialism to contain Afrikans in colonies on its own land, for its own parasitical purposes.

The population census assists us in identifying the six principle internal colonies for Afrikans in Britain. In order of numerical concentration they are: Lambeth, Brent, Lewisham, Haringey, Hackney and Southwark. In all of these areas we find that the social conditions of Afrikans are consistently inferior to those of the indigenous Europeans. The main difference between the British internal colonies and the British settler colonies in Afrika is that Afrikans are in the minority in Britain, which reduces our capacity to achieve revolutionary change.

In his book *A Concise History of Warfare*, arch imperialist warmonger and war Lord Field Marshall Bernard Montgomery explains the thinking behind the containment strategy. He says:

> "In war, the enemy is plain and clear. In peace, a nation is confronted with a more insidious foe: the weakness within, from which alone great nations fall ... the danger from within is always present and must be kept in subjection." (Montgomery 2000, p. 19)

British imperialism has learned from its history. In 1939 when Britain declared war against Germany, the Irish Republican Army (IRA) declared war against Britain. In his book simply entitled *MI5*, Nigel West (enemy agent and journalist) reveals how the IRA, applying what they called their 'S-plan', went on a bombing spree. In London, bombs went off in Stonebridge under the North Circular road, Willesden railway bridge and power station, Hammersmith bridge was struck twice, public toilets received sporadic bombings and cinemas were randomly bombed with tear gas.

They launched random attacks on post boxes, forcing British capitalism to open up all of their post boxes in a desperate attempt to regain public confidence. Victoria and Kings Cross stations, three banks in Piccadilly Circus and Madam Tussaud's waxworks all received their attentions. Beyond London, Birmingham, Manchester, Coventry,

Liverpool and the little known Tralee were in receipt of sporadic attacks. This caused widespread public and official confusion internally at a time when British capitalism was conducting a war externally.

Afrikans in Britain have never resorted to this kind of armed struggle. Despite this fact, Afrikans in the internal colonies in Britain are clearly perceived as the enemy within that must be kept in subjection. It is against this background that a multi-fronted attack has been launched against Afrikans in Britain, using a three phase strategy aimed at:

- Destroying and totally eradicating our existing liberation orientated organisational infrastructure,

- Creating bogus leaders and organisations in and around the Afrikan community. This is designed to distract our energies away from fighting for our genuine liberation; instead, our minds are channelled towards attempting to reform British capitalism. This con trick is promoted to generate within us the vain hope that it is possible to make British capitalism nicer or in some way more palatable, and

- Attacking the community itself with a view to destroying any foundations which could potentially lead to the re-emergence or development of any future progressive organisations

An unrelenting attack has been launched against progressive Afrikan organisations in Britain. Some Afrikans, working on behalf of our enemy, join progressive organisations and behave in ways that subvert or destroy them. Bogus organisations, often funded by British capitalism, are set up in the Afrikan internal colony to distract potentially conscious Afrikans from joining our most progressive formations for self defence. Deceptive propaganda is routinely unleashed against liberation organisations, often with the assistance of Afrikan 'Uncle Toms', with the aim of undermining the community credibility of Afrikan self help initiatives. We find also that facilities are priced out of the reach of grass roots organisations and counter rallies are used to undermine grass roots mobilising initiatives.

To cap the process, bogus leaders are thrust upon the Afrikan community using both overt and covert methodologies. This bogus leadership is not elected within the Afrikan community, nor is it representative of the views of the Afrikan community. In fact a number of cunningly deceptive methods are used to put the bogus leaders in place. Often, under labels such as 'equal opportunities' or 'managing diversity', they receive their appointments via British capitalist institutions with a proven track record of anti-Afrikan activity.

These include institutions such as the Labour party, the Liberal-Democratic party and even the Tory party. Local authority structures, government and quasi-governmental institutions and multi-national companies are often used to put these characters forward and so too are state funded voluntary sector organisations. A favoured method of bringing these 'Uncle Toms' to prominence, is to give them a Knighthood, an MBE, an OBE or a CBE.

The role of the bogus leader is to impose the ideas and desires of British capitalism's dominant groups on the Afrikan community. They operate as the paid agents of the enemy, programmed to destroy Afrikan based self help activities, whilst at the same time promoting Afrikan self hate and increased confusion in the Afrikan internal colony. To assist them in their acts of treachery, they receive state funding and considerable amounts of publicity aimed at raising their profile both within the unsuspecting Afrikan community and also the community of indigenous Europeans.

Whilst some of the traitors fully understand the extent of their evil undertakings against their own people, the sad irony is there are others that remain ignorant of the damage and mayhem that they are heaping onto their own people. The most unconscious of them may even be under the delusion that they are, in some way, being helpful to their people. Regardless of their level of consciousness however, the bogus leaders are all clear in their understanding that British capitalism has the power of veto over their appointments as leaders. In common with many of the neo-colonial heads of state in Afrika, they are therefore wholly owned and controlled by the not so hidden hand of British capitalism.

The attack is then targeted more generally at the entire Afrikan community. Afrikan internal colonies are flooded with hard drugs, which are indisputably not grown in any Afrikan country. This is designed to dampen the consciousness of our community, rendering even the embryo of organisation unworkable. Afrikan internal colonies are flooded with guns, again not produced in any Afrikan country. This heightens the enemy's desire that Afrikans should be in a constant state of disunity, internal slaughter, mayhem and total confusion fostering a condition of divide, so that they can continue to rule us.

These revelations may appear unbelievable to some readers, but conclusive evidence is presented by some of the unapologetic secret agents themselves. Two self confessed traitors of the Afrikan nation Philip Etienne and Bernard Maynard in their book *The Infiltrators*, reveal how they participated in the police unit known as special operations 10 (SO10) by carrying out undercover 'investigations' against their own people in the Afrikan internal colony.

These practices are not new and have been used to attack Afrikans throughout the world. In his *Handbook of Revolutionary Warfare*, **Nkrumah** demonstrated the pattern of the attack. He warned us that:

> "Imperialism constantly infiltrates revolutionary opposition groups with agents, 'special police', and others, compelling such groups to arm even before they have attained the organisational stage of armed struggle." (Nkrumah 1980b, p. 54)

The traitors Etienne and Maynard, steeped in their abhorrent unapologetic arrogance, boastfully testify that the British capitalist police unit SO10 has gone overseas to recruit known multiple murderers and drug dealers. They have calculatingly transplanted these characters into the Afrikan communities here. These police 'agent provocateurs' have then systematically abused innocent Afrikans, up to an including raping, stabbing and shooting us, as a part of carrying out their police duties of flooding our community with hard drugs.

This kind of environment provides sufficient justification for capitalism to unleash a terror campaign, using its police firing squads (i.e. its armed internal military wing or 'first line of defence'), against the Afrikans contained in the internal colony. Indicative trends are that the unwarranted and unprovoked murder of Afrikans by the police becomes increasingly common place, whilst Afrikan young people are deliberately stopped and searched by the police several times more than any other group. Also, whilst expenditure on public services is being reduced in real terms, we notice a real terms growth in police budgets. These are some of the trends that help to confirm the calculated extent and intent of the organised state violence perpetrated against law abiding Afrikan communities in Britain.

An economic and social assault is also launched against Afrikans as a way of ensuring that we are rendered totally defenceless. It follows that unemployment levels amongst Afrikans are constantly higher than all other groups, which further impoverishes the community. Afrikan children are expelled from school at a much higher rate than any other group, diminishing our prospects for future organisation.

Add to this poor housing and high levels of homelessness; poor health facilities and the onslaught of the mental health industry, it becomes clear that Afrikans are held in a state of siege. People in a siege environment are bound to focus solely on survival. This forces them into a day to day, hand to mouth living mode and away from a longer term planning mode aimed at collective development and advancement. These are just some of the signs that indicate the racist containment (or subjugation) policy of successive British governments.

It is not our purpose to reproduce the British government's own statistics which provide overwhelming evidence of the disparities enforced by them against the interests of Afrikan people. The pattern of imposed evil is clearly discernible: we find that Afrikans are over-represented in every social situation that is bad, and under-represented in every social situation that is good.

In addition, the British government operates a system of multiple deprivation scales which it claims is designed to assist in the allocation of resources to different areas of the country. This allocation has built within it the assumption that any area with a high proportion of Afrikans is automatically poor, precisely because of the presence of Afrikans. It is on this basis that it allocates 'extra funding' to these localities.

The government's 'extra funding' is never received by self determining

Afrikan community organisations. Instead, local racist institutions and agencies use the money to launch further public and voluntary sector attacks on Afrikans, whilst pretending to assist us. We note that the Caldecot centre (a government run sexual health clinic) in South London has been publicly accused by its own staff of a range of disgusting practices including deliberately injecting Afrikan patients with venereal diseases.

The British government's own research is increasingly revealing its own racist policies. Faced with the overwhelming weight of the evidence confirming unfair practices against Afrikans in Britain, the British establishment has been grudgingly forced to the point where it has, with the utmost reluctance, acknowledged the existence of institutional racism. Though this level of acknowledgement represents a tiny step in the direction of truth, it massively underestimates the volume, nature and extent of the systematic acts of wickedness perpetrated against Afrikans in Britain.

These barbaric acts of wickedness are implicit within the British capitalist system itself. British capitalism cannot survive without racism and to that extent the term 'structural racism' moves us a little closer to the truth than 'institutional racism', which limits its analysis to mere elements of capitalism or cogs in British capitalism's wheel.

Against the acrimonious background of British capitalism's relentless catalogue of crimes against humanity, sincere Afrikan liberation organisations will have to address a number of potent issues, if they are to demonstrate a value to the brutally exploited and oppressed Afrikan communities in Britain. The initial test for sincere Afrikan liberation organisations is whether they can do anything to reduce the level of the barrage of abuse that is, as a matter of course, heaped on the Afrikan community in Britain. An additional test is whether it can overturn or repel the tide of racist ill-treatment and in the final analysis, whether they can contribute to the overthrow of the capitalist system that perpetuates the evil suffered by Afrikans.

6.2 A collective purpose for Afrikans
6.2.1 A basis for Afrikan unity
An analysis of the historic and contemporary situation of Afrikans across the world reveals a catalogue of horror unrelentingly inflicted upon the

mothers and fathers of humanity. However, it would be inappropriate for us as Afrikans to wallow in our undeserved suffering. Instead, it is more meaningful for Afrikans to address the question of how we can transform our situation to one which is free from exploitation and the oppression which it automatically engenders.

The suggestion here is that Afrikans should focus our energies on creating a situation where we are a self determining people, operating within a social, political and economic system based on justice. It is proposed that three basic principles should guide that justice: *Humanism* – that the welfare of ordinary people is taken as our highest material priority; *Egalitarianism* – that all human beings are equal in essence and despite differences in particular attributes, nobody can claim superiority to anybody else; and *Collectivism* – that the needs of the people as a whole are more important than the desires of any individual or subgroup and that we work together to solve our problems.

Since capitalism is diametrically opposed to justice and just principles for Afrikans and anybody else it does not like, a critical objective for us must be that of achieving fundamental change in our situation. This means a revolutionary change to remove capitalism which is the principal barrier disqualifying us from self determination.

If we can achieve a level of agreement around the notion of Afrikans having a right to determine our own future and that imperialism (i.e. capitalism in its international form) is our principal enemy, then we must address the issue of how best to apply our energies. In other words, what are the best tactics to be applied to achieving self determination? One of the critical questions for Afrikans in Britain to answer is, what particular role can we play in achieving Afrikan self determination globally?

To help us with this analysis we will make a concise illustration of relationship between capitalism, imperialism and neo-colonialism using theft as the common denominator. Crudely interpreted, capitalism is an inherently evil system of organised theft within a nation. *Capitalism* exists when a small band of people in an industrial nation, systematically steal as much wealth from their fellow nationals as they can get away with and at the same time dominate them to prevent them from getting their wealth back; *imperialism* is capitalism in its international form (i.e. theft from and domination of the people of other nations); and *neo-colonialism* is the modern method by which international capitalism (i.e. imperialism) steals the wealth and dominates the peoples of other nations, using an indigenous internal elite class dominated by traitors, who betray the interests of their fellow nationals.

6.2.2 Neo-colonialism: Afrika's principle enemy
Writing in Samuel Ochola's *Minerals in Afrikan Underdevelopment*, Bhagat gives more flesh regarding what is meant by the term neo-colonialism:

> "The principle task of those who man the neo-colonial state apparatus is to facilitate plunder by the imperialist monopolies. The comprador classes and the functionaries of the state apparatus become the junior partners of the imperialists. In keeping with their status, the monopolies give them crumbs. This is not to say that all Afrikan regimes are simply comprador in the sense that they enjoy no relative independence. They do enjoy a degree of relative independence at times but always under the umbrella of imperialism, that is, so long as they do not fundamentally change the overall interests of imperialism.
>
> Imperialist oppression, exploitation and plunder on the one hand and the crumb grabbing of their allies in the neo-colonies on the other means terrible hardships for the masses which gives rise to the discontent amongst them. The neo-colonial regimes basically use two methods to deal with the situation. One is to unleash terror and the other is to attempt some reforms." (Ochola 1975, p. x)

This raises the question of who exactly are the people that man the neo-colonial state apparatus as imperialism's junior partners. Echidime in his book *An Appeal to Fellow Nigerians: Why You Should be a Socialist* gives some description to what he describes as the 'domestic agents' working for the success of the neo-colonial domination of their own people. He identifies them as being mostly:

"obahs, chiefs, and their off-spring; erstwhile politicians and ex-judges, ex-army colonels, generals and police commissioners; senior civil servants and bishops; university dons and ex-presidents and secretaries of the trade unions, and even of university student unions who hoard directorships in the form of retainers for these foreign devils. The directors of the mass media, newspapers and television studios, are thick in the racket ... so called importers and contractors ... the bureaucrats who inheriting the colonial administrative salary and tax structures, which are unrelated to the needs of the ordinary citizen, and whose chief expertise consists of how to spend the oil revenue. Then there are the whole breed of hustlers waiting in the wings hoping to clutch at foreign exchange to sell in the underground market at multiples of that rate and then reinvest the multiples of that rate and the proceeds in more foreign exchange at the official rate and so on." (Eschidime, p. 32)

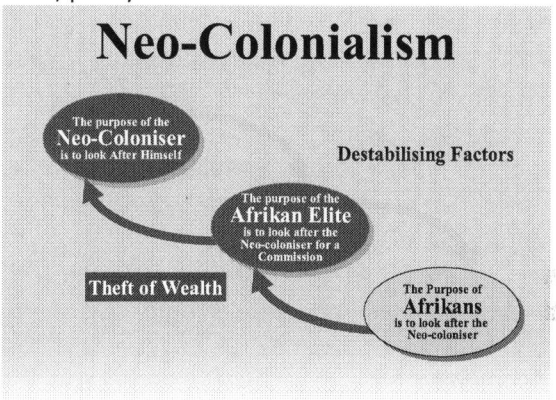

Neo-Colonialism

- The purpose of the **Neo-Coloniser** is to look After Himself
- **Destabilising Factors**
- The purpose of the **Afrikan Elite** is to look after the Neo-coloniser for a Commission
- **Theft of Wealth**
- The Purpose of **Afrikans** is to look after the Neo-coloniser

Brother Omowale

It is vitally important for us to understand that neo-colonialism is at the centre of all of the problems that we currently face as Afrikan people. For this reason it makes sense to further illustrate the impact of neo-colonialism. If a nation has its boarders defined by somebody else; if a nation cannot protect these boundaries from the entry of an aggressor; if a nation cannot control its economy, its political structures and its cultural institutions, then it is no longer a nation, it must be something else and that something else is a neo-colony – a powerless entity, a pretend nation, which exists only to serve its masters at the imperialist centres (i.e. US Satan, Britain, France etc.).

Every pretend nation in Afrika is a neo-colony. Every pretend nation in the Afrikan Diaspora is a neo-colony. Every group of Afrikans contained in the imperialist centres exist in an internal neo-colony. They are collectively arrested, all unable to practice self-determination and all have 'high profile' Afrikan puppets whose strings are operated by the imperialist enemy, which maintains a veto over their tenure in office.

So long as Afrikan countries remain neo-colonies, the wholesale theft of Afrikan resources will continue and intensify. For this reason, **Kwame Nkrumah**, in his book *Handbook of Revolutionary Warfare*, identifies the neo-colonial mechanisms of imperialism as the number one enemy of Afrikan people. Neo-colonialism ravages Afrikans wherever we are in the world. He says that fighting its mechanisms must be treated as the highest priority of all Afrikans because of the life sapping effect neo-colonialism is having upon us as a people.

In addition, he suggests the achievement of Afrikan unity as the other great priority and outlines a formula for achieving unity in both thought and deed. Firstly, all of the Afrikan forces fighting against imperialism (movements, parties and governments etc.) must engage in coordinated collective action through joining an Afrikan umbrella organisation. The close collaboration flowing from working in the Afrikan umbrella organisation would then lead to a second, qualitatively higher phase. The umbrella organisation will develop into a continental wide (including the Diaspora) Afrikan political party which will control a continental wide military wing for defence purposes.

On 24/2/1966 **Nkrumah**'s government was deposed by an anti-democratic, unconstitutional and unlawful coup d'etat. The coup was a conspiracy between the unprincipled and treacherous supporters of neo-colonialism in Ghana itself, combined with the undermining and conspiratorial 'hidden hand' of the capitalist centre's murderous intelligence agencies. This catastrophic event gave the neo-colonial forces control of what was the effective centre of Pan-Afrikanism. It also caused **Nkrumah** to reconsider the best approach to achieving Afrikan unity.

It had also become clear by that time that the sabotaging neo-colonialist minority enemy within the continental Afrikan community was now in control of the then recently formed Organisation of Afrikan Unity (OAU). This exposed a problem of fundamental proportions for those people concerned with achieving genuine Afrikan liberation. Namely, the relative weakness and lack of autonomous political organisation and structures of us as ordinary Afrikan working people, (including unemployed people) pursuing our fully justified quest for freedom.

This point is illustrated more lucidly as the central thesis made by Elenga M'buyinga in his book *Pan-Afrikanism or Neo-colonialism*. He demonstrates that Pan-Afrikanism and neo-colonialism are totally incompatible; that they are diametric opposites; that they are the antitheses of each other; that to support one automatically means to destroy the other; that where one dominates, the other must fight for its very survival. He recognises that any action taken by neo-colonial regimes in Afrika are designed to strengthen their own power base and at the same time destroy and cripple their opposite Pan-Afrikanist initiative. The OAU had developed into a higher collective form of neo-colonial control over Afrika, hell bent on destroying Pan-Afrikanism.

Nkrumah recognised the danger implicit in the development of a continental wide anti-Afrikan governmental agency, which is effectively what the OAU had become. His proposal was aimed at giving some protection to ordinary Afrikan people against imperialism's internal onslaught against us. He proposed the formation of a continental wide Afrikan government as a mechanism to supersede the enemy controlled OAU and to operate as a further catalyst to unity amongst anti-imperialist forces in Afrika. In his book *The Conakry Years* he said that:

> "Such a government could be established over the heads of the independent Afrikan states. Membership or citizenship of the Union will be based on individuals and not on states. And the government doesn't have to seek diplomatic recognition. It will work through its individual citizen membership.... Such a Union government will cut across the confusion and pandemonium reigning in Afrika, since it will function independently of Afrikan states which the Union government consider as zones." (Nkrumah, 1980d, p. 331)

The continental wide government had now become vital, because the expressed desire for unity amongst ordinary Afrikan working people was now being suppressed by the very governmental agencies, installed in Afrika by imperialism that masqueraded as our domestic and international advocates and leadership.

Revolutionary Actions

Revolution
→ Fight Neo-Colonialism & Imperialism
→ Afrikan Unity & Afrikan Organisation

Brother Omowale

The continental wide government and political party were conceived as the mechanism for: guiding our army's fighting role against neo-colonialism; managing the reconstruction of Afrika's political economy; and safeguarding Afrika and Afrikans from any and all future attempts to enslave and subjugate Afrikans with a view to stealing Afrika's wealth or for any other purpose. These protective Afrikan institutions will be vital in helping Afrikans to effectively organise in order to achieve and maintain a self-determining status in the world.

This analysis is suggesting that Afrikan people as a whole should actually stand *for* something i.e. self determination. At the same time it is suggesting that Afrikan people should stand *against* something i.e. imperialism. There is no contradiction between these two aims which are inversely related and complementary. On the one hand we build our own strength from within and on the other hand we fight our external enemy and its allies.

6.2.3 Afrika: Our centre of gravity

Whilst all Afrikans should be involved in both parts of this approach, our location in the world has a key determining effect on where we should lay our emphasis. During one of his London lecture tours Yousef Ben Yochanen made the following remark:

"I don't give a damn if you have a golden toilet bowl in

another man's nation, you've got nothing. It is only when you have your own nation that you can demand anything 'cause you're it." (Ben Yochanan, Lecturing on Kemetic Culture, London)

The analysis is clear, Afrikan self determination must have its centre in Afrika. The self determination base cannot be in Britain or any other part of the Afrikan Diaspora. The role that Afrikans in Britain can play in the self determination part of our strategy is partially determined by our geographical reality. The priority for Afrikans in the Diaspora, is to provide all possible support to the Afrikan masses at home (our centre of gravity) with all the means at our disposal. The only real issue is what forms such support should take.

A geo-political analysis also reveals that Britain is one of the capitalist/imperialist world centres. This means that Afrikans based here are located in the heart of the imperialist enemy infrastructure. The imperialists are well aware of the significance of our location in strategic terms. The warmonger Montgomery's words are again helpful to our analysis:

> "In war, the enemy is plain and clear. In peace, a nation is confronted with a more insidious foe: the weakness within, from which alone great nations fall ... the danger from within is always present and must be kept in subjection." (Montgomery 2000, p. 19)

Our enemy is admitting that we are well placed to play a significant role in bringing their entire system down. In addition, they are reserving an extra degree of oppression for Afrikans to terrify us as a means to dissuading us from taking the actions necessary for bringing their system down. Even if there are question marks regarding our ability to destroy imperialism from within, there can be little doubt that Afrikans can plan or be a part of processes that will cause substantial disruption to the enemy's imperialist infrastructure.

In his book *Handbook of Revolutionary Warfare*, **Kwame Nkrumah** identifies the critical historical role of Afrikan revolutionaries located in the Diaspora. He points out that, with effective organisation, Afrikans outside the continent can:

> "... play an important part in the liberation movement by means of sabotage and subversion at the very core of the capitalist-imperialist states." (Nkrumah 1980b, p. 62)

Any disruptive actions that take place in the heart of imperialism are bound to reverberate throughout the imperialist infrastructure, thereby loosening the grip of its neo-colonial tentacles on the imperialist periphery. Since Afrika is a part of the imperialist periphery, disruptive action here will contribute to an improved environment for our sisters and brothers in Afrika to engage in actions designed to take charge of our land, resources and labour. It will provide an impetus for revolutionary change.

Afrikans in Britain are massively outnumbered and relatively powerless. It follows that a full frontal assault on this imperialist centre would be tantamount to suicide. The battle against imperialism, in this terrain, is likely to take on an unarmed quasi-guerrilla warfare format: a programme of civil disobedience where Afrikans and other oppressed peoples can plan and decide the type of engagement.

Guerrilla warfare is an anti-slavery fighting technique practiced for centuries in West Afrika. It was further developed by Afrikans in the Caribbean as a technique of resistance and revolution. Our enslavement under imperialism meant that we needed a reliable method to fight for our liberation thereby ensuring that we could determine our own destiny. During his revolutionary development in the Caribbean, Che Guevara benefited from this wealth of knowledge and codified it for the benefit of revolutionaries everywhere. In his book *Guerrilla Warfare*, Guevara describes the primary characteristic of the guerrilla soldier in the following terms:

> "... he should preferably be an inhabitant of the zone. If this is the case, he will have friends who will help him; if he belongs to the zone itself, he will know it (and this knowledge of the ground is one of the most important factors in guerrilla warfare); and since he will be habituated to the local peculiarities he will be able to do better work, not to mention that he will add to all this the enthusiasm that arises from defending his own people and fighting to

change a social regime that hurts his own world." (Guevara, 1969, p. 48)

This fits well with the experience of Afrikans based in Britain, with elders who have spent 40+ years of their lives in this terrain and younger Afrikans who have spent all of their lives here.

Racism makes Britain a hostile environment for Afrikans even when we observe capitalist laws scrupulously. That hostility is bound to increase for any Afrikan openly participating in a programme of civil disobedience. The risks to the wellbeing of dedicated Afrikan cadre engaging in this calibre of action are real. It follows that no stone should be left unturned in ensuring the safety and survival of participants. Guevara highlights the importance of this point in the following words:

> "As soon as the survival of the guerrilla band has been assured, it should fight; it must constantly go out from its refuge to fight." (Guevara, 1969, p. 30)

One way of appearing to survive in this hostile environment is to do nothing at all. Another way is to sit in a room, talking amongst ourselves, but stopping short of actively fighting British capitalism, which is our geographical imperialist front. These approaches are based on the false notion that if we 'behave ourselves' or 'keep our heads down' that imperialism will leave us alone. Guevara does not support such cowardly inactivity. Instead his words make it clear that *in addition to ensuring our survival*, we must constantly go out and fight imperialism. Against this background, sincere Afrikan liberation organisations must provide Afrikan people with a mechanism for confronting British capitalism on terrain where it would rather not fight.

The supply of resources to our sisters and brothers fighting for revolutionary change at home is another significant contribution that Afrikans in Britain can make. Our close proximity to advanced technology and finance for instance, means that we can facilitate the supply of materials critical to the success of our people's fight on the ground in Afrika. This must however, be regarded as secondary to the role of disruption in the heart of imperialism, since imperialism's actions are literally killing us off as a people. It is also clear that imperialism has the capacity to send more resources to its allies in Afrika than we are able to send to ours.

6.3 *Ukombozii* Statement on Reparations
6.3.1 They all owe us
The enslavement of Afrikan people created unprecedented levels of wealth for the imperialists who controlled the slavery system. As part of their agenda of stealing other peoples' wealth they managed to usurp Afrikan people's labour without having to pay. The imperialists then used the massive quantities of wealth that they accumulated from slavery as capital to invest. These investments were the cause of many new beginnings including: a proliferation in the development of technological inventions in Europe; the creation of factories in Europe; the development of mass production in Europe; the development of industrialisation in Europe; the birth of capitalism as a social, political and economic system; the birth of the capitalist phase of world history; and the birth of modern racism (Bottomore, 1981, p. 96).

These changes also meant that the newly created mass producing factories of Europe needed labour in order to operate effectively. This new need was hindered by the fact that the labour of European peasants was tied to the land in a form of bondage called serfdom. The requirements imposed by the newly emerging capitalist system meant that the European peasants had to be released from serfdom by their Lords and Masters (Bottomore, 1981, p. 133/134). Their release was one of the essential ingredients that brought capitalism into existence. It was the release of European peasants from serfdom that gave birth to the European working class (i.e. proletariat). The European working class was created by the new capitalist elite for its own diabolical purposes. The European working class was also born out of the terrible suffering of enslaved Afrikan people.

The European working class was created precisely so that the capitalists could exploit them as a means of making profits. In order to resist this exploitation the working class was forced to organise for self defence. Trade unions are the result of the European working class' organised struggle against capitalism - the same capitalist system that was created by and profited from anti-Afrikan slavery.

Trade Unions which were the European working class' legitimate response to capitalist exploitation have at their root the terrible suffering of enslaved Afrikan people. The outcome of this process is that European working class suffer capitalist oppression on the basis of class; Afrikan people suffer double oppression – class and race; and Afrikan women suffer triple oppression – class, race and gender.

Slavery & The Working Class

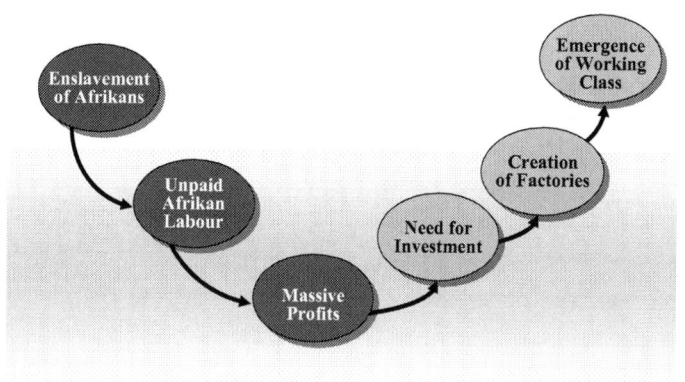

Brother Omowale

In short, if there was no slavery there would be no capitalism. If there was no capitalism there would be no working class. If there was no working class there would be no Trade Union Movement. Capitalism, the working class and Trade Unions all owe their existence to the enslavement of Afrikan people. They are all indebted to and owe reparations to Afrikan people, from whose genocidal scale suffering (i.e. exploitation and oppression) they arose. They were all born out of the terrible suffering of enslaved Afrikan people.

6.3.2 A business case for reparations

If we view capitalism as a business and apply its own cash flow analytical technique to measure its development, the results are very illuminating from a reparations perspective. Typically, businesses go to banks to secure a loan in order to get going. The loan helps by covering start up costs and keeping its cash flow within acceptable boundaries.

If that loan did not exist, the business would accrue unmanageable debts and go out of business before it gets off the ground. The loan is therefore absolutely essential to the successful business and all capitalists recognise that they are indebted to the bank and are absolutely required to repay the loan. In fact, failure to repay would be a breach of capitalism's laws, bringing with it the very real prospect of court proceedings, bankruptcy and exclusion from engaging in running other capitalist businesses.

This raises the obvious question of where did capitalism get its loan in order to come into being. The answer is simple, it came from the blood, sweat and tears of Afrikan people. The unpaid labour stolen from Afrikan people produced massive volumes of money in the form of profits from slavery. That accumulated money was the 'loan' that 'kick started' capitalism, making it viable. It was the 'loan' that ensured capitalism didn't fail from the off. It is the 'loan'/debt which the laws of capitalism would otherwise demand must be repaid. Capitalism's consequence for non-repayment is bankruptcy and even imprisonment.

6.3.3 The first instalment is 243 years overdue

The wicked enslavers made some attempt at keeping records that give some indication of the extent of their indebtedness to Afrikan people. For instance:

> " ... Dalby Thomas declared that every person employed on the sugar [forced labour camps] was a hundred and thirty times more valuable to England than one at home. Professor Pitman has estimated that in **1775** West Indies [forced labour camps] represented a valuation of *fifty million pounds sterling*, and the [wicked enslavers] themselves put the figures at *seventy millions* in **1788**. In **1798** Pitt assessed the annual income from West Indian [forced labour camps] at *four million pounds* as compared with one million for the rest of the world." (Du Bois, 1996, p. 59 – **Author's emphasis**)

By boastfully testifying the value of their gains for their crimes against humanity in the years 1775 and 1788, the wicked enslavers have given an indication of the loan forcefully extracted from Afrikan people's labour. We need to be clear that this is for labour, it covers in part our ancestors sweat, but not their blood and tears. It is an indicator of the 1 in 5 who made the *Maangamizi* crossing and lived, not the 4 in 5 murdered in the genocide along the way. It indicates the loan forcibly extracted from Afrikan people by wicked British enslavers, not the hordes of other wicked non-British European imperialist enslavers. Nor does it include their debts for their colonial and neo-colonial crimes against humanity.

The equation for calculating compound interest is: **P(1 + r/n)$^{(nt)}$**, where **P** *represents the principal,* **r** *the annual interest rate,* **n** *the number of times interest is compounded per annum* and **t** *the number of years.* The given principle is £50m and £70m respectively. If we were working with a British loan we might choose a modest 5% as our interest rate. However, the loan was forcefully extracted from Afrika. It is therefore more appropriate to use an indicative Afrikan interest rate. More precisely, it should be an average interest rate of all of the areas of Afrika colonised by Britain. Afrikan interest rates are much higher. Some economies have been subjected to prolonged periods of hyper-inflation precisely because the continent was ravaged through slavery and its updated forms. An ultra modest interest rate of 20% will therefore be applied for the purpose of this calculation. 1775 to 2018 is 243 years and 1788 to 2018 is 230. To keep things simple, we will require only one compounding of interest per annum.

Utilising the figures provided by the wicked enslavers and their ideologues the equation for the years under consideration are as follows:
- 1775 is £50m(1 + 0.20/1)$^{(1*243)}$
- 1788 is £70m(1 + 0.20/1)$^{(1*230)}$

Our initial demand to the British imperial state is quantifiable as:

- £50m(1 + 0.20)$^{(243)}$ + £70m(1 + 0.20)$^{(230)}$

- £50m (1.20)$^{(243)}$ +£ 70m(1.20)$^{(230)}$

Trusting that the spreadsheet can handle the weight of the calculation, this in Quintillion[1] i.e. (10)^{18} become:

- £870,989,250 Quintillion + £113,968,450 Quintillion

---

[1] Million = (10)^6, Billion = (10)^9, Trillion = (10)^{12}, Quadrillion = (10)^{15}, Quintillion = (10)^{18} & Sextillion = (10)^{21}

Giving a grand total of:

- **£984,957,695 Quintillion** (alternatively expressed):

- **£984,957,695,000,000,000,000,000,000** (alternatively expressed):

- **Nine hundred and eighty four million, nine hundred and fifty seven thousand, six hundred and ninety five quintillion pounds.** (a little shy of 1 Sextillion pounds)

This then is the bill for the first financial instalment of Afrikan people's reparations demand against British imperialism, plus or minus a few Quadrillion, payable in gold. It is only a limited claim at this stage in order to start the ball rolling. The wicked enslavers should consider this easy payment plan approach an act of good will on the part of the aggrieved Afrikan people to whom they are immensely indebted. The bills for the other years and other missing elements will, in due course be calculated and forwarded.

These monies must be paid without any further delay. This particular instalment is already at least 230 years overdue. Further delays will cause it to continue to compound at a rate of 20% per annum reaching a figure of £37,760,914,064 Quintillion (£37.8 Sextillion) in the year 2038 in the event of delayed payment.

The Reparations Value Table ending this chapter illustrates the current per annum charges. Afrikan people reserve the right to raise the interest rate in the event of further unreasonable repayment delays. The terms are 28 days net, taxable only by the people of Afrika.

An equivalent calculation is carried out with the 1798 revenue figure provided by the wicked enslavers' then Prime Minister and the well known £20m subsidy paid to Britain's wicked enslavers as a reward, designed to assist them in changing the form of their anti-Afrikan wickedness. The latter became due on 1st August 1838, the date British imperialism alleges it abolished slavery. The £4m revenue figure brings forth a reparations value of a mere £10,518,023 Quintillion rising to £403,235,763 Quintillion in 2038 in the event of further payment delays; the £20m reward/subsidy produces a modest reparations bonus of £3,578,115 Quintillion rising to £137,176,338 Quintillion in 2038. These have not been included in the initial demand.[2]

Numerical Denominations

	21	18	15	12	9	6	3
Thousand							1 000
Million						1 000	000
Billion					1 000	000	000
Trillion				1 000	000	000	000
Quadrillion			1 000	000	000	000	000
Quintillion		1 000	000	000	000	000	000
Sextillion	1 000	000	000	000	000	000	000

Brother Omowale

Afrikan people are a collective people and it goes without saying that those of us enslaved, colonised and neo-colonised by British imperialism will share our first instalment payment with our sisters and brothers the world over, pending the successful outcome of their initial payments. Working on the premise that there are approximately 1.6 billion Afrikan people in the world, this means that **each individual Afrikan person in the world has a personal stake of £615,598,559 Billion** i.e. **six hundred and fifteen million, five hundred and ninety eight thousand, five hundred and fifty nine billion pounds** in British imperialism's first instalment reparations repayment.

It should also be noted that this element of the reparations i.e. the debt is independent of whether British imperialism's conduct was right or wrong, moral or immoral, legal or illegal – the recipient of a loan is not absorbed of their duty to repay on the basis of whether or not they are a nice person or a criminal. This is strictly business – the loan was extracted and as with any loan, must be repaid. Furthermore, if it is British imperialism's position that its forcibly extracted loan was legal,

---

[2] Figure not adjusted to account for changing value of money (inflation).

then this is additional confirmation of its legal obligation to pay. If, for some inexplicable reason, British imperialism opts to avoid repaying its debt, then it is depriving Afrikan people of the sums forcibly extracted – with intent. That would render its actions/inactions, illegal theft. The natural course is for stolen property to be taken away from a thief caught in or after the act. It is then returned to its rightful owner – in this case, Afrikan people *en masse*.

6.3.4 Reparations is one small 'r' in the 'Revolutionary armoury'

The more astute will by now have noticed that British imperialism will experience considerable difficulties in paying even the first instalment of what it owes Afrikan people. This pattern will obviously be repeated throughout the other brands of imperialism that carried out and in most cases, still carry out anti-Afrikan genocide programmes. All of them will experience difficulties in making good even the first instalment of their debt.

The only solution therefore is revolution. Reparations then constitute one small 'r' in the 'Revolutionary armoury'. The purpose of revolution is to advance humanity from one phase of history to the next – from the current backward phase to a future more advanced one – where the world is not ruled by genocidal maniac lying thieves and the quality of life is better for all.

As evidenced by the foregoing text, humanity is currently in the capitalist phase under the control of maniacs. The role of revolution is to assist humanity to reach the next historical phase – socialism – an era of liberation where the overwhelming majority, freed from the clutches of the maniacs will rule their own lands in their own best interests.

It is the role of all counter revolutionaries to delay humanity's historical progress to socialism. By contrast, it is the role of all revolutionaries to ensure that humanity advances to socialism in the shortest possible timescale. That is how you can tell the revolutionary from the counter-revolutionary. The true revolutionary is working to repair humanity. For Afrikan people 'catching so much hell' from capitalism, it should be, but isn't always obvious that their freedom requires a revolutionary path. However the hard truth is, the only way to achieve reparations is via revolution.

European beneficiaries of the genocidal scale enslavement of Afrikan people have an even more difficult task. The only way that they can pay their reparations is by committing what the great Afrikan revolutionary Amilcar Cabral called 'class suicide'. Their revolutionary duty is to urgently destroy from within the very system that grants them crumb scale privileges over and above Afrikan people. If they are not actively engaged in that task (and by far the majority are not), they are part of the problem in need of repair.

Revolution requires the sweeping aside of all imperialisms, ridding the world of capitalism. The destruction of the capitalist system is not a quest for some kind of warped pleasure from tearing things down, nor is it destruction for destruction's sake; it is to clear from all exploited peoples' paths the proven destructive capitalist system, so that the whole of humanity can enjoy a better future based on humanist principles.

Reparations Value Table

	Capital Amount £50m 1775 + £70m 1788 Quintillion	Revenue Amount £4m in 1798 Quintillion	Subsidy Amount £20m in 1838 Quintillion
2018	984,957,695	10,518,023	3,578,115
2019	1,181,949,234	12,621,628	4,293,738
2020	1,418,339,081	15,145,953	5,152,485
2021	1,702,006,897	18,175,144	6,182,983
2022	2,042,408,277	21,810,173	7,419,579
2023	2,450,889,932	26,172,207	8,903,495
2024	2,941,067,919	31,406,649	10,684,194
2025	3,529,281,502	37,687,979	12,821,033
2026	4,235,137,803	45,225,574	15,385,239
2027	5,082,165,364	54,270,689	18,462,287
2028	6,098,598,436	65,124,827	22,154,744
2029	7,318,318,124	78,149,792	26,585,693
2030	8,781,981,748	93,779,751	31,902,832
2031	10,538,378,098	112,535,701	38,283,398
2032	12,646,053,717	135,042,841	45,940,078
2033	15,175,264,461	162,051,409	55,128,094
2034	18,210,317,353	194,461,691	66,153,712
2035	21,852,380,824	233,354,030	79,384,455
2036	26,222,856,989	280,024,835	95,261,346
2037	31,467,428,386	336,029,803	114,313,615
2038	37,760,914,064	403,235,763	137,176,338

List of Mentioned Sources
1. Bhagat, H in Ochola. Samuel Agonda, (1975), *Minerals in Afrikan Underdevelopment*, Bogle L'Ouverture Pubilcations Limited
2. Blum. William, (2003), *Rogue State*, Zed Books Limited
3. Bottomore. Tom, (1981), *Modern Interpretations of Marx*, Basil Blackwell Publisher
4. Chomsky. Noam, (2003), *Power and Terror: Post 9/11 Talks and Interviews*, Turnaround Publishers Services Limited
5. Du Bois. WEB, (1996), *The World and Africa: Inquiry into the part which Africa played in World History*, International Publishers Company Incorporated
6. Etienne. Philip & Maynard. Bernard, (2000), *The Infiltrators*, Penguin Books
7. Echidime. S., (1981), *An Appeal to Fellow Nigerians: Why You Should be a Socialist*, E. Stanley Impex Company (Publishing) Limited
8. Fanon. Franz, (1990), *The Wretched of the Earth*, Penguin Books
9. Guevara. Che, (1969), *Guerrilla Warfare*, Pelican Books
10. M' buyinga. Elenga, (1982), *Pan-Afrikanism or Neo-colonialism: The Bankrupcy of the OAU* Zed Press
11. Montgomery. Bernard, (2000), *A Concise History of Warfare*, Wordsworth Edition Limited
12. Nkrumah. Kwame, (1980a), *Consciencism*, PANAF Books Limited
13. Nkrumah. Kwame, (1980b), *Handbook of Revolutionary Warfare*, PANAF Books Limited
14. Nkrumah. Kwame, (1980c), *Neo-Colonialism: The Last Stage of Imperialism*, PANAF Books Limited
15. Nkrumah. Kwame, (1980d), *The Conakry Years*, PANAF Books Limited
16. Ovenden. Kevin, (1992), *Malcolm X: Socialism and Black Nationalism*, Bookmarks
17. Poulman. Linda, (2003), *We Did Nothing: Why the truth doesn't always come out when the UN goes in*, Penguin Books Limited, (English Translation)
18. Rodney. Walter, (1981), *How Europe Underdeveloped Afrika*, Howard University Press
19. Toure. Sekou, (1977), *The Strategy and Tactics of the Revolution*, The State Office, Republic of Guinea, English 1st Edition, Volume XXI
20. West. Nigel, (1983), *MI5*, Triad Granada

Decoding Slavery & Anti-Slavery Systems:
Their Principles, Origins and Development

7 Decoding slavery & anti-slavery systems: Their principles, origin and development

7.1 The fundamental basis of human relationships
Amilcar Cabral in his book *Return to the Source* teaches us that economics at its essence is the relationship between people and nature. He also shows us that politics at its essence is the relationship between people and people (Afrikan Information Service, 1973, p. 41: Mc Culloch, 1983, p. 84). It is the relationship between people and nature that fundamentally determines the relationship between people and people. At the same time, the relationship between people and people gives direction to the relationship between people and nature. All social systems produced by human beings are fundamentally based on the relationship between people and people on the one hand people and nature on the other. Together these two sets of relationships determine all other types or categories of human relationship. In other words, all human relationships are reducible to some permutation of economics and politics.

Nature is older than people, it existed before people. People were created out of nature and are completely contained in both time and nature. Since people are contained in nature, politics must be contained in economics. In other words all politics is economics; however because the rest of nature exists outside of people, the rest of economics must exist outside of politics - therefore not all economics is politics. Economics is therefore bigger than politics; politics is really a part of economics, but it is the critical part of economics that determines the direction and levels of success of economic activity.

Relations in Context

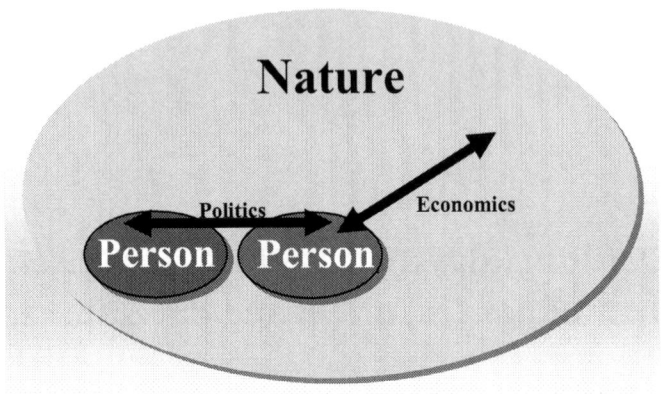

Brother Omowale

7.2 Human beings cannot exist outside of nature
7.2.1 Nature has four elements
Nature is composed of 4 different elements: air, water, fire (the sun) and earth (the land) – each of these elements act on and are essential to human life (Toure, No. 88, p. 133). Together they produce all of the vital ingredients which living creatures need to survive. Human beings through their consciousness have the capacity to interact with all of these elements and create even more things that they need to enhance their prospects of survival and beyond that the quality of their lives. All of these elements therefore provide a potential base for power, because they are each vital to life.

Our dependency on nature's air is total. For instance, if human beings are without air for 5 minutes, they die. However, there is no viable method for containing, controlling or claiming ownership of the air. We cannot use access to the air as a basis for claiming other people's wealth from them. We cannot make other people totally dependent upon us for access to the air. No group of human beings have been able to claim personal control of the air. Human beings are completely surrounded by the air and instinctively draw the air that they need in order to breathe. In that simple sense, the air belongs to everyone.

A similar case can be made for sunlight. If the world were deprived of sunlight for any significant length of time, plant life would die off. This would have a catastrophic affect on the food chain and would result in the extinction of human and other forms of life higher up the food chain. No one can own or control the sun. We cannot get close to the sun. We cannot even look at the sun without harming ourselves. We cannot use the denial of access to the sun as a basis for claiming other people's wealth from them. Most importantly, we cannot block other people's access to the sun in order to make them dependent upon us. No group of human beings have been able to claim control or 'ownership' of the sun. Sun rays come via the sky and all human beings experience the benefits of it in some way or form. In that sense the sun belongs to everyone.

It is also observable that our dependency on nature's water is total; if human beings are without water for 5 days they die. Some control can be exerted over water which is on the ground. However, it is impractical to prevent people from catching rain water and making use of it. We cannot generally use the denial of access to water as a basis for claiming people's wealth from them. We cannot generally make other people totally dependent upon us for access to water on a consistent basis. No group of human beings have been able to claim total personal control of the world's water supply. Water falls from the sky and anybody with an appropriate container can catch it and drink it. Again, in that simple sense water belongs to everyone.

7.2.2 Land is unique amongst nature's elements
Our dependency on nature's land is also total. If land did not exist, human life would be altered beyond all recognition. In fact human life would be extinguished because everything that is necessary for human survival is either on the land, comes into contact with the land or is in the land. Land differs from the other elements in that the wealth contained in the land is relatively accessible to people and exchangeable between people. The resources contained in the land are useful in human societies. Systems can be put in place by some people to block other people's access to land and its contents. Some people can and

historically have claimed 'ownership' of land and have used the land as a basis for claiming other people's wealth from them. Since land is essential to life the land 'owners' have been able to use their power over the land to stifle other people's development. Historically the 'ownership' of land had such a profound affect that it gave the alleged 'owners' the power of life and death over the other people on the land. Systems of land ownership eventually meant that the land did not belong to everyone in the sense that the other elements did. It was usurped by a small sub-group of humanity.

Land, which can also be thought of as the planet or the base of nature also existed before people. In fact people come from the land and live on and off of the land. Furthermore, whilst people are wholly dependent on the land for their very existence, neither the land nor nature relies upon people for their existence. If people are dependent upon the land for their existence and that land is 'owned' by somebody else, it means that the people become dependent upon the 'owner' of the land. The 'owner' of the land therefore becomes all powerful to the point of even being able to decide on matters of life and death for the people on 'their' land. This is the kind of reasoning that brought Malcolm X to the realisation that 'Land is the basis of all independence' (Breitman, 2002, p. 21). This statement is true because everybody fundamentally depends on the land for their survival, but unlike the other elements of nature, it can be controlled by a sub-group of humanity.

7.3 People, land and the development of principles
7.3.1 Some characteristics of land

This calibre of relationship with the land generated a set of **matriarchal principles** that governed human relationships. Since nobody claimed personal 'ownership' of the land: everybody shared in the wealth produced out of the land, everybody remained dependent on the land but because it was not personally 'owned' nobody became dependent upon anybody else. As a direct result of this scenario three **matriarchal principles** developed: firstly, the welfare of the people was treated as more important than individual 'ownership' of the land i.e. the source of wealth. People's welfare therefore became society's highest priority - this generated the principle of **humanism [People before property]**. Secondly, the people began to notice that by working the land together, they each gained more than they would have gained had they worked by themselves. This encouraged them to work together to satisfy their joint needs - this generated the principle of **collectivism [We before me]**. Thirdly, since adults were generally not dependent upon any other adult, everybody recognised that they were neither superior nor inferior to anybody else. They were all equal in essence - this generated the principle of **egalitarianism [We're all equal in essence]**.

It is important that we do not mix up egalitarianism and equality. They are not the same. There are different approaches to equality. One such approach is elitism, which is the approach that openly rejects equality i.e. I get all the shoes and you get none. Another is equalitarianism, which is the approach that demands that everyone should be treated identically, regardless of their needs i.e. we all receive size 4 shoes. Egalitarianism is the approach that draws according to ability and allocates according to need i.e. we receive the shoes that fit our feet. Clarity on these differences is important because:

> " ... no society can be founded on the equality of its members, although some societies are founded on egalitarianism which is something quite different." (Nkrumah, 1980f, p. 441)

Egalitarianism recognises that though we are not and cannot be equal in form, we are all valuable and equal in essence.

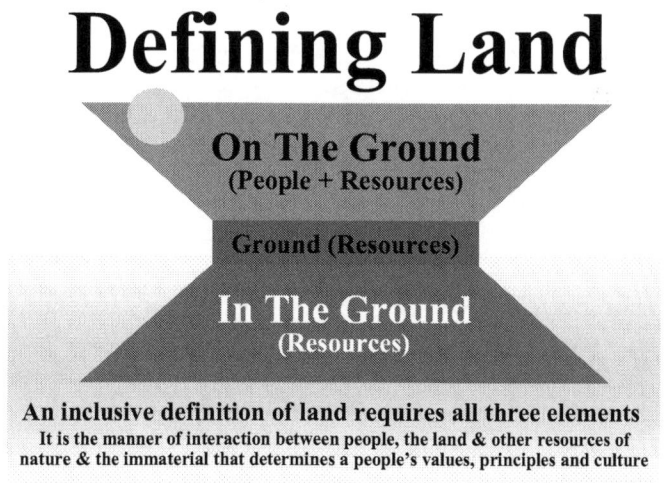

Defining Land

On The Ground
(People + Resources)

Ground (Resources)

In The Ground
(Resources)

An inclusive definition of land requires all three elements
It is the manner of interaction between people, the land & other resources of nature & the immaterial that determines a people's values, principles and culture

Brother Omowale

It is also important to note that land operates on the feminine principle. For instance, farmers recognise land as having similar characteristics to a woman's womb. The land is fertilised by water, in a manner similar to the way in which the sperm of a man fertilises the egg in a woman's womb. Trees, fruits and vegetables come out of the ground in a manner similar to the way in which human beings come out of the woman's womb. When human beings live in a manner that complements the principles of land, their behaviours generate **matriarchal principles**. Conversely, when human beings behave in ways that run counter to the principles of land their behaviours generate **patriarchal principles**.

7.3.2 The establishment of the true principles of humanity

As human beings we come from the land, are a part of the land and in essence belong to the land. The land provides us with what we need; we are like parasites on the land, depending on it for our needs and our survival. In early human societies it was accepted that the land owned the people. At that stage it never occurred to anybody that people could 'own' the land (Nkrumah, 1979, p. 21). To claim private 'ownership' of the land would have been a bit like two fleas arguing about which one owns the dog. If anything the dog owns the fleas, but the fleas could never truly own the dog. People in this frame of thinking understood that if the land was 'owned' at all, it was collectively 'owned'.

When the land is collectively owned, nobody is landless and everybody has an equal right to: (i) Stand on the land; (ii) Eat the produce of the land and (iii) Build their housing on the land. The only necessary condition is that they must all agree on how to allocate portions of the land between them. Nobody else owns us and we are each powerful (and collectively substantially more powerful). Other individuals cannot block our access to the wealth of the land and use it to control us. In this situation, there can be no separation into *classes* with opposing *class* interests. There is just one *class* and everybody is in it. Everybody gives what they can to that *class* and everybody receives what they need from that *class*. All peoples started off thinking and behaving in this way. When people accepted that they were owned by the land, rather than claiming individual 'ownership' of it, access to the land was free for everyone and as a result human beings were all free from enslavement. Under these circumstances no human being claimed 'ownership' or control of any other human being; slavery was non-existent.

This calibre of relationship with the land generated a set of *matriarchal principles* that governed human relationships. Since nobody claimed personal 'ownership' of the land: everybody shared in the wealth produced out of the land, everybody remained dependent on the land but because it was not personally 'owned' nobody became dependent upon anybody else. As a direct result of this scenario three *matriarchal principles* developed: firstly, the welfare of the people was treated as more important than individual 'ownership' of the land i.e. the source of wealth. People's welfare therefore became society's highest priority - this generated the principle of *humanism [People before property]*. Secondly, the people began to notice that by working the land together, they each gained more than they would have gained had they worked by themselves. This encouraged them to work together to satisfy their joint needs - this generated the principle of *collectivism [We before me]*. Thirdly, since adults were generally not dependent upon any other adult, everybody recognised that they were neither superior nor inferior to anybody else. They were all equal in essence - this generated the principle of *egalitarianism [We're all equal]*.

When matriarchal principles are dominant in a pre-industrial setting, the social system created is called communalism. Under communalism, it is not possible for slavery to thrive. All human societies, without exception, were originally communal societies. Every section of the human family started off in this way. Communalism, with its matriarchal principles was the social system of Afrika before the invasion of alien cultures. Even after the alien invasions communalism did not disappear, instead it retreated to the countryside and can still be found in Afrikan villages to this day (Afrikan Information Service, 1973, p. 49). Communalism does not stand as an isolated system it is part of a family of social systems which includes socialism and communism. What they have in common is that they operate on the basis of matriarchal principles.

7.3.3 The change to anti-human patriarchal principles
As has already been demonstrated a people's principles are derived from the way in which they interact with land (and land is feminine). Since everybody is dependent upon the land for their survival and existence, if some of the people successfully claim 'ownership' of the land, they simultaneously claim 'ownership' of the other people on the land. This is what happened historically. The culprits gained control of

the land for themselves and amassed their own personal wealth at the expense of other members of the group (Nkrumah, 1980e, p. 14).

When the land is privately 'owned', landless people must ask the land 'owner's' permission before they can do anything on the land. If they stand on the land, they trespass; If they pick fruits to eat, they steal; They cannot build a house without permission because they have no foundation upon which to build. They must ask permission of the land 'owner' for anything that they need to do. They are therefore dependent upon the land 'owner' for their needs. They must pay the land 'owner' what he wants in order to get permission before they can satisfy their own needs. The land 'owner' has power over the landless: The freedom of the landless is, in all practical terms, taken away by the land 'owner'. The landless are enslaved by the land 'owner's' 'ownership' of the land upon which they have to stand. Landless people are effectively 'owned' by the land 'owners'.

In this situation, two distinct **classes** emerge with opposing interests. The **land 'owners'** want to use 'their ownership' of land to take the wealth of the **landless**. The **landless** want to keep their wealth by changing the land 'ownership' system to permanently ensure that their wealth will never be taken away from them. In addition, other **landless** and **small land 'owning' classes** develop in between the **major land 'owners'' class** and the **landless class**. Their **class** position is based on how closely they align themselves economically with either the **major land 'owners'** or the **landless**.

These processes actually happened in some parts of the world and when they did, three **patriarchal principles** developed as a direct result of the land 'owners'' selfish actions: firstly, the more the landless people produced, the wealthier the land 'owners' became. Eventually, 'ownership' of property became more important to the land 'owners' than the welfare of the other people on the land - this calibre of behaviour produced the principle of **exploitation [property before people]**. Secondly, the very act of selfishly claiming the land for themselves meant that they were thinking of themselves before they were thinking of the welfare of the other people on the land - this mode of behaviour produced the principle of **individualism [me before we]**. Thirdly, taking control of the land made them more powerful than the other people on the land. The other people owned nothing and therefore became dependent upon them as the land 'owners'. This dependency caused the land 'owners' to view the other people on the land as inferior - this mindset produced the principle of **elitism *[I'm better than you]***.

Allocating The Land

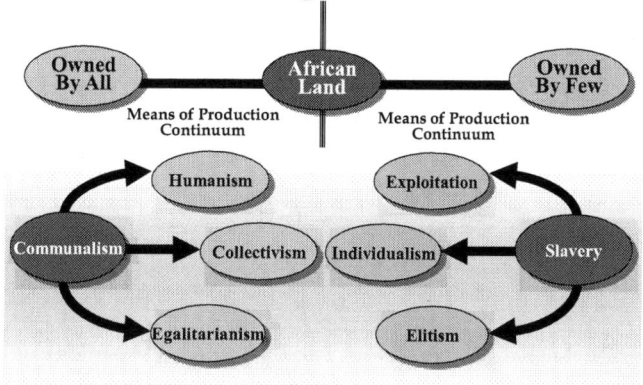

Brother Omowale

These **patriarchal principles** are the core principles of **slavery**. Wherever these anti-human principles are found, they manifest themselves as some version of **slavery**. **Exploitation** is the central principle of **slavery** and like **slavery** it is anti-human and anti-nature in its very essence. Wherever we find **exploitation** we find **elitism**; wherever we find **exploitation** we find **individualism**; wherever we find **exploitation**, **elitism** and **individualism** we find **slavery**. **Exploitation** is the sign that **slavery** is present; it is the common denominator of all forms of **slavery**. The reason why we can truthfully assert that **slavery** has not been abolished, but rather has changed form, is because **exploitation** has not yet been defeated. **Slavery** will only be truly abolished when **exploitation** is banished from the earth forever.

7.4 The origin, development and methodologies of slavery
7.4.1 Exploitation – the common denominator of slavery
Samora Machel (Machel, 1973, p. 26/7) explains that from the moment that people began to produce more than they consumed, the problem of what to do with the excess existed. The first phase of **exploitation** happened when an individual or a small group of people claimed 'ownership' of the excess produced by the whole group. They were in effect 'stealing' from the other members of the group because the others had also participated in the process of producing the surplus.

This sometimes subtle form of **exploitation** happened in varying degrees in all parts of the world. This was the subtle beginning of slavery.

7.4.2 Women were the first 'slaves': Exploitation and its impact on Afrikan women

When the exploiting sub-group made its move to steal the surplus from the rest of the group, women hardly participated in the process. It is not that women were not interested in having a say in how the surplus was distributed, but given that their basic needs were met, women were much too busy caring for their families to fight the budding thieves for the surplus. As a result of their love, kindness and dedication, women were not oppressed into doing some of the things, including serving others, which later turned out to be to their social disadvantage. Women willingly made some concessions for the benefit of their families and the community as a whole. Women's generosity was then taken advantage of and used against them by men. Men took advantage of the fact that women tended to have a higher level of family 'constraints'. This led to men's subjugation of women with little rebellion (Sankara, 2004, p. 260).

As a result, women found themselves by-passed in the quest for what became private property. This proved to be a great disadvantage to women because private property became the foundation of power in early societies. Private property came about through the theft of the group's surplus and simultaneously brought with it the enslavement of women who were too busy doing other things to fight for it. It was at the stage in the historical process, when surplus was monopolised by a minority sub-group that a subtle form of sexism was born and simultaneously, women became the 'first slaves'. The enslavement of women was to intensify later. However, once women fell into the trap of enslavement, it became necessary for men to oppress them in order to keep them there. Once this was 'achieved', more oppression was exerted and further concessions were forced from women by men. This is the proof that the European concept of 'race', a term used to justify European racism was unconnected with slavery at the point of slavery's origin. In other words, sexism is older than racism.

Using the group's surplus as the only basis for enslavement had its weaknesses. For instance, enslaved people who were dissatisfied could go somewhere else out of the reach of those that stole the surplus and start again. This early form of slavery was therefore incomplete because it ultimately relied on the enslaved person accepting their subordinate position because of their emotional bond with the group. Enslavers therefore had to move to a more secure system. They eventually moved from claiming the whole group's surplus to the next stage of claiming 'ownership' of the whole group's land. This was an important development because these societies were agriculturally based, meaning that the land was the actual source of the surplus.

In the second phase, the **exploitation** sharpened: The individual or small group successfully claimed 'ownership' of the land that their people lived on. This went beyond merely 'stealing' produce from the larger group. Since they 'owned' the land that their people lived on, they ended up owning everything on the land, including the rest of their people. This calibre of **exploitation**, known as feudalism was more pronounced in Europe than any other part of the world. Slavery therefore intensified as the minority sub-group monopolised 'ownership' of the land. They used their 'ownership' of the land to steal the labour of the other people in the group. Full blooded slavery was an internal group phenomenon before it became employed by one group against another.

The third phase of **exploitation** formed the ultimate foundation for racism. It linked the concept of race to **exploitation** and is often falsely portrayed as the origin of slavery. This third phase happened in two stages. In the first stage, one nation of people stole the physical bodies of members of other nations. The enslavers were then in a position to hold the stolen people in bondage whilst extracting their labour by force. This system of **exploitation** is sometimes referred to as 'chattel slavery'.

In the second stage the process of **exploitation** intensified as one nation of people physically conquered and took control of the land of another nation of people. Their 'ownership' of the other people's land put them in a position to 'own' and control the other people. This calibre of **exploitation** is known as colonisation (Nkrumah, 1980e, p. 14). It was practiced by European imperialist nations against Afrikan nations and others. Crudely interpreted, **Exploitation** in this context is the process of 'stealing' other people's resources and enslaving them. In effect it separates a nation of people from their land, other associated production mechanisms and the product of their labour.

The position of Afrikan women reached a new low point when European imperialism arrived on Afrika's shores and colonised the land; with the invasion of European imperialism Afrikan men became the slaves of European men and women. Afrikan women, who were already partially enslaved by Afrikan men, were fully enslaved and became in Sekou Toure's word's "the slave's slave" (Toure, Tome X, p. 265; Toure, undated, p. 9).

7.4.3 How exploitation led to oppression
When a people find that their resources are being 'stolen' or have been 'stolen', they resist: They try to get their resources back. The *exploiter* must then resort to using a combination of force and trickery to retain the 'stolen' resources (Rodney, 1981, p. 65). The use of force is to prevent the *exploited* people from rising up to take their 'stolen' resources back. The use of psychological processes utilising tools such as their religious institutions, their education system, their media mechanisms, their drug economy and the mental hospitals is to deflect the *exploited* people from even thinking about rising up to take their stolen resources back. All of these processes are *oppressive*. *Oppression* in this context is the process of committing systematic acts of physical and mental 'terrorism' against an *exploited* people.

7.4.4 How oppression led to domination
When the processes of *oppression* have been so successful that the *oppressors* can affect virtually total control over the *oppressed* people, the point of *domination* has been reached. The subjugation of the *oppressed* people is now nearing completion. However as **Amilcar Cabral** (Afrikan Information Service, 1973, p. 43) points out, this level of subjugation can only last until the subjugated people's culture has sufficiently recovered for them to throw off the *oppression*.

7.4.5 How domination led to humiliation
When the *dominated* people are unable to defend themselves and are obliged to obey their *dominators* to the point of carrying out tasks that devalue them as human beings, the point of *humiliation* has been reached. Their *oppressors* can do with them as they choose and overt resistance is almost undetectable. The degrading nature of their

oppressor's abusive practices reduces them to a sub-human status in the eyes of their *oppressors*.

7.4.6 How humiliation led to alienation

At the material level, the humiliation of the people is achieved when the product of their labour is taken away from them i.e. owned and controlled by their exploiters, oppressors, dominators, humiliators.

At the a-material level, when the *humiliated* people internalise their *humiliation* and begin to accept that they and others like them are something less than human beings, the point of *alienation* has been reached. One of the signs of the *alienation* of Afrikan people in British society comes in the form of their exclusion from society's decision making processes. In some cases they may not even dare to imagine that they could have a role in the running of this or even their own society, which in turn generates both apathy and lethargy (Machel, 1974, p. 43).

Process of Subjugation

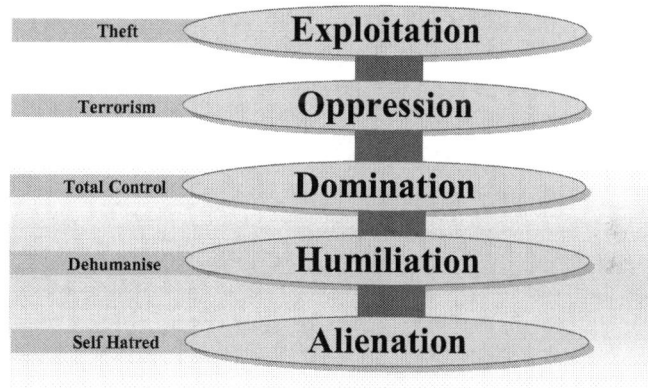

Theft	**Exploitation**
Terrorism	**Oppression**
Total Control	**Domination**
Dehumanise	**Humiliation**
Self Hatred	**Alienation**

Brother Omowale

An even more intense form of *alienation* becomes apparent when *alienated* Afrikan people begin to display signs of hating themselves. Self hatred, the most tragic manifestation of *alienation* can take many forms. However, in the worse cases it brings suicidal behaviours. Behaviours that can involve Afrikan people taking their own lives or murdering others in their community that look like them (Fanon, 1990, p. 203/211/240; Afrikan Information Service, 1973, p. 45).

7.5 Linking exploitation and divisive barriers amongst Afrikan people

This is a summary of the conditions of the various systems and consequences of enslavement that have affected and continue to affect Afrikan people around the world. All Afrikan people, regardless of geographical location have been subjected to the same historical and psychological process of exploitation, oppression, domination, humiliation and alienation. This exploitative process undermines the very fabric of unity amongst Afrikan people. It creates an environment in which it appears 'natural' for Afrikan people to hate and mistrust each other. It appears 'natural' for Afrikan people to think that other Afrikan people are not worthy enough to work alongside them. This is a condition that some commentators have described as 'mental slavery'.

7.6 Property relations: The source of all systems of slavery

We are now in a position to clarify the role that private property plays in the enslavement process. When the surplus of the group was taken over by a sub-group, it became private property; when the land was taken over by a sub-group it became private property; when all aspects of the means of production were taken over by a sub-group it too became private property (Sankara, 2004, p. 261/2). Once these changes took place, property relations underpinned the relationship between individuals, families, groups, organisations, institutions, social systems and all permutations of these different aggregates. It followed that private property imposed the master/slave relationship i.e. the owner/owned relationship on people in their various groupings; it was the source of exploitation between all peoples:

- When exploitation was practiced between women & men of the same nation it expressed itself as sexism, patriarchy and the patrilineal system;
- When exploitation was practiced between men of the same nation it expressed itself as class, class struggle and class conflict;
- When exploitation was practiced between women of the same nation it expressed itself as class, class struggle and class conflict;
- When exploitation was practiced between men and men, women and women or women and men of different nations it

expressed itself as racism, colonialism and because Europeans carried out the invasions, 'white supremacy'.

Social class, sexism and racism are the three primary forms by which slavery has manifested itself on earth. Of these, the worse manifestation of slavery has been the various systems of slavery imposed on Afrika and Afrikan people by European imperialism over the last 500 years. Within that orchestrated process of European imperialist genocide, Afrikan women who were subjected to triple oppression (i.e. oppression on the grounds of sex, class and race) suffered most of all.

7.7 Slavery and anti-slavery social systems

Principles are founded on people's relationship with nature. They provide a framework for the dominant ideas of a society. They are the highest expression of the mode of operation in a society and structure all activities in that society. They are universal in character and therefore override the personal values of individuals in the society. They are reflected in an integrated and complimentary set of attitudes which become dominant in the society. Society's principles are manifested in the behaviours of its people through the way that they treat other people (their sisters and brothers) and relate to nature (their mother). They are directly determined by the society's dominant mode of production (Afrikan Information Service, 1973, p. 50).

Slavery, Feudalism, Capitalism, Imperialism, Colonialism Settler colonialism and Neo-colonialism are related systems because they share the same set of anti-human patriarchal principles – in their essential and central ideas they are the same; all of them are variant forms of slavery. Communalism, Socialism and Communism are also essentially the same and are related to each other through a common set of ideas and matriarchal principles. The two sets of principles are diametrically opposed to each other, they are the anti-theses of each other; to support one automatically means to destroy the other; where one dominates, the other must fight for its very existence.

Under communalism and related systems the principles of ***humanism [people before property]***, ***collectivism [we before me]*** and ***egalitarianism [we're all equal]*** become dominant. Under slavery and related systems the opposite principles of ***exploitation [property before people]***, ***individualism [me before we]*** and ***elitism [I'm better than you]*** dominate. The principles of communalism and its related systems are superior to those of slavery because they encourage people to work jointly towards achieving benefits that are common to all of them. By contrast the principles of slavery and its related systems are inferior because they force the majority of people to work with little or no benefit for themselves whilst others i.e. the 'owners' of property benefit greatly from their efforts.

Principles & Systems

Matriarchal	Patriarchal
Principles:	**Principles:**
Humanism (People before property) Egalitarianism (We're all equal) Collectivism (We before me)	Exploitation (Property before people) Elitism (I'm better than you) Individualism (Me before we)
Systems:	**Systems:**
Communalism Socialism Communism	Slavery　　Feudalism Colonialism　Capitalism Settler colonialism　Imperialism Neo-colonialism

Brother Omowale

7.8 Afrika's experience of slavery - in brief

Afrika gave birth to the communal social system which successfully operated in Afrika for thousands of years (Nkrumah, 1980e, p. 13). In that sense, Afrika was free from slavery. Afrika first experienced the principles associated with slavery as an internal change when some parts of the continent moved from communal living to the beginnings of feudal social systems (Toure, undated, p. 7). This happened in two stages: firstly, the whole group's surplus produce was usurped by 'leaders', 'elders' and others giving themselves superior positions in the community (Machel, 1973, p. 26/7); secondly, the 'leaders' and 'elders' began moving towards claiming 'ownership' of the land, but this process was never completed. However, Afrika's most profound experience of the principles associated with slavery was an external intervention by Europeans with an imperialist intent. It came in the form of a genocidal assault against Afrikan people which resulted in the murder, rape and enslavement of millions of Afrikan people (Sankara, 2004, p. 198/9).

The principles inherent in slavery intensified and then took the form of colonialism. The Afrikan continent was divided up between competing capitalist interests at the so called Berlin conference. The conference took place from October 1884 to February 1885; it was used to prepare agreements between European imperialist enslavers before they launched further savage attacks against Afrika and Afrikan people. As the anti-Afrikan genocide worsened, millions more Afrikan people were murdered, raped and enslaved with out and out war, the theft of land, indoctrination, peonage and taxation being employed as some of the tools in the process.

The principles associated with slavery have now transformed into neo-colonialism – an even more vicious form of enslavement where a class of Afrikan people were specifically created and used to oppress other Afrikan people on behalf of imperialism. Millions more Afrikan people are being murdered, raped and the Afrikan micro-states created via the Berlin conference are being enslaved by the policies of the World Bank, the IMF the WTO and the UN. Afrikan people are now inflicting the face to face damage on each other whilst the capitalists manage the process through bogus leaders, puppet governments and proxy wars.

Development of Capitalism

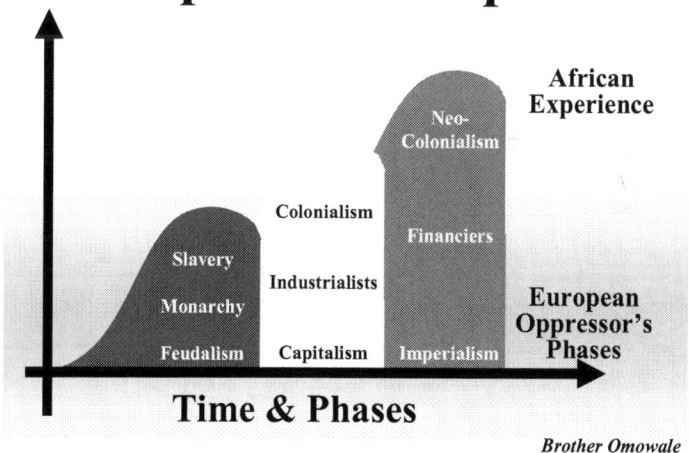

Brother Omowale

7.9 Defeating slavery – a brief note on the future

In order to sort out the current mess and defeat slavery, it is necessary to embrace two critical objectives: the first is the reclaiming of traditional Afrikan culture with its nature based scientific methodologies and anti-slavery, pro-humanity communal principles; the second is to develop a strong state supported by a strong industrial framework so as to be able to produce what we need in order to survive and thrive as well as ward off future potential aggressors. This analysis points us towards what some people have called socialism, a social system that many of us have been indoctrinated and misled into believing is alien to us and bad for us.

What we have not generally been told is that Afrikan traditional beliefs are founded upon the deep, prolonged systematic and scientific observation of nature's processes and patterns and the principles of Afrikan communalism i.e. humanism, collectivism and egalitarianism are identical to the principles of socialism. Socialism differs from communalism in two major respects: firstly, the socialist society maintains the use of state machinery. It is impossible for any nation to exist in the current epoch of history without state machinery. The state machinery would be used under socialism to promote the matriarchal principles of Afrikan culture as well as to prevent the re-emergence of capitalism and its anti-human patriarchal slavery principles. Examples of significant attempts already exist in Afrikan history (Toure, 1979, p. 297-358). Secondly, socialism exists in an industrial setting i.e. there must be mass producing factories under socialism and these components cannot exist under communalism. Again attempts have been made in this direction by Afrikan nations, only to be thwarted by the hidden hand of European imperialism (Nkrumah, 1968, p. 83).

Put another way the essential difference between Afrikan communalism and socialism is the existence of state machinery and industrialisation. Socialism cannot operate without the existence of the state and communal systems have not yet reached that stage of political development. Similarly, socialism cannot exist without industrialisation and communalism which has not yet reached that stage, is pre-industrial. In other words, when communalism is practised in an industrialised economy controlled by national political state machinery, it is called socialism. It is the relationship between communalism and socialism combined with Afrika's history of communalism that makes Afrika a continent already adapted to socialism. Indeed, Nkrumah reminds us that socialism is the modern day guardian of the principles of communalism (Nkrumah, 1980f, p. 444).

There is no doubt that Afrika and Afrikan people gave birth to the principles inculcated in the system that others have now labelled 'socialism'. Though Afrika has never directly experienced socialism which requires a strong united state and industrialisation, it has a long and strong history of communalism. Through communalism Afrikan people have been living by socialist principles for millennia before foreigners came along and claimed to discover it. **Samora Machel** for instance confirms that he came across the ideas that some Europeans call socialism, in Afrikan culture. These ideas were part of his childhood and upbringing which he experienced long before he came across the ideas of Europeans who are incorrectly treated as the 'discoverers of socialism' (Christie, 1989, p. 123).

Matriarchal Systems: Compared

System	Principles	Agriculture	Industry	State
Communalism	Matriarchal	Yes	No	No
Socialism	Matriarchal	Yes	Yes	Yes
Communism	Matriarchal	Yes	Yes	No

Brother Omowale

Industrialisation and state mechanisms also help to clarify the basic distinction between socialism and communism. A communist social system can only emerge after a period of socialism has existed. These two social systems therefore belong in different epochs of history and cannot exist in the same place at the same time. This partly explains why it is that the system of communism has never existed anywhere in the world. The historical development of humanity is not yet ready for it. Communism like socialism maintains mass producing factories which result from industrialisation, but the state machinery eventually becomes redundant and is withdrawn. The communist society is essentially the same as the socialist society; the main difference being that the machinery of the state is present under socialism and is absent under communism (Cabral, 1974, p. 78).

The communist society with its matriarchal principles is therefore essentially the same as the traditional Afrikan communal society except that the communist society has mass producing factories, whilst the Afrikan communal society does not. The essential difference between Afrikan communal and communist social systems is the level of technological development. It follows therefore that the essential difference between the traditional Afrikan society and the communist social system is the difference in their respective levels of technological development. The traditional Afrikan society is therefore even closer to the communist social system than it is to the socialist system. Communism therefore draws on the matriarchal principles inculcated in the culture of Afrika and then Afrikan culture, using technology as a tool, will adapt what others have called Communism so that it works for us in Afrika's modern environment.

Having a discussion on how the various social systems relate to each other can operate as a valuable tool in the process of raising our collective consciousness. However, since such a discussion can appear quite abstract, it brings with it the danger that we can engross ourselves in a discussion about the 'labels' applied to systems and their 'meanings'. This can distract us from dealing with issues of real substance that have developed as a result of practical work. **Cabral** summarises the confusions caused by discussions about the 'labels' given to social systems as follows:

> "To have ideology doesn't necessarily mean that you have to define whether you are communist, socialist, or something like this. To have ideology is to know what you want in your own condition." (Afrikan Information Service, 1973, p. 88/9).

Afrikan principles and ideology which come out of Afrikan culture do not need to conform to the 'labels' that have been created by other cultures (Cabral, 1971, p. 21). Nonetheless, we do need to clearly understand where Afrikan principles, ideology and culture stand in relation to the pro-slavery and anti-slavery social systems of the world.

7.10 The Afrikan Personality and its humanist ideology and culture

The opposing sets of *3 core principles* form the second highest/deepest dialectic of the *4 Dialectic analytical tool* i.e. the humanist v exploitation cluster of principles - the *ideological dialectic* (Pert-em-Hru, 2017c, p. 191 & 274). Amongst other things, Nkrumah uses the following quote from Mazzini to explain the relationship between principle and ideology:

> "Every true revolution is a programme; and derived from a new, general, positive and organic principle. The first thing necessary is to accept that principle. Its development must then be confined to men who are believers in it, and emancipated from every tie or connection with any principle of an opposite nature." (Nkrumah, 2009, p. 56)

Ideology and principle are two of a number of related linkages on different planes. At the level of their material building block, the opposing sets of *3 core principles* are the anti-thesis created in the core (i.e. the nucleus) of the atom as the protons apply nuclear force to get away from each other, but are held back by the binding force of the neutrons; At the level of nature, they are the masculine and feminine principles; at the level of society, they are the humanist and exploitative cluster of principles; At the level of culture, they are the opposing ideologies which vary in form according to the stage of human economic and political development. Principles at the natural and social level are therefore ideologies at the cultural. An ideology then is a principle (or set of principles) that define a particular society. The fact that it parallels the most potent force at the atomic level, is an indication of its explosive power.

Taking the primacy of 'the dot' as our starting point, from the above it is possible to deduce that the dialectical nuclear forces in the atom - as source, generate the opposing principles in nature and society, which in turn generate the ideological dialectic in culture. In other words, when we multiply the a-material unexploded atomic forces of the atom by billions, they develop into a-material principles and when further multiplied by billions, they develop into a-material ideologies. We can further deduce that the relationship between the proton (material) and the neutron (material) equates to the relationship between the people (material) and the land (material) in nature (material + a-material).

Every individual, community or nation operates on the basis of one of the opposing sets of *3 core principles* (i.e. humanist or exploitative cluster) – this is its ideology. In the case of Afrika the humanist/matriarchal principles which flow naturally from our culture are our ideology. Another expression for our ideology is the **Afrikan Personality** (Nkrumah, 2009, p. 79; Pert-em-Hru, 2017c, p. ?) It varies in form according to the stage of human economic and political development: It is communalist in the pre-industrial setting; socialist in the industrial; and communist in the industrial, where the state mechanism has been dispense with. It is automatically in revolutionary confrontation with social systems driven by the exploitative **3 core principles**, namely: slavery, feudalism, capitalism and 'its hand maidens' colonialism, neo-colonialism and settler colonialism.

Out of this analysis flows the **3 core principles analytical tool**. This tool can be used to identify the ethical basis of any and all social systems and groups. Furthermore, by assessing a person's actual behaviours against the principles as yardsticks, it is possible to determine where they stand in relation to the social system of their day. Indeed **Nkrumah's, Sekou Toure's** and **Amilcar Cabral's** combined works, together codify the matriarchal/humanist core principles as the essence of Afrikan culture/ideology. This is precisely what the **Afrikan Personality** is. It follows that Afrikan people living in capitalist, colonialist and neo-colonialist settings can adopt and practice the principles inculcated in the **Afrikan Personality** for a level of protection from the ideological moral decay surrounding them. It can also help to drive them to personally contribute to a revolutionary solution to their predicament. By contrast, in a socialist environment it complements and reinforces the social order.

Having a discussion on how the various social systems relate to each other can operate as a valuable tool in the process of raising our collective consciousness. However, since such a discussion can appear quite abstract, it brings with it the danger that we can engross ourselves in a discussion about the 'labels' applied to systems and their 'meanings'. This can distract us from dealing with issues of real substance that have developed as a result of practical work. **Cabral** summarises the confusions caused by discussions about the 'labels' given to social systems as follows:

> "To have ideology doesn't necessarily mean that you have to define whether you are communist, socialist, or

something like this. To have ideology is to know what you want in your own condition." (Afrikan Information Service, 1973, p. 88/9).

Afrikan principles and ideology which come out of Afrikan culture do not need to conform to the 'labels' that have been created by other cultures (Cabral, 1971, p. 21). Nonetheless, we do need to clearly understand where Afrikan principles, ideology and culture stand in relation to the pro-slavery and anti-slavery social systems of the world.

7.11 Afrikan people will abolish slavery for ever
Afrikan people have abolished every system of slavery that alien cultures have put in their path. In abolishing chattel enslavement and colonial enslavement, they found that their efforts led not to the end of slavery (as was hoped), but to the transformation of slavery into its current neo-colonial form. Nonetheless, overcoming these barriers represented tremendous successes as milestones in the overall struggle against exploiting and enslaving systems. These successes would not have been possible had Afrikan women not come to the forefront of the liberation struggle. As we overcome the internal dimension of enslavement, part of which holds Afrikan women back, we release their energy to help combat the externally imposed systems of enslavement. Afrikan people's fight against slavery is therefore both internal and external.

Kwame Nkrumah has explained that we are now at the final frontier in the struggle to abolish the systems that enslave human beings. Once Afrikan people defeat neo-colonialism we will have inflicted a death blow on exploitation and the other anti-human patriarchal principles of slavery forever (Nkrumah, 1974, p. ix-xxi). In order to ignite the revolutionary transition that will take humanity from the anti-human patriarchal principles of neo-colonialism to the pro-humanity matriarchal principles of Afrikan culture, the Afrikan masses will need to unite. That unity will need to be based upon two crucial premises: firstly a collective fight to the death against neo-colonialism and its destructive intrigues and simultaneously a reclaiming of our Afrikan identity and the principles of Afrikan culture.

References

1. Africa Information Service, (1973), *Return to the Source: Selected Speeches of Amilcar Cabral*, Monthly Review Press
2. Breitman. George, (2002), *Malcolm X speaks*, Pathfinder
3. Cabral. Amilcar, (1971), *Our People are our Mountains: Amilcar Cabral on the Guinean Revolution*, Committee for Freedom in Mozambique, Angola and Guine
4. Cabral. Amilcar, (1974), *Revolution in Guinea: An African People's Struggle*, Stage 1
5. Christie. Iain, (1989), *Samora Machel: A Biography*, PANAF Books
6. Fanon. Frantz, (1990), *The Wretched of the Earth*, Penguin Books
7. Machel. Samora, (1973), *Mozambique: Sowing the Seeds of Revolution*, Committee for Freedom in Mosambique, Angola & Guine
8. Mc Culloch. Jock, (1983), *In the Twilight of Revolution: The Political Theory of Amilcar Cabral*, Routledge and Kegan Paul
9. Pert-em-Hru. Omowale R, (2017c), *Pan-Afrikanism: From Programme to Philosophy*, Ukombozii (www.Ukombozii.org)
10. Nkrumah. Kwame, (1968), *Dark Days in Ghana*, Lawrence and Wishart
11. Nkrumah. Kwame, (1974), *Neo-colonialism: The Last Stage of Imperialism*, PANAF Books
12. Nkrumah. Kwame, (1979), *Towards Colonial Freedom*, PANAF Books
13. Nkrumah. Kwame, (1980e), *Class Struggle in Africa*, PANAF Books
14. Nkrumah. Kwame, (1980f), *Revolutionary Path*, PANAF Books
15. Rodney. Walter, (1981), *How Europe Underdeveloped Africa*, Bogle-L'Ouverture
16. Sankara. Thomas, (2004), *Thomas Sankara Speaks*, Pathfinder
17. Toure. Sekou, (1979), *Africa on the Move*, PANAF Books
18. Toure. Sekou, (No. 88), *Revolution, Culture & Pan-Africanism*, African Democratic Revolution – The Party-State of Guinea
19. Toure. Sekou, (Tome X), *The Doctrine and Methods of the Democratic Party of Guinea*, The Democratic Party of Guinea
20. Toure. Sekou, (undated), *Women in Society*, All-African Women's Revolutionary Union

Index

'Anthony Liar Blair' 216
'shitting' in people's mouths 51
3 core principles 270, 271, 272
8th West India regiment 171
Abolition Matrix 124, 125, 129
abolition of slavery .. 85, 90, 92, 93, 96, 97, 98, 99, 100, 101, 102, 103, 105, 114, 117, 118, 119, 120, 123, 124, 129, 153, 164, 168, 178, 197, 198, 200
Abolition Society..90, 92, 95, 98, 99
Aboriginal people 21
addiction to gambling 106
Afrika ... i, 17, 20, 21, 22, 23, 24, 25, 26, 31, 50, 58, 60, 61, 62, 63, 64, 66, 69, 70, 73, 74, 76, 78, 79, 209, 210, 211, 212, 213, 214, 215, 216, 217, 218, 219, 222, 223, 225, 230, 232, 233, 234, 235, 236, 237, 247
Afrikan .... vii, 85, 86, 88, 89, 90, 91, 92, 95, 96, 97, 98, 99, 100, 101, 102, 103, 104, 105, 113, 114, 115, 116, 117, 118, 119, 120, 121, 122, 123, 124, 125, 129, 130, 131, 132, 133, 134, 135, 136, 137, 138, 139, 140, 141, 142, 143, 144, 145, 146, 147, 148, 149, 150, 151, 153, 154, 156, 158, 159, 163, 165, 166, 167, 168, 169, 170, 171, 172, 173, 174, 175, 176, 177, 178, 179, 188, 189, 190, 191, 192, 193, 194, 195, 196, 197, 198, 199, 200, 201, 202, 204, 209, 210, 211, 212, 213, 214, 215, 216, 218, 219, 220, 221, 224, 225, 226, 227, 228, 229, 230, 231, 232, 233, 234, 235, 237, 238, 239, 247
Afrikan Brigands 174, 175, 176
Afrikan chiefs 68
Afrikan freedom fighters .. 119, 129, 130, 139, 142, 143, 144, 145, 146, 147, 148, 169, 199
Afrikan history 268
Afrikan identity 273
Afrikan liberation 228, 233
Afrikan maroon community 37
Afrikan Maroon community 166, 167, 168, 170, 171, 173
Afrikan Maroon war 166
Afrikan Maroons 149, 165, 166, 167, 168, 170, 171, 172, 173, 176, 177, 180
Afrikan nations ... 22, 71, 72, 73, 74, 115, 131, 132, 133, 134, 135, 136, 214
Afrikan people 17, 18, 19, 20, 21, 22, 23, 24, 25, 26, 27, 29, 30, 31, 32, 33, 34, 35, 36, 37, 39, 40, 42, 45, 46, 47, 48, 49, 50, 51, 57, 58, 59, 60, 61, 62, 63, 64, 65, 66, 67, 68, 69, 70, 71, 72, 73, 74, 75, 76, 77, 79, 80, 85, 86, 89, 90, 91, 92, 95, 96, 97, 99, 100, 101, 102, 104, 105, 113, 114, 115, 116, 118, 119, 120, 121, 122, 123, 124, 125, 129, 130, 131, 132, 133, 134, 135, 136, 137, 138, 139, 140, 141, 142, 143, 145, 146, 147, 148, 149, 150, 151, 154, 163, 165, 166, 167, 168, 169, 170, 171, 172, 174, 175, 176, 178, 179, 188, 189, 190, 191, 192, 193, 194, 195, 196,

197, 198, 199, 200, 201, 202, 209, 210, 213, 216, 219, 221, 232, 233, 234, 237, 238, 239, 263, 264, 265, 266, 267, 268, 273, 298
Afrikan Personality 270, 272
Afrikan resources 211, 232
Afrikan strikers 170
Afrikan warrior women 28
Afrikan women. 104, 144, 171, 239, 260, 262, 265, 273
Afrikan women's foetuses 32
Afriphobia 80
Agaja Trudo 69, 70, 71, 76, 77, 131, 132, 133
aggressors 134
Agnes Bronte 103, 109
alcohol 22, 73, 74, 91, 135, 136
Alcohol 135
alcoholic 106
Algeria 222
a-material 263
American Indians ... 62, 63, 79, 174, 178, 193, See American Indian, See American Indian
Amilcar Cabral 251, 262, 274
Ancient Ghana 9
Ancient Mali 9
Anderson 23, 25, 26, 27, 28, 29, 31, 32, 51, 74, 80
Andre Rigaud 154, 156
Angelique 171
Anthony 'liar Blair' 36
Anthony 'Liar Blair' 20
anti-Afrikan 225
anti-Afrikan slavery racket 107
Antigua 143, 149
anti-human 257, 259, 265, 268, 273
anti-imperialist 97, 150, 233
anti-slavery 89, 90, 91, 97, 102, 103, 104, 105, 116, 118, 120, 122, 123, 125, 128, 129, 133, 136, 137, 140, 148, 149, 165, 177, 178, 188, 189, 236

Apollo 172, 173
Arabs 63
Archahaye 160
aristocratic landed gentry 106
Aristotle 11
Armet Francis 25
arms 216, 217, 219
Arthur Thistlewood 97
Aruba 197
Ashante 22, 73, 135
Ashantiland 49
Asia 63, 78, 79, 214
Asians 64
assiento 68
Auschwitz 80
Ayuba Diallo 121
Baga 76
Baga people 137
Balla 171
Bambara 73, 134
bankruptcy 240
baracoons 23
Barbados 33, 51, 145, 148, 149, 176, 177, 202
Barcelona 10
Barclay's Bank 19
Barkindo 69, 76, 80
Battre Bois 172
Beckles 31, 33, 39, 40, 43, 48, 51, 52, 64, 69, 81
Ben 36, 81
Ben Jochannan 10
Berlin Conference 218
Bernard Montgomery 223
Bini 70
Bini people 131
Black Caribs 178
Black Jacobins 93, 109, 203
Black Joke 27
Blackamoors 10
Blum 215, 247
bodily fluids 25, 27

bondage..86, 90, 95, 102, 103, 104, 114, 118, 137, 139, 141, 142, 145, 177, 194, 238
Bonny 146
Borno Kanem 9
boycott of sugar 120
boycotts 123, 147
Breaking the silence 24, 31, 32, 49, 73, 75
Breitman 254, 274
Brigadier Commander Lamartiniere 157
Brigands.... 175, 176, 177, 178, 202
Bristol 24, 52, 62, 75, 76, 77, 82, 138, 205
British vii, 85, 86, 87, 88, 89, 90, 91, 92, 95, 96, 97, 99, 101, 102, 104, 109, 113, 114, 115, 116, 117, 118, 119, 120, 122, 123, 129, 130, 131, 132, 133, 134, 135, 136, 137, 139, 141, 142, 144, 145, 146, 147, 148, 149, 151, 153, 154, 166, 167, 168, 169, 170, 171, 172, 175, 176, 178, 179, 188, 189, 190, 191, 192, 193, 197, 198, 199, 200, 201, 202, 203, 204, 205, 216, 222, 223, 224, 225, 226, 227, 228, 237
British imperialism... 20, 22, 37, 51, 64, 67, 68, 71, 73, 74, 77, 78, 79, 85, 86, 87, 89, 90, 95, 102, 104, 113, 114, 115, 116, 117, 119, 120, 129, 130, 132, 133, 135, 136, 141, 147, 149, 151, 167, 171, 176, 179, 188, 189, 191, 197, 198, 200, 201, 202, 223
British seamen 91, 107
burned alive 50
Bussa 177
Bussa rebellion 177
Buxton 101, 119
Cabral 269, 270, 272, 273, 274
Calabar 138, 143

Calypso 171
cannibalism 51
cannibalistic 21
cannibals 21
capitalism . 136, 194, 196, 201, 209, 215, 222, 223, 224, 225, 226, 228, 229, 237, 238, 239, 268
Capitalism 52, 81, 229, 265
capitalist killer institutions 212, 213
capitalist system 228
Caracalla 10
Caribbean18, 33, 51, 52, 63, 64, 66, 81, 236
Caribs 149, 177, 178
Carruthers 33, 62, 80
cash flow 239
Castle Bruce 171
castration 51
Chaim Weizmann 79
chaining people to decomposing dead bodies 51
Chandler 62, 80
Chantelle 171
chattel enslavement. 17, 19, 46, 47, 49, 50, 51, 61, 62, 68, 85, 86, 114, 124, 191, 273
chattel slavery 18, 19, 21, 45, 60, 61, 62, 77, 78
Che Guevara 236
Chevalier 50
child sexual abuse 45, 52
child slavery 106
Chinese 63, 78
Chinweizu 78, 81
Christianity 91, 104
Christie 269, 274
Christophe 156, 158, 160
Cicero 172
Clairvaux 160
class 42, 58, 59
class struggle 264
Clemence 172
coastal battles 131, 137, 140
Codrington forced labour camp 177

Cole 79, 81
Collectivism 59, 229
colonel Grogan 211
colonial enslavement 115, 197
colonial troops 148
colonialism212, 223, 230, 231, 232, 233, 247
Colonialism................................265
Commander Charles Belair 159
communalism....257, 265, 268, 269
communism 257, 269
compensation 102, 166, 195
compulsory deportation 17, 18, 22, 24, 51, 62, 63, 64, 67, 69, 71, 74
concentration camps 23, 24
Congo 218
Congo Ray 172
consciousness ..122, 123, 125, 126, 177, 225, 226
conspiracies........................116, 176
containment..............222, 223, 227
Coomba 42
Corbett 155, 156
Cordova 10
Corn Laws.............................88, 89
coup 232
coup d'etat................................232
Crete a Perrot............................157
culture 25, 61, 62, 74, 79, 262, 267, 268, 269, 270, 273
Curacao 197
Dahomey 70, 71, 76, 131, 132
Dalby Thomas............................240
De Bow's Review 49
deconstructed the truth............108
Defile 155
dehumanisation 20, 36, 51
Democratic Party of Guinea 274
Dennis 27, 51
deportation .. 23, 32, 57, 63, 64, 65, 66, 67, 69, 70, 72, 74, 75, 76, 77, 80, 92, 95, 98, 99, 101, 120, 131, 133, 134, 135, 136, 137, 140, 147

Dessalines 156, 158, 160
Dessalines 'the ferocious' 155
destabilisation 22, 24, 59, 73
destabilisation of Afrikan governments.......................... 24
destruction of the Afrikan family 24
Diano.. 172
Diaspora.............. 59, 218, 232, 235
Diop 5, 10, 14, 21, 51, 61, 62, 81
diplomacy 76, 77
Diplomacy 127, 128
diplomatic 115, 120, 122, 123, 124, 127, 128, 132, 133, 200, 202, 233
diplomatic activity 115, 127
disembowelled 30, 32
disembowelling..................... 30, 51
Domestic slavery......................... 61
Dominica.. 148, 168, 170, 171, 172, 173, 203, 204
Drapetomania 49, 52
drug addict................................. 90
drugs 225, 226
Du Bois 9, 10, 12, 13, 14, 94, 240
dungeons 23, 25
Dutch 22, 73, 135, 136, 199
DynCorp 217
Eastern Caribbean 150
economic . 102, 125, 126, 128, 130, 150, 191, 192, 193, 194, 200, 201, 215, 221, 227, 229, 238
economics................... 18, 251, 252
Egalitarianism 59, 229, 255
Egypt..................................8, 11, 14
Elephant..................................... 172
elitism 255, 259, 265
Elitism 59
Elmina 146
enslaved............ 258, 260, 262, 267
enslavement .20, 21, 22, 24, 31, 32, 33, 36, 43, 46, 47, 48, 49, 57, 58, 60, 61, 62, 66, 67, 69, 71, 75, 76, 78, 85, 86, 89, 90, 91, 95, 97, 98, 99, 102, 104, 114, 115, 116,

122, 124, 129, 130, 132, 133, 136, 137, 140, 141, 148, 150, 165, 168, 176, 190, 191, 194, 195, 냄196, 197, 200, 236, 238, 239, 256, 260, 264, 266, 267, 273
enslaving. 57, 60, 64, 70, 74, 77, 78, 79, 90, 115, 122, 131, 133, 136, 141, 153, 192, 197
Eudoxus 11
Europe 209, 211, 220, 247, 261, 274
European imperialism ... 18, 57, 60, 61, 64, 65, 66, 67, 68, 70, 78
exploitation 104, 123, 130, 151, 194, 212, 215, 222, 229, 230, 238, 239, 258, 259, 261, 262, 264, 265, 273
Exploitation................................... 59
false imprisonment..................... 24
Fante............................ 22, 73, 135
Ferguson 18, 62, 68, 81
feudalism 261
Finch 8, 9, 11, 14
foetus... 30
food contaminated with urine, saliva and feces................... 51
forced labour camps 116, 170, 171, 172, 176, 189, 190, 191, 193, 198, 201
France 214, 231
Francis Barber........................... 121
Francis Drake 63
Francois Capois......................... 163
French............................. 26, 67, 68
French colonies......................... 153
French Commissioner............... 153
French imperialism .. 116, 150, 151, 153, 167
French Jacobin Commissioner . 168, 169
French revolution 150, 166, 168, 179

friends of Afrikans and Asians Society 100
Fryer . 22, 51, 60, 61, 62, 63, 67, 68, 70, 72, 81
Gambia 139, 192
Gambia River............................ 139
Garvey 298
GATT.. 213
Gavrus 41, 51
General Agreement on Tariffs and Trade 213
General Maxwell Taylor 218
genocidal.. 114, 115, 140, 141, 151, 173, 189, 190, 191, 194, 210, 216, 221, 239, 266
genocide. 18, 28, 33, 62, 69, 78, 79, 80, 265, 267
George Bridgewater..................121
Germany....................................223
Ghana 146, 232, 274
Gibal Tarik 10
Gibraltar 78
Glele 69, 76
globalisation 215, 216
Goa 10
Gold Coast 22, 73, 135
Goree 172
Gourmond 9
Granville Sharpe 119
Great Pyramid of Gizeh 12
Greece...................................11, 12
Greg...172
Grenada.... 148, 168, 170, 178, 179, 197, 204
Gros-Morne.................................49
Guadeloupe...... 116, 148, 149, 150, 159, 168, 169, 175, 176, 178, 179, 204, 205
guerrilla 136, 148, 166, 176, 178, 236, 237
guillotine 169, 175
guinea pigs 41
Guinea-Conakry........................137
gunpowder into the 'arse'...........51

279

guns 22, 31, 71, 72, 73, 74, 133, 134, 135, 136, 144, 214, 226
Guyana 149
Haiti .. 33, 37, 42, 49, 67, 93, 95, 96, 97, 99, 116, 148, 149, 150, 151, 153, 156, 164, 165, 167, 168, 179, 199, 220, 221
Haitian revolution 96, 99, 149, 150, 151, 188
Hall 172
Hamilcar Barca 10
Hannibal 10
Hart 33, 44
Hecth 79, 80, 81
Hector 48
Henriette St Marc 162
Henry Christophe 149
heroism 18, 49, 50
Hill 172
Hippocratic oath 11
history 210, 215, 220, 223
Hitler 80
Hochschild 42
Homo Sapien Sapien 5, 20
Honduras 178
Honychurch 18, 24, 52, 63, 81
horrors of slavery 21, 50
hot wood on the buttocks 34
House of Commons 89, 92, 99
Hughes 168, 169, 171, 175, 176, 178, 179
human trafficking vii, 24, 26, 27, 31, 49, 75, 76, 78, 90, 96, 115, 118, 125, 137, 138, 139, 140, 141, 142, 143, 144, 145, 147, 197
Humanism 59, 229
IBRD 212
ideology 270, 272, 273
Ignatus Sancho 121
IMF 212, 213, 214, 215, 267
imperialism. 86, 209, 210, 211, 212, 213, 214, 215, 216, 217, 218, 219, 220, 221, 222, 223, 229, 230, 232, 233, 234, 235, 236, 237
Imperialism 212, 213, 215, 216, 218, 219, 226, 247, 265, 274
imprisonment 146, 148
Indians 62, 63
Individualism 258, 259, 265
Individualism 59
industrialisation 268, 269
infanticide 51
institutional violence 32
institutionalised cruel treatment 51
International Monetary Fund ... 212
involuntary human medical experimentation 51
Irish Republican Army 223
Ishango bone 8
Isokrates 11
Jacko 172
Jamaica .33, 37, 39, 48, 51, 81, 108, 122, 148, 149, 165, 167, 168, 177, 196, 203, 204
James 32, 33, 34, 35, 36, 37, 43, 44, 46, 50, 52, 77, 81
James Byrd Junior 46
James Rogers 138
Jean Jacques Dessalines 164
Jean Louis Polinaire 170
Jean Zumbi 172
Jenne 10
Jerusalem District Court 80
Jesus of Lubeck 63
Jewish leader 79
Jews 79, 80
John Ystumllyn 121
Johnson 166
Jonathan Strong 121, 122
Joseph Knight 121
Juba 172
Julien Fedon 179
Julius Soubise 121
junkie 106
Jupiter 172
Justice 22, 52, 63, 67, 68, 70, 73, 81

Karenga 24, 52
Kemet 9, 11, 12
Kenya 8, 211, 222
kidnappers 115, 131, 132, 136, 137, 138, 139, 140, 141, 143, 144, 145, 146, 147, 192
kidnapping 17, 21, 22, 24, 25, 32, 51, 57, 60, 62, 63, 64, 65, 66, 67, 68, 69, 70, 71, 72, 73, 74, 75, 76, 77, 80, 85, 86, 90, 91, 92, 95, 98, 99, 100, 101, 113, 114, 115, 118, 120, 124, 125, 131, 132, 133, 134, 135, 136, 137, 138, 139, 140, 141, 147, 191, 193, 197, 202
Kikuyu people 211
Lamartiniere 157
land ... 252, 253, 254, 255, 256, 257, 258, 261, 262, 264, 266, 267
Latif 9, 14
Legar Felicite Sonthonax 168
Lewis 172
Liverpool 75, 138, 224
Lloyds of London 19
London 104, 109, 120, 121, 132, 138, 139, 143, 203, 223, 228, 234, 235
Louis Michel Pierrot 152, 163
Luke Collingwood 28
Maangamizi .. 17, 19, 20, 50, 58, 69, 80, 96, 105, 113, 114, 115, 116, 119, 124, 125
Mabouya 172
Machel 259, 263, 266, 269, 274
Maco 172
Madam Pageot 160
Magny 157
Malcolm X 247, 254, 274
Man eating dogs 36
Manchester 223
Marie Clair Heureuse Felicite Bonheur 155
Marie Jeanne Lamartiniere 157
Marie-Rose 171
Marin Pedre 170, 175, 178
Marissante Dede Bazile 155
Maroonage 116, 172, 174, 177
Marrow 46
Martin 31, 32, 52, 61, 69, 81
Martinique 149, 150, 168
Mary Prince 38, 39, 47, 120, 121, 122, 205
Matamba 136
matter 298
Mc Culloch 251, 274
mercenaries 217
Mexico 68
micro-states 267
Middelburgs Welvaren 143
military . vii, 99, 125, 127, 128, 130, 136, 148, 150, 156, 165, 166, 167, 168, 169, 178, 188, 189, 192, 196, 199, 200, 202, 215, 217, 218, 226, 232
military bases 197
misogynistic 105
Moise 155, 156
monarchy 19
Monomotapa 9
Montego Bay 166
Montserrat 149
mothers and fathers of humanity 21, 50
MPRI 217
murder ... 24, 33, 34, 36, 40, 44, 46, 51, 62, 266
Mutapa 9
mutilation 29, 35, 37, 44, 51
Mutilations 34
Nanny Grig 177
Nanny of the Afrikan Maroons .. 177
nature ... 87, 99, 122, 126, 127, 128, 173, 209, 211, 222, 228
Nazi Germany 80
Ndongo 136
neo-colonial 212, 213, 214, 215, 225, 230, 232, 233, 236

281

neo-colonialism 212, 222, 229, 230, 231, 232, 233, 234
Nevis 149
Nicholas 172
Nico 172
Nigeria 131, 138, 143, 146, 192
Nile Valley 8
Nkrumah 20, 218, 226, 232, 233, 235, 236, 247, 255, 256, 258, 261, 266, 268, 273, 274
Noel 172
non-violent 141, 177
Nova Scotia 167
Nubia 8, 9, 10, 12
Nzinga 136, 137
OAU 233, 247
Oba Akensua 70, 131
Oceania 79
oil 231
Olaudah Equiano. 21, 120, 121, 122
Old Calabar 75, 76, 138
oppression 215, 229, 230, 235
organise 234
Ottobah Cuguano 120
Ovenden 215, 247
Oyo 71, 132
paedophile 106
paedophilia 45, 51
Palmer 166
Pan-Africanism 274
Pan-Afrikanism 232, 233, 247
Parkinson 166
Parliament ..... vii, 88, 90, 91, 92, 93, 95, 98, 99, 104, 113, 118, 147, 148, 153
Patrice Lumumba 214
Peckham Ladies Anti-Slavery Association 102
Peiterse 79, 81
peonage 196
Pert-em-Hru .... vi, 298
Petion 160
Pharcelle 172
piracy .... vii, 86, 90, 91, 101, 142

Pitman 240
Pitt 90, 91, 92, 96, 97, 98, 99
Plato 11
political 87, 103, 104, 123, 125, 127, 128, 130, 133, 135, 148, 150, 192, 199, 201, 214, 215, 229, 231, 232, 233, 234, 235, 238
politics 81, 251, 252
Pope Alexander VI 63
Portuguese 68, 136, 200
pouring burning wax 51
principles ... 59, 251, 254, 256, 257, 258, 259, 265, 266, 267, 268, 270, 273
prison 142, 143
prisons 27, 46, 60
privacy 26
privatisation 216, 217, 218
Privatisation 216
Privy Council 98, 191
propaganda attack 57
proxy states 134
proxy wars 219
Public castrations 31
Pythagoras 11
Quakers 90
Quashie 172
Queen Elizabeth I 63
Queshebah 177
racism .. 18, 20, 41, 50, 80, 211, 228
racist 20, 28, 36
Racist 98, 100
rape ... 28, 31, 38, 39, 40, 42, 43, 44, 45, 51
raped 28, 30, 37, 39, 42, 45
rebellions . 147, 148, 158, 176, 177, 189, 190, 192
refugees 169, 217, 219
reparations 211
resistance 17, 18, 20, 29, 31, 33, 59, 77, 81
revolution 236

revolutionary ... 223, 226, 229, 236, 237
revolutionary change223, 229, 236, 237
revolutionary Jacobins 96
Rhodesia 222
Richard Hart............................... i
Roatan 178
Robert Wedderburn . 121, 122, 123
Robin 172
Robinson................................... 37
Roderick Johnson....................... 46
Rodney....52, 66, 69, 70, 73, 76, 77, 81, 211, 247
Rome 12
Rudolf Kastner 80
Rwanda 219, 221
Sadistic tortures....................... 34
Sahara 8
Saint Domingue 156
Samuel Cartwright 49
Samuel Stribling................. 76, 138
Sandie 172
Sanite Belair............................ 159
Sankora 10
Sarah 44
Satan imperialism 215
scientific socialism 298
Seaboard rebellions................... 31
Segu 73, 134
Sekou Toure 211
self defence 224
self determination 229, 234, 235
Sengeh Pieh 31
Senghay Pieh 142, 145, 146
Septimus Severus 9
Sexual assaults........................... 32
sexual molestation 51
Shepard ..21, 36, 38, 39, 44, 47, 52, 64, 69, 81
siege of Jacmal........................ 155
Sierra Leone 139, 147, 167, 176, 192
Sims 40, 41

Slav 62
slave trade.... 58, 63, 67, 68, 69, 70, 71, 74, 77, 86
slavery 212, 251, 256, 257, 259, 260, 261, 264, 265, 266, 267, 268, 270, 273
slavery' 85
Smith 166
socialism 257, 268, 269
Socialist 108, 230, 247
soldiers . 91, 96, 139, 141, 154, 156, 164, 166, 168, 170, 171, 175, 178, 188, 201, 218
Soliel..172
Songhai..9
Sonthonax 168
South Afrika..............................222
South America...........................214
Spanish 67, 68, 78
Spanish imperialism 151, 179
Spanish West Indies 68
Special Warfare 218
S-plan 223
St Croix 149, 199
St Dominigue 153, 159, 164
St John 149
St Lucia 148, 168, 170, 174, 175, 177, 178, 202
St Vincent .. 149, 168, 170, 177, 178
Strip beatings 44
struggle 224, 226
Struggle 274
sub-human 18, 20, 21, 47, 50, 51
subsidy 195
Sudan 10, 219
Sun Tzu 189
Susanna Strickland 38
Suzanne Bele 159
Suzanne Simone Baptiste L'Ouverture 158
Swaziland 9
Tackey 149
Tanzania 8
Tate & Lyle 19

terrorising 22
terrorism 17, 18, 19, 21, 35, 37, 43, 46, 47, 49, 50
Texas 46
the Afrikan Queen 76
The Afrikan Queen 24, 138
the Americas . 17, 24, 33, 64, 65, 79
the Amistad 142, 145
The Amistad 31
The Asia 167
the Brig-Rachell, Leetch of Boston
.... 144
the Creole 158
the Felicity 142
the Hawk 146
the Henry 143
the Hero 158
The Jewish Agency 80
The Jolly Bachelor 139
the Marlborough 142, 146
The Marlborough 31
the Neptunius 142, 145
The Neptunius 31
the new world order' 216
The Perfect 139
the Robert 142
The Robert 137
The Rupert 32
the Sally 143
The Sally 32
the Thomas 142, 144
The Thomas 31
the Vigilantie 144
the Washington 145
The William 143
The Zong 27
Thistlewood 39, 40, 48
Thomas Clarkson 118
Timbuktu 10
time 251, 253, 269
Tobago 149
Tomba 76, 137
Tortola 149

torture 17, 19, 24, 29, 30, 31, 35, 36, 37, 39, 40, 43, 44, 47, 49, 51, 210
Toure 212, 247, 252, 262, 266, 268, 274
Toussaint... 154, 155, 156, 158, 168
Toussaint L'Ouverture 154, 168
Trade Unions 238, 239
trafficking 26, 63, 64, 70, 77
Tranquille 171
trans-Atlantic 140, 201
trans-Atlantic slavery 106
trans-national corporations 215
traumatised Afrikan children 29
Treaty of Tordesillas 63
treaty of Utretch, ... 68
Trelawny 167
Triangular trade 64
Trinidad 149, 193
triple oppression 41, 265
Uganda 13, 219
Ukawsaw Gronniosaw 121
Ukombozii 298
umbilical cord 30, 44
UN 212, 214, 215, 247, 267
unity 264, 273
Upper Nile 8
uprisings... 115, 116, 142, 148, 149, 150, 165, 168, 176, 188, 189, 190, 194, 202, 220
US Satan... 146, 213, 214, 215, 217, 218, 219, 220, 231
Van Sertima ... 5, 8, 9, 10, 12, 13, 14
Victor Hughes ... 169, 170, 172, 179
Victorie 171
Virgin Islands 149
virginal speculum 40
wage slavery 102, 194, 196
Walter Rodney 211
Walwin 28, 32, 52, 69
war 22, 70, 71, 73, 79, 93, 123, 127, 128, 131, 133, 135, 142, 144, 147, 150, 154, 166, 167, 170,

172, 175, 176, 178, 217, 218, 221, 223, 224, 235
West Afrika 135, 137, 236
West Indies 75
Whipping 34
white slave................................... 62
Wilberforce.................................. 85
William Cuffay 97, 121, 123
William Cuffey 121, 122
William Davison 97, 121, 123
William Potter.......................... 139
William Wilberforce. 85, 87, 88, 90, 103, 105, 109, 114, 116, 124
Williams................ 25, 52, 66, 73, 81
working class 87, 88, 115, 119, 141, 147, 188, 189, 190, 238, 239
World Bank 212, 213, 214, 215, 267
World Trade Organisation.........212
WTO 212, 213, 215, 267
Young Chatoyer........................178
Zambia..9
Zimbabwe..............................9, 140
Zionists 79, 81
Zombie 172

Author: Brother Omowale

Spoke some home truths in Britain's Parliament on 17th January 2017. Some sections of the media went berserk as a consequence. Click link for presentation:
https://www.youtube.com/watch?v=Sp-ylYnzbg8

Publications written by
Brother Omowale

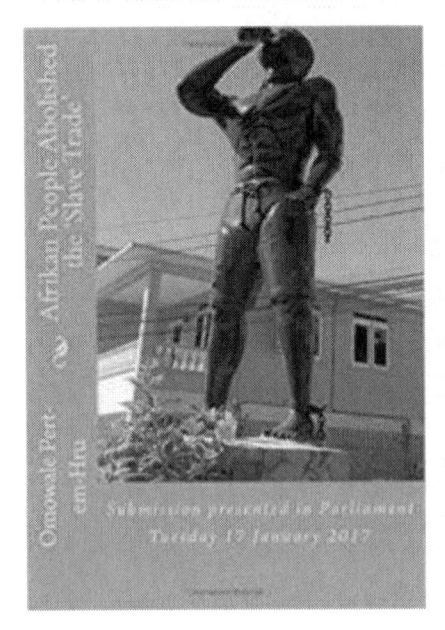

Pan-Afrikanism
From Programme to Philosophy:
An outlook on Liberation

An Introduction to the Programme, Guiding Strategies, Economics, Politics, Ideology and Philosophy of Ukombozii

Ukombozii
www.ukombozii.org

Pan-Afrikanism
The Battlefront:
Afrikan Freedom Means Defeating Neo-colonialism

Ukombozii
www.ukombozii.org

Omowale Pert-em-Hru — Afrikan People Abolished the Slave Trade
Submission presented to Parliament, Tuesday 17 January 2017

Omowale Pert-em-Hru — Horrors, Responsibilities and Origin of Slavery
Background for the Parliament Debate

Pan-Afrikanism: From programme to philosophy

"Pan-Afrikanism: From programme to philosophy" is the only book in the world to provide clear lucid and simple explanations of the liberation strategies of Marcus Garvey, Kwame Nkrumah and Malcolm X. Historians have been naturally concerned with reporting facts of the lives of these great Pan-Afrikanists, but it is for activists to contextualise them in liberation strategies and action plans - a process kick started in it. In addition:

1. It provides a clear succinct explanation of international capitalism's parasitical dependence upon Afrikan people;
2. It provides a clear simple explanation of scientific socialism, relating it to Afrikan principles and culture;
3. It introduces the notion of the greater cycle of revolution which examines and locates revolution not as an incident, but as a process in the context of the entirety of human history;
4. Through an examination of universal principles, it locates the material base of the two opposing sets of ideologies driving human activity and identifies the natural position of Afrikan culture in that milieu; and finally,
5. Through a newly devised set of dialectical tools, it provides a powerfully clear philosophical analysis of matter as a basis for uncovering and understanding the universal laws required for Afrika's liberation.

"Pan-Afrikanism: From programme to philosophy" is a long overdue and much needed source book on the theory of Pan-Afrikanism. For people new to Pan-Afrikanist activism or those who simply want to understand what Pan-Afrikanism is, this book provides clear theoretical guidance. For seasoned cadres and veterans of the Pan-Afrikanist movement, it is a checkpoint/frame of reference for assessing, orientating or even refocusing the trajectory of their activities. Ideally should be studied collectively in groups, particularly those genuinely working towards the liberation of Afrika and her people in the context of worldwide revolution.

Pan-Afrikanism: The Battlefront

When we (Afrikan people) were oppressed under slavery and colonialism our ancestors knew it; they knew that they had to remove these oppressive systems in order to be free. Now we are living in the neo-colonial phase of history and most of us don't know what it is. If we don't know it, we can't understand it; if we can't understand it, we can't consciously do anything to challenge it; if we can't do anything to challenge it, we can't get rid of it; if we can't get rid of it, we're stuck in it; if we're stuck in neo-colonialism, Afrika can't be liberated and we won't be a free and self determining people. The critical task before us therefore, is to raise our collective consciousness of neo-colonialism and how to defeat it in Afrikan communities everywhere. *"Pan-Afrikanism: The Battlefront"* raises our consciousness to better equip us for Afrika's liberation.

"Pan-Afrikanism: The Battlefront" provides a thorough analysis of neo-colonial mechanisms and processes by which the capitalist system arrests Afrikan development in the contemporary world. By facilitating a grounded understanding of how those mechanisms hold us back, it lays the foundation for Afrikan people's corrective actions. It seeks to enhance our understanding by:
1. Introducing readers to some basic concepts of war;
2. Explaining how Afrika's resources was the hidden reason behind World Wars I and II;
3. Linking neo-colonialism to its roots in the enslavement and colonisation of Afrikan people, exposing it as their modern manifestation;
4. Examining the origin, development and intricate workings of neo-colonialism and its adverse impact on Afrikan people;
5. Exposing how a wavering neo-colonialism is altering its form in a desperate and increasingly vicious attempt to increase its life span;
6. Exposing the appointment of President Obama, as an act of counter-insurgency and containment against Afrikan people in quest of liberation; and
7. Exposes Zionism as settler colonialism and genocide, which whilst operating as a junior, but powerful partner in imperialism, actively undermines the interests of Afrikan people.

"Pan-Afrikanism: The Battlefront" should be treated as an introductory and grounding text, laying the foundation for a fuller understanding of the essence of the economic and political problems confronting Afrikan people in the world today. As with the other books in the series, it should be studied collectively in groups, particularly by groups genuinely working towards the liberation of Afrika and her people in the context of worldwide revolution.

Afrikan People Abolished the 'Slave Trade'

British imperialism owes each and every Afrikan person in the world a whopping £615,598,559 Billion first instalment i.e. six hundred and fifteen million, five hundred and ninety eight thousand, five hundred and fifty nine billion pounds - each. The premises/assumptions, formula and calculations are openly stated in *"Afrikan People Abolished the 'Slave Trade'"*.

By combining economic, political and military analysis on the geographical plane, *"Afrikan People Abolished the 'Slave Trade'"* introduces the new **Abolition Matrix tool**, which revolutionises the readers ability to accurately and properly analyse and assess the impact of forces leading to the defeat of slavery. The **Abolition Matrix tool** is supported by a gender balanced, contextually rich rendition of the Haitian revolution. In addition it:

1. Provides a brief insight into the glorious history of Afrikan people before the enslavement era, illustrating how Afrikan genius advanced humanity;
2. Graphically outlines the outrageously inhumane treatment issued to Afrikan people by the wicked enslavers of European imperialism;
3. Examines the thesis that Afrikan people's enslavement was self-inflicted, providing evidence of Afrikan resistance usually excluded from that debate;
4. Exposes evidence indicating William Wilberforce was an anti-abolitionist subversive government agent, tasked with undermining the whole abolition movement and process;
5. Provides lucid, clear and succinct examples of named Afrikan warriors, whose actions forced the abolition of slavery and the misnamed 'Slave Trade';
6. Contextualises slavery as the origin of imperialism's colonisation and neo-colonisation processes; and
7. Identifies the origin and core principles of slavery and anti-slavery social systems, proving that slavery has no implicit connection with Afrikan people and their culture.

"Afrikan People Abolished the 'Slave Trade'" should be treated as an introductory/grounding text, laying the foundation for a fuller understanding of the primary and critical role of Afrikan people in abolishing slavery and the misnamed 'Slave Trade'. As with the other books in the series, it should be studied collectively in groups, particularly by groups genuinely working towards the liberation of Afrika and her people in the context of worldwide revolution.

The Horrors, Responsibilities and Origin of Slavery has now been incorporated into *Afrikan People Abolished the 'Slave Trade'*.

Publications written by
Brother Omowale

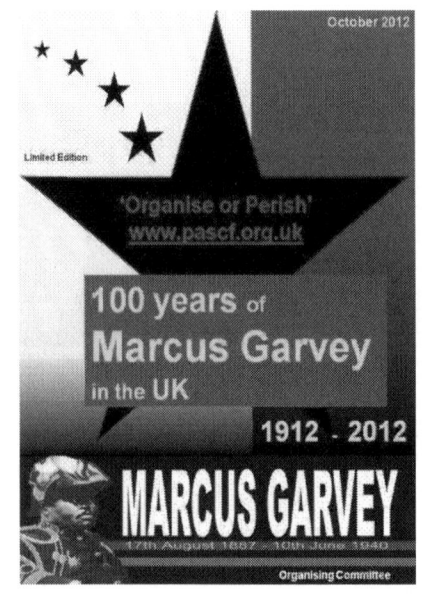

The Beautiful Black Afrikan People Went for a Walk
Written for children and adults alike, *The Beautiful Black Afrikan People Went for a Walk* gives a simple, cogent and clear account of the early history of Afrikan people and humanity, presented as a metaphor. Potently written, it clears the fog of centuries of misinformation, turning the perspectives of 'orthodoxy' upside down. It is an important learning tool for people of all races, pointing all in the direction of hidden historical truths.

100 years of Marcus Garvey in the UK
Written to commemorate the 100th anniversary of Marcus Garvey's first arrival in Britain, *100 years of Marcus Garvey in the UK* contains Garvey's autobiographical account of his organising activities. It summarises and recounts aspects of his history whilst there. It briefly summarises the essence of Garvey and the UNIA and shows how he successfully married his Christian beliefs with his Pan-Afrikan vision. Finally, it recounts the early history of the Marcus Garvey Organising Committee, set up in Britain in the early 2000's.

Strategically selected quotes from Marcus Garvey
Strategically selected quotes from Marcus Garvey is intended as a handbook for members of Pan-Afrikan organisations, other activists and students to assist them in the speedy assimilation of Garvey's key strategic ideas. Beyond that it is hoped that it will also contribute by performing a similar role in the wider Afrikan community and among friends and supporters of the wider Afrikan liberation struggle, popularising his ideas in the process.

Centenary of World War, the UNIA and 'Race First'
As its title implies, *Centenary of World War, the UNIA and 'Race First'* was written as a commemoration of those 3 important events in Afrikan people's and broader humanity's history. It presents evidence supporting the thesis that Marcus Garvey was the greatest Afrikan grassroots organiser of the twentieth century. It exposes a fake debate which occurred in Britain shortly before the centenary year which misleadingly claimed - in opposition to the historical record - that 'Marxists' cannot be members of the UNIA. It concludes by identifying the origin of 'Race First' as an idea and term, demonstrating that it was brought into the UNIA by what the fake debate wrongly labelled 'Marxist members' of the UNIA.

Publications written by
Brother Omowale

The Beautiful Black Afrikan People Went for a Walk

Omowale Ru Pert-em-Hru, 1998

For further information about publications contact:

+44 7914 750 753 or

Ukombozii@gmail.com or

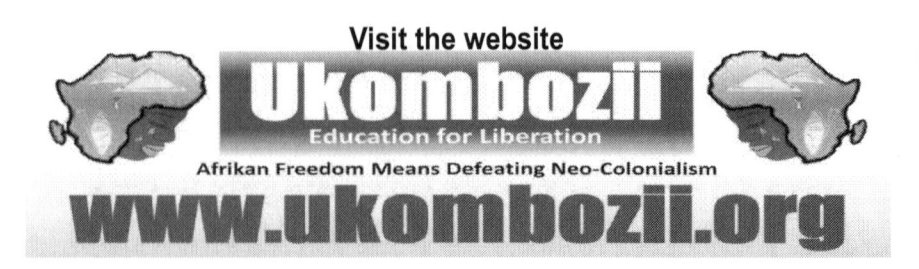

Visit the website

Ukombozii
Education for Liberation
Afrikan Freedom Means Defeating Neo-Colonialism
www.ukombozii.org

About the Author

Omowale Ru Pert-em-Hru is committed to the restoration of justice for Afrikan and other oppressed people of the world. He is the founder of Ukombozii and the Pan-Afrikan Society Community Forum (PASCF) its forerunner. He also founded the Marcus Garvey Annual Memorial Lecture (MGAML). He has been involved in student and community activism since the 1990's.

Ukombozii is a Revolutionary Pan-Afrikanist organisation. In acknowledging the primacy of matter it is philosophically materialist. It seeks to make a contribution to the unification, liberation and development of Afrika and Afrikan people under scientific socialism. It regards the achievement of this objective as Afrikan people's contribution to the worldwide revolutionary movement.

Printed in Great Britain
by Amazon